Edmund Ware Smith

FOR MAINE ONLY

Other Books by Edmund Ware Smith

A Tomato Can Chronicle (Derrydale Press)

Tall Tales and Short (Derrydale Press)

The One-Eyed Poacher of Privilege (Derrydale Press)

Further Adventures of the One-Eyed Poacher (Crown Publishers)

Rider in the Sun (A novel, Lothrop, Lee & Shepard)

From Fact to Fiction (a textbook on short story writing, with Robeson Bailey, D. Appleton-Century)

The One-Eyed Poacher and the Maine Woods (Frederick Fell, Inc.)

A Treasury of the Maine Woods (Frederick Fell, Inc.)

FOR MAINE ONLY

by Edmund Ware Smith

FOREWORD BY DONALD EIPPER

WITH ILLUSTRATIONS BY MAURICE DAY

New York, Frederick Fell, Inc., Publishers

Published simultaneously in Canada
by George J. McLeod, Limited, Toronto

Manufactured in the United States of America
by H. Wolff, New York

DESIGNED BY SIDNEY SOLOMON

Acknowledgments

For the privilege of re-publishing certain of the stories and essays in
this volume, the author is grateful to the editors of Ford Times, New
England Journeys, Derrydale Press, Crown Publishers, Field & Stream,
True Magazine, Outdoor Life, Esquire, Collier's, and the Saturday Evening Post.

Dedication

As an expression of admiration and gratitude, this book is dedicated to the Honorable Percival P. Baxter who gave fifty mountain peaks and two hundred thousand acres of wilderness to the people of Maine and the nation . . . "to be forever held . . . forever left in its natural, wild state . . ."

E. W. S.

Contents

Foreword, *by Donald Eipper*   9

PART ONE: *Woe in the Wilderness*

Last Trip Together   17
The Tenderfoot Who Wasn't   24
Old Lady in Waiting   41
Weather Prophet   58
Owed to an Old Woodsman   72

PART TWO: *Meat, Fish, and Potatoes*

Jake's Rangers vs. Spring Fever   89
A Rifle Named "Sleighbells"   105
The Fish With a Sense of Humor   121
The Vanishing Trout Pool   133
Potatoes: Maine vs. Idaho   146

PART THREE: *Religion, Rum, and Rascality*

The Warden, the Rum and the Preacher   151
Diary of Death   166
The One-Eyed Poacher Conquers Holiness   182
Man Hunt in Mopang   195
Breath in the Afternoon   216

PART FOUR: *Pine Tree Towns*

Dahlonega, Georgia   233
Greenville   239
For Eastport—Till We Meet Again   244
Poland Spring   249

PART FIVE: *Maine Variety Package*

Spring Drive   259
The Genteel Interval   267
The Outermost Henhouse   270
America's Voice Has Changed   276
The Snorkel Bird   282
Summer Hazard   285

Foreword

A FOREWORD to a book is often treated like a commercial on TV in that many people skip it in their eagerness to get on with the play. This is not unreasonable treatment, particularly when there have been several previous books each with a foreword eulogizing the author. There is a limit to eulogizing without becoming repetitive. Edmund Ware Smith, who ran away to become a cowboy at the age of fifteen, probably because there were blue genes in his blood, has been called author, lecturer, teacher and editor as well as woodsman, guide, explorer and professional fly casting performer; I can add carpenter, cabinet maker, and anthroponomist to the list, which is foundation enough for one author.

An anthology of his stories adds up to the natural history of the Pine Tree State. He deals with the forests and mountains, the lakes and streams, and above all with the inhabitants of the remote places; their beauty and tranquility, excitements and dangers, drama and humor.

Oddly enough he was introduced in his youth to the denizens of the Maine woods by a Dennison of Massachusetts who had a much beloved camp on Dobsis Lake in Maine. The introduction resulted in infatuation, growing ultimately into passion. Meanwhile he travelled extensively on this continent, accumulating a fund of information on wild life in country and city.

A few years ago in a fit of abberation he was enamoured
with Florida and bought a place on the Gulf coast. He had met
a friend there who after spending some sixty-five years in the
deep woods of Maine had retired to Florida where he was very
happily raising strawberries and selling real estate. The two
things Ed likes least are raising strawberries and selling real
estate, which he did not attempt to do, but he succumbed to the
magic of the climate. Within two years he began to wonder
why he was there, and not coming up with any good answer
promptly sold out and settled in Damariscotta, Maine. There
he is trying to erase the taint of contamination from land to the
South and West that he might have acquired in his travels, so
that he may be accepted as a blood-brother down-Easter.

His mania for Maine is resulting in a fine series of factual
and delightfully imaginative fictional stories to perpetuate for
posterity the virginal deep woods against the inroads of mech-
anized civilization.

I like his character studies. The trinity of Uncle Jeff Coongate, old Zack Bourne, and Fiery Dagger rum enables the full
scope of Ed's imagination to come into play. Breathing mayhem
and murder in every word to camouflage their tender hearts
these delightful old rascals concoct wily schemes to outwit the
game warden. Sometimes they succeed. On one occasion they
rescue a warden from drowning, who thereupon discovers an
illegal moose hung in Zack's woodshed. This poses a pretty
problem for the warden, eventually solved with a little subtle
aid from Jeff, Zack, and Fiery Dagger in a combination play.
This poacher-game warden feud is on a sporting basis with the
penalties fixed by law; purely a battle of wits without blood-
shed other than that spilled on occasion by a deer or moose.

There have been sections of country where the closed season
on game meant the open season on wardens. I recall from many

years ago a warden on a small Canadian salmon stream that my wife and son and I fished frequently. One day Al, then about thirteen years old, was hiking along the trail upstream to fish a remote pool when he fell in with the warden headed for the same pool. Within a couple of hundred yards of the spot, the warden halted the procession, blew a loud blast on a whistle and sat down for five minutes. They then proceeded through the woods to the pool which was deserted and serene. That warning blast from the warden might have been an act of self preservation.

This feeling of the woodsman's inalienable right to kill a deer in any season would be upheld by Uncle Jeff Coongate on grounds that "it ain't anyways sinful; moose and deer ain't even once mentioned in the Ten Commandments." Pursuing that theme you ask if he believes in a life hereafter and expects to end up in heaven. The answer is that he "ain't aimin' to go to heaven—too much harp-playin' and I ain't musical. I expect to go to hell where it's more home-like."

The title "For Maine Only" might seem to exclude not only the sister States but even all women and children. But don't hesitate on that account for Ed Smith has fascination for all people whose hearts are stirred by the contrasting serenity, peacefulness, and drama of the wilderness. His stories and narratives of personal experience will stir up memories of your own expeditions in the woods or, lacking these, kindle a longing to experience the magic spell of woodlore; you may find yourself lured into a wilderness adventure.

We on the outside think of New England as an entity. The natives of those States agree that New England is a superior section of the U.S.A. but the individual pretends that his own State is just a cut above the other States; the New Hampshire man has said that you always know it as soon as you step across the border into Vermont because the people seem a bit stupid; the State-of-Mainer may say that if you are somewhat balmy move to New Hampshire where nobody cares how odd you are. The Vermonter after listening to the man from Maine explain that Poland Spring water is the purest in the world because it has a bacteria count of minus two asked him which two bacteria were missing when they called the roll. I always liked the legend about Connecticut making wooden nutmegs to sell the sister States though Ed Smith says that is pure libel. He does not say whether it is libelling Connecticut with the label of dishonesty or defaming the nutmeg purchasers by the insulting inference of gullibility.

While the Florida venture had been a short term winter project, for ten years Ed stretched the Summer season to six months of the year to live deep in the Maine woods in a log cabin on the shore of Mattagammon Lake not far from the Canadian border. The cabin on a little rise of woodland over-looking the lake matched and blended with the beauty of the setting. Except for some native help with the log framing, Ed and his wife Mary built it with their own hands and it was a lovely accomplishment. The impact of suddenly coming upon this single bit of human culture after a journey of fifteen miles through uninhabited forest is difficult to describe.

To many people, envisioning a struggle for life in the wilderness under primitive conditions, this project might seem appalling—a coon-skin cap exploit. What Ed and Mary achieved was a luxurious home uncluttered by too many luxuries, a relaxing, restful place—beautiful—and stimulating. In sight of the front porch was the motorboat (for access to the nearest road two miles across the lake) moored to the small dock and a canoe overturned on the shore. When you had time and in-

clination there were lakes and streams to be explored and fish
to be caught.

Back of the camp wandered an old woods road long abandoned except for the occasional hunter or trapper in the fall
of the year. Walking quietly along this trail you might often
surprise a deer or moose, a partridge, or even a very shy black
bear.

That was the setting Ed chose for gathering material and
atmosphere for stories of the Maine woods. It was not a lonely
life, for they were much too busy and too appreciative of their
surroundings for loneliness. In addition to household chores
there was, during the first years, the cabin to be finished, furni-
ture to be made by the expert cabinet maker of the family, and
a garden which Mary hewed out of the forest behind the cabin.
Not to mention Ed's writing, upon which depended bread and
butter. Mary was no mean carpenter herself when it came to
equipping the kitchen. Her mechanical tendencies were evident
at the age of about fourteen when I was told of her having
completely dismantled a phonograph of the side-winder type
which was not functioning properly. When it came to putting
it together again the loose parts had become so involved that
it took the whole family working in shifts two days to assemble.
I believe this story because in the first place it was my wife who
told it and in the second place it was my phonograph.

Then there was the weekly trip via motor boat and auto-
mobile to the General Store and Post Office at Shin Pond.
Mary's garden and hens supplied fresh vegetables and eggs but
other necessities came the long way from town. The return
crossing at night in the sometimes heavily loaded motor boat
could be wet and even hazardous with a strong wind blowing.

Despite the remoteness visitors were not deterred. The

Smiths' friends travelled for days by car, plane, and boat for the sake of a few days with Mary and Ed. They came with the swallows, though the lure was not Fiery Dagger rum. Fortunately accommodations were limited to one guest room, with no nearby motels. Unless you brought a sleeping bag and tent, bookings were strictly in advance. But the presence of guests did not interrupt the writing, for each day Ed would disappear into his study for hours at a time and it was perfectly understood that he was writing; of course he may have been having a nap, but how else can authors dream up their stories?

Ed Smith is fun to be with—in person if possible, otherwise in his books. No back-slapper (which you will discover in this volume) he has a gift for understanding people. This with his wide knowledge of woodcraft, his deep feeling for Maine, and sense of humor, is the foundation of this book.

DONALD EIPPER
Gatineau, P. Q., Canada

Part One

WOE IN THE WILDERNESS

Last Trip Together

MY OLD MAN laid there in his bunk in the cabin, an' the swamp robins never stopped singin'. First off, it hadn't seemed right for nothin' to be singin', but lookin' at it another way, I was glad of them robins goin' it. Maybe they remembered how he always loved their song an' thought he could hear it now. They was everywheres around in the woods by the lake. They made it seem like the old man might wake up pretty quick, an' say: "Web—hear them robins? Storm 'fore night. Better load me an' start."

It was twenty-eight mile to Privilege, an' I knew I ought to get a move on, but couldn't seem to. There was things of his in the cabin I couldn't bear to touch, things as much a part of the old man as his hands was: his paddle, his hewin' axe, his watch, an' the pen he wrote in the diary with.

Mr. Rogers, the New York sportsman that we built the cabin for, he wanted the diary kept regular, an' Father hadn't missed a day till this one. I went over to the table where the diary lay open with his pen in the middle of it. The date was May 21. I dipped the pen an' wrote down how it happened:

> *Jim Rivers and son Web here since the ice cleared hewing sills and peeling spruce for the addition. He complained bein tired, said when we was done work he would lay abed the next morning to seven o'clock. Last nite we was all done, and this morning I couldnt raise him from sleep, as he must of past away durin the nite.*
>
> *We are leaving 8 a.m. bound for Privilege. Wind southwest, clear, temp. 58°. This entry by his son Web Rivers.*

Father was heavy an' didn't handle good. I had to joggle him an' bump him 'round wrappin' him in the tarp, but I wrapped him fine'ly, an' toted him down to the shore an' laid him on the beach by my canoe.

I walked back to the cabin to close up an' get a few things. I got my tea boiler an' some tea, an' dippers for us to drink out of. I took my old man's paddle to use on the trip down. Seemed like if I used his paddle, he would be helpin' me, like all the other times.

I put everythin' inside the cabin that the porcupines might chew up. After I locked the door, I went down an' took the middle thwart out of my canoe so he could lay out straight. Then I loaded him an' started for the outlet.

It was our last trip together, an' in some ways the best we ever had. I could really be some use to him now, it seemed. All he'd ever showed me an' told me was clear in my head, an' I had to do the talkin' an' thinkin', an' make the decisions for the both of us.

Off Mink Carryin' Place, there come a blustery breeze. "Father," I says, tuggin' at his feet, "you come to the stern a little. She's bow-heavy." After he come back, she handled good in the cross-chop.

His paddle was sure a good one—thinned down at the handle an' throat, an' the blade edged so 'twould knife the water without a sound. Many's the dry doe we'd sneaked onto an' shot in closed time with him paddlin' with this very paddle, still as a cat on a cushion. He was a good woodsman, my old man was, an' he showed me everything I know.

At the outlet where the lake emptied into the Little Mopang River, I went ashore to cut a pole to set down river with. "You wait here," I says to him. "I won't be long."

I found a dry spruce, good an' springy, knotted it off smooth, an' we started again. On the quick water, I aimed to show him everything he had learned me. "Take the left channel, the way the water is," he seemed to say, an' he sure must of been proud, the way I handled her on Ellum Stump Rips, an' the Elbows, an' Hell's Gate. I was good that mornin', an' we made a fast run. I never realized how fast till we come to the long deadwater. I unwrapped the tarp an' took out his watch, an' it was only five minutes past ten. Twelve mile in two hours!

"It's too fast, Web, an' you ain't had no breakfast."

"That's so! I never thought about it. Where'll we boil her this noon, Father?"

"Same place."

"By that rock across Chancery Portage?"

"Yes, sir. That's where. It'll be out of the wind, an' we can see the lake there."

We come down lacin' the suds over the last pitch of rips, an'
I throwed the pole away. It was all lake or deadwater from
there, an' his paddle made the canoe jump. I lugged him across
Chancery Portage, an' only set him down once when my heart
got poundin' so I was scared it wouldn't hold out. But it made
me 'shamed to set him down. "You used to lug me across when
I was little. So now it's your turn, Father."

"But there ain't no hurry, Web. Take it easy, boy. We got all
day."

When I come with him to the shore of the big lake, I
looked out an' seen a black cloud in the northwest. I figured he
was right about them swamp robins predictin' a storm, so I set
him down comfortable agin' a big pine that would shelter him
while I went back for the canoe. I had to take a little time put-
tin' the middle thwart back in, but she carried faster that way.
The shower broke while I was on the way over, but I was dry
under the canoe, an' I knowed he was all right there under the
pine. I found him just as I left him.

I took my belt axe, split some kindlin' off a cedar stub, an'
before I had a fire goin' the rain quit, an' it come off hot an'
muggy. Flies commenced to hatch all along that shore, an' the
big trout an' salmon come boilin' up two or three foot out of
water. I never see such a sight in my life.

"I seen it like that just once before—on the west shore of
Otter Lake." He'd told about that lots.

"Say, Father! If Mr. Rogers was here now with his friends,
an' their fly rods!"

"You want to set that down in the diary. It's them things he
wants set down there, Web."

The tea water boiled, an' I throwed in half a handful, let
her boil up once more, an' set her to one side. I spilled in a little
cold water, an' when the tea settled I poured the dippers full. I

picked up my dipper, an' put it to my mouth an' said: "Wow! Jesus!"

"Hot, ain't it?"

While I was waitin' for it to cool, Father moved. I heard him, an' looked, an' he had slid a little way down the tree trunk, like somethin' had disturbed him. I looked all around to see what was wrong, an' seen my mistake. I had left his paddle layin' in the hot sun.

"Well, it was rainin' when I got the canoe over, an' I never thought," I says, an' shoved the blade in the water so it wouldn't warp.

"You want to keep them things in mind, Web."

After we'd had our tea, I took out the middle thwart again an' laid him out comfortable full length, an' shoved off for the last eight mile down lake.

It was a wonderful time durin' that last stretch, best we ever had. Everywheres on the shore of the big lake was places where things had happened to us, an' we got talkin' about 'em, an' laughin'.

" 'Member in there back of Caribou Rock, an' us layin' quiet with a hind-quarter, an'—"

"Yes, an' them two wardens in the canoe went by not two rod from us, an' never suspicioned."

Pretty quick we rounded Leadmine Point, an' there was an open place in the trees on shore. "That's where we was bark-peelin' two springs ago, an' them jeesely yellow jackets drove us to hell out, 'member?"

"Yes, an' it was right here—no, maybe farther north— where the squall hit that time. 'Member?"

"I never thought we'd make it that time, Father. Never thought we'd get ashore."

We were away offshore from Leadmine now, an' you could

see just where the Injun Village was by the sun on the white
cross on their church. I kep' lookin' over there a long time, till
he said:

"Web, you keep clear of them young squaws, boy, or you'll
hate the smell of sweet-grass the rest of your life."

I laughed, an' the sound set two loons to hollerin', an' then
I said: "By God, Father! How'd *you* know about that?"

"You just mind what I tell you."

The loons hollered again, so I laid the paddle on the gunwales, wet my hands in the water, an' whistled to them. Then
we started again, an' pretty quick the houses in Privilege come
into view, dancin' a little in the distance across the water.

I leaned forward an' says: "What time is it?"

"You take my watch an' quit botherin' me."

So I took it out from his pocket, an' looked, an' it was only
quarter past one. "Say, did you wind her?"

"I wound her last night. She's goin' all right."

"It ain't only quarter past one. I thought it must of stopped."

"No, time don't stop. It's the fastest we ever made it down,
Web. It's too fast. You're beat out. Do like I say, now, an' slow
down. There ain't no hurry."

My arms shook clear'n to the shoulders, an' my belly felt
crawly, but I didn't feel played out to speak of. Still an' all,
every time I give a rake with his paddle, I could hear the water
sing along her bows, an' I guess we was travellin' fast.

When we got 'way down below Genius Island, I seen a
man on the public landin' at Privilege. He begun to walk back
up the hill, but turned an' seen our canoe comin', an' stopped in
his tracks. I was maybe a quarter-mile or so away, but he stayed
there watchin', like he seen somethin' queer.

There was a dog layin' in the sun on the landin', an' he
stood up an' shook, an' looked, with his nose up high.

When I looked toward the hill again, the man was comin' back down to the wharf. He met another man, an' they come on down together. Some others come out of the boathouse, an' stood; an' two more that was on the dam come over an' stood.

For a minute, I couldn't figure what the trouble was. I says: "Quite a crowd gatherin' there, Father," an' never a sound from the old man.

Now, with them standin' there an' starin' on the landin', I knew. They stood there like crows around a wing-broke hawk, only they wasn't cacklin'. They was almighty still. I sided in to the landin', an' felt myself get dizzy, an' reached out an' grabbed the edge of the landin'. I got my balance, an' looked up into the faces of them God-damn devils standin' there. It was *them* made me see where he hadn't talked at all, an' how all the time it was just me answerin' my own self!

The Tenderfoot Who Wasn't

AS SOON as they got off the train at the flag station, Mercer began to deride the place, its dilapidation, even its unknown inhabitants. But Mr. Reuben Usher, who at sixty had never been in the wilderness, said quietly: "The stillness doesn't frighten me. I like it."

"You wait, Reuben," Mercer said. "The real stillness is when we get in the canoe—on the lake."

"And if it were noise I liked, then would you also know where were even finer noises?" said the old man, in a most patient voice.

"Humph," growled Mercer. "Like to buzz this dump in a plane."

Mercer chuckled in his thought of startling the natives. Strident in the belief that he was a sportsman, he wore a heavily checked shirt, an exaggerated belt, and high laced boots. He was fat, bluff, permeated with his own heartiness. But on the splintered platform of the flag station, his uniform looked fake.

"Seems good to get the old woods clothes on again," he said, flexing his huge arms. "I wish young Ireland would hurry up. I told him nine o'clock in the *morning*. But time means nothing to these backwoods guides."

Mr. Usher remembered that he had come here by promise

of the very timelessness which Mercer now impugned. He was glad in this new and tranquil environment, even though he felt ill-equipped to comprehend it. He felt a trenchant yearning to know, and to participate; and he pointed to some swallows mustered on the telegraph wires, and said: "Look, isn't that a storm warning?" Somewhere he had read that the congregating of swallows foretold a storm, and this small knowledge would be his contribution.

"Doesn't mean a thing," said Mercer, glancing contemptuously at the sky. "Not a cloud. It's clouds that count."

"I must have been misinformed."

"Takes experience to read weather right, Reuben. Of course I've been at it a long time. Were you worried about the canoe trip on the lake?"

"Maybe—maybe I was thinking of that, deep down."

Mercer strode away along the platform, and the old man looked wonderingly at the forest. He discovered it to be both beautiful and melancholy, and he resented the railroad tracks which had cut through it. Precocious, incredible tracks! He reflected that only twelve hours ago he had been at peace in the roaring twilight of the North Station, Boston. He had felt at home, consoled, one of a myriad beings bustling under a roof. But here—he was not quite sure. He was fascinated, troubled, wary, and profoundly reverent.

He looked beyond the tracks at the slow uncoiling of the river. Somewhere in his immense talk, Mercer had mentioned a rapid named Slewgundy Heater. Mr. Usher looked up the river as far as he could see, then down, believing he might be rewarded with a glimpse of this savage-sounding place. But from one direction the river flowed deathlessly out of the forest, and in the other as deathlessly into it. He was refreshed by the supernal stillness of the river's flowing.

In front of a shack on a slope, a sequestered prophet chopped wood. The old fellow seemed vastly unannoyed with this work, and the blows of his axe belonged. Never had Reuben Usher heard the "chock" of an axe in a clearing, yet by some miracle the sound was familiar. The odors of spruce and woodsmoke made him tingle, and he wished slyly for the nostrils of a hound so that he might sniff, and isolate even finer ingredients.

Thinking reverently of the forest, Mr. Usher saw how little of its meaning books might convey. After sixty years he felt on the brink of a new and more beautiful kind of life. He understood people, the management of industry, toil in the cities of the world. He knew music, literature, and painting, and he felt that music alone might construe the talents of the river, the forest, and the sky.

Now from the telegraph wires, the swallows twittered and made brief nervous flights, reminding Mr. Usher of his newness here. Again came Mercer in his brown, emphatic boots. Mercer trod auspiciously, and was a prophet of weather.

"Here comes Ireland!" the big man said. "He'll do anything for me. I knew his father well."

The earnest ears of a horse showed on the skyline, then horse, wagon and man were visible on the dusty road. Mercer was stimulated by Ireland's approach. "Well, how do you like it, Reuben?"

"It's good," said Mr. Usher, softly.

"You'll catch on. Wait till you get on the lake and hook your first trout. Ever been in a canoe much?"

He had told Mercer several times that he knew nothing of canoes, but he repeated patiently: "Just once, in the park, when I was a boy."

Mercer chuckled as if his knowledge of canoes were occult

and patented. "This is the real stuff." Then, lowering his voice in confidence, he said: "You ought to have bought high laced boots and woolen pants."

The old man looked gravely at his linen trousers, his new white sneakers, and his shaker sweater.

"Mark you as a tenderfoot right away," said Mercer, disapprovingly.

"I am a tenderfoot."

"Yes—but you don't want them to think so."

When the wagon drew up, Mercer gave the horse a dusty slap, and was first to greet Steve Ireland.

"Hello there, Stevie. Knew your old man well, so we'll start right off with first names, eh? Mine's Al. Al Mercer."

"Yes," Steve said. "I've heard of you Mr. Mercer."

"Brought my friend Usher—Reuben Usher. He's interested in a little rest in this country you fellows have got up here. How are the trout biting?"

"Ought to pick up a few."

They climbed into the wagon and started toward the lake, and the wheel-sounds were muffled in the dust. Everywhere the sun shone on deserted fields, and on the leaves of Spring.

Mr. Usher noted that Steve was young, lank, and sinewy. He looked straight ahead, and listened calm-faced to Mercer's outbursts of lore. Steve was not uncommunicative. He was reserved, quietly and courteously withholding his personality, as if he felt too many men had tried to get acquainted with him in seconds. As they passed a farm, Steve looked long at an old cow which lay on the grass. He looked from the cow to the sky, then straight ahead again. "Cow layin' down in the mornin'," he said. "Storm 'fore night."

"Not today, Stevie," contradicted Mercer. "Not a cloud in the sky. I was telling Reuben, it's clouds that count."

Steve nodded, and Mr. Usher felt a deep affection for his swallows.

Before they reached the lake, a buck deer cleared the road ahead of them in a single leap. Astonished, Mr. Usher rose from his seat, as if with longing to capture and suspend this flash of beauty. For him all the forest was enriched by the live, wild thing which was a part of it.

At first sight of the deer, Steve's eyes had darkened in a quick and savage joy. Steve Ireland was a native hunter; and, crouched on the wagon seat, he had gestured fiercely, saying: "God! Look at him! Look! Look!" Then he sat back, sighing, relaxed, his lips wrinkling in a dreamful smile. Damp beech leaves on a long ridge, a fire no bigger than the bottom of a tea pail, liver broiling on a stick, and that buck hanging by his gambrels from a bent sapling. Peace and plenitude were Steve's. He wanted only things which were probable of fulfilment, and he did not wonder whither he was going, or why. Here was this buck, working in his country! He looked artlessly around him, saying in his mind: "I'll hunt this ridge, come fall. I'll dump that critter on his nose before a lynx gets him. God A'mighty, I can taste the gravy now, and the drool a-gatherin' in my mouth a'ready."

"Lot of deer up around Jackman," Mercer informed. "That's the place to see deer. Ever up around Jackman, Stevie?"

"No."

"You ought to try it there some time."

Through the trees the lake shone with abrupt radiance, like daylight at the end of a tunnel. Mr. Usher climbed from the wagon, and walked with boyish eagerness to the sand beach. He stood there, a silver sheen of hair curling from under his hat. He felt strangely beholden to something. He could not remember when he had felt both awe and gratitude simultaneously. Was it the long mystery of distance? The remote and dusky shores? The boulders atop themselves in trembling mirage? Or was it simply the hovering paternity of earth and sky? Oh, he would bring his children here, and show this to them, watching while it penetrated them as it penetrated him.

Beneath a dignified spruce, Mercer babbled and assembled fly rods. Steve unhooked, and hung the harness on a tall gray stump. He waved to the horse, and said: "Go it, old Crawnch! Go it, boy!" The horse shook, and trotted up the road, its destination private.

At the edge of the forest, Steve rolled a green canoe to his shoulder and brought it down to the beach. He thrust the bow into the water, loaded the duffel, and took a long steady look into the northwest.

"How far is it to camp?" asked Mr. Usher.

"They call it eleven miles. I guess we're all set, sir." Steve leaned on his paddle, and while he waited, stared again at the sky. The cloud was there, all right—black, and low down in the horizon.

Mr. Usher stooped and touched the gunwale of the canoe. "This is all new to me, you know," he said.

Mercer, having finished with the rods, came down in time to overhear this. "Don't worry, Reuben. A canoe'll scare you to death before it'll drown you. Right, Stevie?"

Steve nodded toward the bow, and said to Mercer: "Will you sit forward, please?"

Mercer stepped in and moved to his position. "That's a fact, though—about canoes, isn't it Stevie?"

Steve's active eyes squinted a trifle as they focussed for an instant on the low-lying cloud. "That's what they say," he said. Bending, he steadied the canoe for Mr. Usher. "Just step in the middle of her. Here, grab my shoulder. And when you set down, rest your back agin the middle thwart an' face towards me."

Carefully the old man did as he was told, and he marvelled at the grace with which Steve shoved off and jumped into the stern, his moccasins making scarcely a whisper on the cedar planking of the craft. Steve's paddle knifed into the water, and the canoe moved out into the lake.

Mr. Usher peered into the water. The sides of boulders loomed, fell away to depth and darkness. Mercer had begun casting, and was making handsome predictions as to the size and number of trout he would take. But it appeared that his prophecies were delayed of fulfilment, and he grew petulant and dismayed, and spoke of great catches in Moosehead Lake, and of rainbows from the Cowichan River on Vancouver Island, and of the merits of many places quite impossible to reach at the moment.

"Why don't you get the canoe out farther?" he said to Steve. "Can't you tell by this time they're not lying in close?"

"Just as you say," said Steve. He had been following the margin of an underwater bar, but he nosed the canoe outward. For a while they fished fruitlessly a quarter mile off shore, and Mercer began again: "This is too far out. I didn't mean this far. Can't you take us where they are?"

Steve angled toward shore until he picked up the shadowy outline of the bar again. It was his job to keep his sportsmen happy, and to do what they said, no matter what. It was also his job to keep an eye on the cloud which stretched long and straight across the northwest. Maybe it was just as well their backs were turned to this cloud. He rolled a cigarette, and had trouble making the paper stick. "I got the driest spit of any man I ever see," he finally remarked, tossing the cigarette away.

In the narrows between two long points, Mercer began to

catch trout. He grew voluble, informative, and obstreperously happy. "See? I told you, Reuben," he said. Everything he said was loud and definite, and his voice re-echoed from the point. Mr. Usher felt curiously glad of this double stating. The stillness was now hovering, oppressive, and Mercer's prattling somehow served as a contact with humanity.

"Got another!" he shouted. "A beauty. Say, how many I got now all together?"

"You got enough," said Steve. "Shall I let this one go?" Paddle balanced across his knees, Steve held the trout under-water in the net.

"Let it go?" protested Mercer. "What's the sense in catching them if you let them go?"

"He'll live. You got more'n you can eat a'ready."

"Let him go," said Mr. Usher.

A few moments later, Mr. Usher felt a violent tug on his line. He had been trying to cast, and, doing rather badly, had allowed his fly to trail in the water. As the trout struck, he had instinctively lifted his rod and hooked the fish. He sat forward, eyes sparkling with delight, his lips spread in an embarrassed smile.

"Steve! What shall I do now?"

"Reel in! Reel in!" instructed the tireless Mercer. "Keep a taut line! How do you like it now, Reuben?"

"You're doin' all right, Mr. Usher," Steve said, peering into the water. "Good fish. Go mighty near two pound."

Suddenly the old man's line went slack, and the spring of the rod whipped the fly clear of the surface.

"Gone! But I don't care, Steve—not if you don't. Really."

Steve grinned at him, and Mercer said: "What did I say about keeping a taut line? You can't catch trout unless you learn the art of keeping a taut line. Right, Steve?"

"Well, it's too bad Mr. Usher," Steve said. "Your first one, too."

"But I'm just as happy. Really, I've never been so happy."

Steve had no time to savor his wish that all men were like Mr. Usher. A puff of wind snapped out of the northwest, and a dark cat's paw fled across the water. The wind reached them all in a cold, quick pressure which put Steve's hatbrim flat against his forehead, and brought the water to his eyes. His lips twitched and tightened as he reached for his hat. He was looking far away at the cloud, and he saw that its lower edge was ripped and lacy.

The canoe emerged between the two points into the widening body of the lake. Distances stretched ahead, and to the right and left. Steve looked measuringly at Cardiff Point. He could duck behind it if things got bad. Or, if the sportsmen wanted to reach camp, he might try for the lee of Munson Island, three miles away. His two passengers sat with their backs to the cloud, and they had not seen it. When the time was right, he would call it to their attention. Anticipating that moment, he gave them each a sharp glance of estimate. Steve had classified them simply as the fat bastard in the bow, and the old man aft of the middle thwart. You could feel the wind pretty good now, he thought—a cold one. The lake was rippling some, too, and the spruce tops waving on Cardiff Point. . . .

Mr. Reuben Usher reeled in his line, and sat thinking, his eyes half closed. The young guide, so close to him in the stern of the eighteen-footer, had a quality which he hoped his own sons might some day possess. This quality, Mr. Usher believed, concerned the patience to remove ten thousand stones from a field, and the reticence to hew in a clearing. What if one transplanted himself permanently into this environment? What would he miss first? One wanted to cry out: "I would miss nothing!" But was that true? Mightn't one long for good music, for his work, or for someone with whom to draw comparisons?

An unfamiliar rocking of the canoe disturbed him. Glancing about, he noted some remarkable changes. Everywhere was motion. The waves marched in sharp, unending echelons, and trees swayed against the sky. In any direction it was a long way to shore, but you could see the swaying of trees, distance or no. Young Steve had changed his course, so that he quartered into the waves. These waves slapped briskly against the starboard bow, and they seemed impious, and direly purposeful.

Down wind came an eerie babel of laughter, and Mr. Usher thought suddenly of ghouls, and glanced apprehensively at Steve.

"Loons," Steve said, serenely. "They do that sometimes when the weather's changing." He stuck his hand in the water and scooped some to his mouth. Wiping his lips, he said: "Better reel in now, Mr. Mercer."

"Reel in? Why should I reel in?" the big man asked.

Steve twitched his paddle. The canoe swung sharply, rolling in the trough of the waves. At this angle, by turning their heads slightly, all three men could see the cloud. Its forward edge was smooth, dense, jet black; and its trailing edge was torn and coppery.

"See that?"

Mr. Usher nodded. His swallows! They had been right.

"Well, what about it?" Mercer asked.

"Wind."

"So what? What's a little wind?"

Mr. Usher observed that the men were shouting, not in anger, but to make themselves heard. The wind pressed hard upon his cheek and howled in his head. He had read of squalls, but there must be a limit, a restriction somewhere on velocity. At a certain point in the wind's acceleration, it ceased its benediction, and became arrogant, menacing, and cold. It knocked the tops from selected waves, and scattered them on the back of one's neck.

"I can make Cardiff Point," yelled Steve, his shirt ballooning, "or I can try for Munson Island. Camp's on the mainland, just beyond Munson. What do you want to do?"

"It'll blow over," said Mercer, reeling in. "You're not scared of a little wind, are you Stevie? Head for Munson Island."

Steve snatched off his hat, placing it on the floor of the canoe, his knee on the brim. The wind tussled his black hair, parting it indiscriminately and showing the white scalp.

"Suit yourself," he said.

The cloud shut off the sun, and the sun's abatement did something ominous to the scenery and to the moods of the men. In the dim light the waves became black and murderous, and their crests hissed, and were dirty white. Steve began to study them steadily, not just once in a while.

Mr. Usher wished they were now about to land on Munson Island; but Munson was an imperishably far distance, and this was so of all shores, and the canoe seemed to be making no headway. He recalled two recent shouts from Mercer, and in these shouts he perceived a special significance which he had not noticed at the time.

One shout had been: "How do you like it now, Reuben?" and this had been in a kind of paper-thin voice, a voice uncertain of itself. The second shout had been directed to Steve: "Why don't you turn and run with it—*any* shore?"

"Swamp over the stern," Steve had answered.

Thereafter, Mercer had been silent, and Mr. Usher realized that Mercer was frightened, and that he himself was frightened, and that of all living men, Steven Ireland was most important. There was something very illogical about their predicament. You could step away from an onrushing train, a tiger, or a madman. But you could not step away from this.

Always Mr. Usher had regarded wind as something wild, free, and magnificent. He saw now that it was also wanton, merciless, and unpredictable. It snapped off the top of any tree at random. It filled the air with frayed leaves, and tumbled crows in their stride. Moreover, it imparted to the lake a cold, coherent lust.

The waves came close and crowding. They came on, towering, toppling, threatening Steve Ireland's precocious vigilance. And the waves applauded themselves by the hiss of their torn crests.

The canoe lurched, and a gout of spray spilled over them, spanked the bottom of the canoe, and cascaded toward the stern. Steve steadied her with his knees, and yelled to Mercer: "Lay down! Lay down! They don't get no smaller if you rise up an' look at 'em. I said lay *down!*"

Mr. Usher's stolen glances toward Munson Island brought nothing but a sickening sight of power beyond belief. They would never make it. And if there were no progress, why continue this teetering, this hypocritical effort to keep the bow of a canoe in one direction? Munson Island was a bait designed by experts in irony. It was a thing toward which to struggle in vain. They had all been very cunningly trapped.

The old man felt that his fear was degrading and shameful; and he wondered how long a human being could live in its concentrated misery. Many times in life he had been startled, momentarily filled with terror. Time was the element which differentiated between fear and fright. Mr. Usher knew that his wish to pray was weak and pitiful, because he knew it was merely the wish to live. But he said in his mind:

"God, please wait a minute if You can. God, what is a minute to You?" He knew it was his finest prayer.

He was wet clear through, and when the canoe heaved under him, he seemed to compress, growing inferior in stature and great in circumference. Whereupon, the canoe pitching downward over a crest, he became a being of only vertical dimension, and all his width was evaporated. He could anticipate these mad sequences by the crackling antagonism in Steve's eyes. Steven Ireland knew exactly how to look at a wave, and the look was not scornful.

The old man began arranging sincere objections to his own drowning. There was too much work left undone. A man should be duly warned and prepared for such a climax as his own death. He should be permitted to order his larger work of life, so that it could be entrusted to an able successor. But it didn't work out that way. Had he actually believed that he would lie down some day in a quiet place and say: "Now I am ready to die"? If so, he had been guilty of false thinking, for it was apparent that one could prepare only for life. In fact much of life was nothing else. Death had its own incalculable volition, and anyone who thought it might procrastinate in his favor was a fool. Munson Island was undoubtedly a beautiful place where men could walk, or lean gratefully against trees and stare out at this cold compendium of hell. What did it matter, now?

Mercer, who had been so boisterous, so braggart in the placid wilderness, lay in the bow, eyes shut, face slack and ugly in its terror.

Steven Ireland knelt in the stern, working. Mr. Usher believed him possessed of all knowledge useful on earth, as well as an amazing sense of balance. Steve must also have an unswerving egotism to engage these waves. His hair was whipped and stringy with spray. Water spilled from him and was blown to vapor. When Mercer moved, a victim of his own panic, Steve yelled: "Lay down!" He yelled so that the cords in his neck strung tight, but his voice was reduced to a whisper in the howl of wind and crashing of the seas.

Without realizing what had happened to him, Mr. Usher had buried his fear in his admiration for Steve. The situation itself belonged to Steven Ireland. He alone was useful and articulate. His patience was an enduring attribute, proof against this wave, the next, and all others. Steve was here against his own judgment, the only judgment which counted. But he wasted no time in thinking he would soon be dead. He did not appear enraged at anyone for getting him into this, yet each paddlestroke must have drawn achingly of his strength. His shirt was a wet skin plastered over his chest. Under it the muscles showed lean and live. He was incurably busy. No sooner would he defeat one wave, than he would be about the outrageous problem of the next. He took no time for triumph, breathing, or oration.

Of a sudden Mr. Reuben Usher came aware of his own returning courage. Winning this fight no longer seemed grievously important—if only he could help Steve. The old man's eyes glowed with his new excitement. He leaned forward, crying out through his numbed mouth: "I want to help!"

Steve's lips curled briefly from his teeth. Without taking his eyes from the waves, without missing a stroke, he reached behind him and tossed an empty lard pail into Mr. Usher's lap.

"Bail her!"

Working joyfully with his lard can, Mr. Usher bailed. In time he developed a great pride in his technique. He found that he could plan his awkward scooping when the canoe was tipped, and thus get nearly a full pail at a scoop. On these great occasions, he would glance warily at Steve, and Steve was infallible and wordless in his gratitude. This moment, felt the old man, was very close to inspiration . . . when one fears nothing, when everything at once seems fine, and in one's heart is the wholesale evidence of truth.

At length they came exhausted into the lee of Munson Island, and now that rest and security were at hand, they doubted the violence of their own adventure. No one, they felt, could have come through alive. They must have been imagining things. But on the mainland, less than half a mile distant, they saw a cluster of motionless men. Then they had had witnesses! Then it was true! Steve wigwagged with his paddle, and all the men on the mainland waved their arms at once, and moved about in a state of excitement.

Steve sided the canoe into a sheltered cove on the island, and held her steady while Mr. Usher stepped out. The old man's legs were cramped and stiff. They buckled beneath him, and he felt himself obliged to fall down. The stones upon which he lay seemed to heave, as if the waves had imparted a habit to them. Steve Ireland bent over him and lent him a hand.

"Mine won't straighten out neither," Steve said. "It's like they're wore away to a couple of danglin' cords, ain't it?"

Steve got his axe from the stern and walked off looking for a dry pine stub. When he had gone, Mercer raised his head and looked around, blinking. Mercer did not disembark from the canoe. Rather, he emerged from it, like some huge and lumpish animal. At the sound of an axe, he glanced along the beach, noting that Steve was well out of earshot.

"That was awful, Reuben," he began.

Mr. Usher scarcely heard, so intent was he upon the nearness of trees, and upon the feel of round stones and earth.

Mercer was regaining confidence and voice. "That was some blow, Reuben. Ireland had no business getting us into that, you know. It's sheer luck we weren't all drowned."

Reluctantly Mr. Usher turned his gaze away from some flies which by a method known only to themselves had congregated in numbers on the calm water.

"What did you say?" the old man asked.

Mercer began to pace the beach, to gesticulate. "I say that young fool has poor judgment. I'm going to see to it that his guide's license is revoked permanently."

"Oh, do they have to have licenses?"

"Licenses? Certainly. Take his license away, and he can't guide, see? Teach him a lesson."

Mr. Usher reached into his shirt pocket for a cigar. Sorrowfully he discovered that his supply had become a dark brown mush, which had stained his shirt. He turned his head slightly, noting that Steve had a fire started between two boulders up the shore. Woodsmoke. The old man's nostrils twitched, and in him there awakened strange longings.

"My fortune is considerable," he said, very soberly. "And I had wished to divide it equally among my sons. But if you should happen to have the boy's license revoked, I shall gladly spend the whole fortune reinstating it."

He knew it sounded foolish, dramatic and pontifical, but he didn't care.

He stood up and walked to the fire which was blazing merrily. Steve knelt close beside it, drying his clothes, and melting the chill from his bones. As Mr. Usher approached, Steve jumped up and handed him an ancient coat, resplendent with elbow patches and assorted buttons.

"By God," he said, evenly, "you put this on."

Mr. Usher did as he was bid, and pointed curiously to Steve's feet. "Do you suppose you could get me a pair of moccasins exactly like yours, Steve?"

"Why, sure. Sheldeye Linton makes them, by the old Britton tan. I give three dollars an' thirty-five for these."

Mr. Usher licked his lips. He leaned against the side of a boulder and stared into the fire. "Was it really a bad blow, Steven?"

"It was real bad."

"Well—tell me this: when you see a lot of swallows together, is that a sign of a storm?"

Steve nodded affirmatively and dropped a piece of split cedar on the fire. The old man smiled, as if he knew his next question were to be boyish, but could not resist asking it.

"Was I any use to you—out there?"

Steve pushed his hat back on his head. He lowered his voice the merest trifle, then bent closer over the fire.

"I wisht they was all like you," he said. "Jesus, I do!"

Old Lady in Waiting

THE OLD LADY was a Catholic, and when she thought of the church nothing was unendurable—not even the cruelty of the wilderness before the coming of spring. As a girl she had dreamed of attending services in the cathedral of Notre Dame, in Paris. She knew all about Notre Dame. It was said to be on an island in the river Seine. The ceiling arched to unguessable heights, mystic in the twilight of stained glass, dusky with the smoke of candles, and haunted with the yearning of ancient prayers.

Realizing as she grew older that she would not see Notre Dame, she had reefed her vision for the nearer view—the shrine in the province of Quebec. But when she knew she was never to set foot in St. Anne de Beaupré, she found consolation in a postcard showing the lighted cross on Mount Royal, farther south.

Now that the old lady had come so late in life to this wild, merciless land, she could worship only at rare intervals. Thus the thing she loved most was all but denied her. At sixty-seven, there remained for old Sarah, wife of Zack Bourne, the slab church in the Indian Village on the lakeshore; and until the ice cleared, even that was unreachable.

At one time, Sarah had been Mrs. Patrick O'Mahoney,

and had lived in a Boston suburb, where within walking distance were a dozen stone churches. During Holy Week, immediately following Mr. O'Mahoney's death, she had attended
mass at all twelve. Shortly after her first husband was buried,
Sarah had gone into housework. She had been at it forty years
when, with tumult and with shouting, Zachariah Bourne came
into her life.

Zack Bourne was a widower of about Sarah's age. Sarah
had met him while he was carpentering on an addition to the
home where she cooked. Zack was many things besides a carpenter. He was tall, stooped, and mammoth-handed. He was
boisterous, kindly, profane, bold, honest and a giant. When his
wrist was infected from the stab of a rusty nail, Sarah had
prayed for him. Zack was no Catholic, but the prayer worked.
He recovered, married Sarah, and took her off with him—back
to the wilderness whence he had come.

Returning to the lakes and forests as caretaker of Mr. Reuben Usher's cabin, was to Zack Bourne like an unexpected
opening of the gates to heaven. He was on the verge of thanking God, when he remembered to congratulate *himself*. Along
the Mopang watershed were many of Zack's boyhood friends—
Ap Ireland, father of Steve, Jeff Coongate, the one-eyed
poacher, old Joe Keegan and others. But to Sarah, who had
never been far from the city, the pilgrimage to the north was a
strange and terrible experience.

When Mr. Usher voiced doubts of Sarah's strength to with-
stand the loneliness, and the deadly waiting for spring, Zack
had replied: "Mr. Usher, never you fear. Old Sarah's tougher'n
a link of boom-chain."

"But I was thinking also of emergencies, Zack. What of
sickness in the winter?"

"She'll pray her way out, like a snowplow bustin' through

a drift." Gesturing with his slab-like hands, Zack had offered irrefutable proof: "Why, God damn it, Mr. Usher—one time a cousin o' hern took sick in San Francisco, an' Sarah lit a few candles, kissed the daylights out of her crucifix, an' prayed her cousin back to life three thousand mile away."

"Are you a Catholic, Zack?"

"Me? Hell, no—but I believe in it."

In the beginning, Sarah felt that anyone living in this ruthless country must be an escaped convict, or have some other sinister reason for renouncing a paved world. Four or five seasons passed before she accustomed herself to the visits of the savage, one-eyed Mr. Coongate, who cursed more fluently even than Zack, and threatened the lives of game wardens near and far. But Uncle Jeff called Sarah by her first name immediately after introduction, and in time quelled her fears with flaming compliments on her cooking, crocheting, and choice of husbands.

"Why, Sarah," said the outlaw, "—anyone that'd marry that old tomcat's pratickly noble."

After that, Zack and Jeff had thumped each other on the back, scuffled a little, and settled down to exaggerating Mopang log-drive adventures, and their own personal superiority from childhood to the present.

Gradually and foggily it came to old Sarah that her giant of a man was actually gentle. He blasphemed, and laid roaring plots against his enemies, but he loved the loons nesting in the cove. He grew sentimental over the bald eagles in the sky, and tolerated the old does who cautiously ate all the lettuce in the garden in the summer.

Whenever Uncle Jeff stopped by on his illegal moose hunts, he and Zack lay in the grass devising fiendish tortures for any game warden that came to mind.

"We could take an' tie Tom Corn in his canoe," Jeff said, once, "an' anchor it in a hundred foot of water off Headworks Island. We'd come by in our canoe ever' hour or so, an' heave rocks into the warden's canoe—jest a few to a time, till it sunk, an' him tied in it."

Uncle Jeff closed his one eye blissfully, but Zack had objected to the scheme: "It'd be a shame to waste a good canoe on a warden, even his own."

"Well, we could locate her by the bubbles."

"No, I got a better way," Zack said, earnestly. "We'd wait till the heighth of fly time, the almighty peak of it. Then we'd tie him bare-nekkid with haywire between two trees, with the wire looped around his neck, an' a turnbuckle rove in. We'd come by when we was a mind to, an' give that turnbuckle jest a little tightenin'—"

"Till his eyes podded out!" sighed Uncle Jeff, in ecstasy.

"By God, yes—an' look: once a day we'd feed him a crust of bread."

"Buttered with—"

Sarah had approached to announce that she was dishing up, and they had better come to the table. Rising, the two assassins exchanged glances of mutual understanding. *They* knew how they would butter the warden's crust.

Sarah no longer lived in terror that they would execute their conspiracies. She had had wardens to meals many times in the last six years. Hadn't Zack talked and joked with young Tom Corn, the very warden he claimed to hate to death? Zack had made Tom a new axe handle, urged a hot mince pie on him, and helped him launch his canoe. After Tom paddled away, Zack had showed signs of being lonely for him, saying: "He's a good fellow, the son-of-a-bitch. Mighty able an' square, that young Tom Corn. He knows damn well there's moose

meat in that pie-fillin'. I hope he fly-blows, an' rots out—
but I wisht he'd come back soon."

Merely to be on the safe side, Sarah continued to pray God
to stay the murderous hands of Jeff Coongate and her husband.
She beseeched Him to reduce the percentage of Zack's swear-
ing, and to prevent his playing cribbage on Sundays. Once,
during Lenten season, Zack had gone two whole days without
smoking. Feeling that the spirit of righteousness had at last
steamed its way into him, Sarah complimented Zack for his
sacrifice. But, irritable from the itch to feel a hot pipe bowl in
his fingers, Zack had turned on her, fuming: "Lissen, ole lady:
I done it to please you, not to please God."

Before freeze-up, as the seventh winter faced them, Zack
sent Sarah back home to visit her old friends. She was gone six,
unbearable weeks. In his loneliness, Zack worked in a kind of
fury. He cut wood in the clearing, and while he chopped and
sawed, he planned surprises to gladden Sarah's return. From
the catalog he ordered a new cook stove, and a radio and battery. He laid congoleum on the kitchen floor, re-chinked the
cabin, and banked the sills with spruce boughs.

To Zack's two hound dogs, Buck and Slats, the new stove
was anathema. They couldn't quite get under it, and had to
sleep by the wood box, where it was drafty, and where, if they
happened to be smelling extra strong, Zack could reach them
with a sharpshooting toe.

When Sarah returned, just before Christmas, Zack hauled
her from Privilege over the ice on a handsled. Along with a
winter's supply of crochet needles, thread, yarn and pattern
books, Sarah had imported a small, outrageous dog. Buck and
Slats had been too boisterous for the old lady. She wanted a
comfortable pet—but no creature such as this had ever been

imagined around Mopang, much less darkened the door of Zack Bourne's cabin.

"Zack—look," Sarah asked, holding up the trifling ball of fur from which glared two impudent and conceited eyes. "Ain't she cute?"

Zack's idea of a dog was something which would run a deer to water if it took two days. Glowering at Sarah's importation, he snorted: "Huh! What you call it, old lady?"

"Rosie," she answered, stroking the creature.

"No—I mean, what kind of an *animal* is it?"

"Why you, Zack! It's a dog!"

"The hell you say. Look out it don't kick you."

"Now, you be nice to Rosie."

"Rosie," Zack growled. "God a'mighty. Rosie. Her ancestors must of been mighty casual strangers."

"Now, Zack."

Fortunately for Rosie, Buck and Slats were off somewhere —doubtless on a deer trail—when Zack had arrived drawing Sarah and her pet on the sled. Sarah's simpering attention to Rosie's welfare diluted Zack's pleasure in displaying the radio, the new stove and the congoleum. But he pointed to them, one by one, and said: "Look at that, an' that, an' that—what I done for you."

"Why, gracious goodness," cried the old lady, her eyes watering. "Just let me get my bearin's a minute. Here—you hold Rosie. Gentle now."

"You sound like a settin' hen," Zack grunted, holding Rosie at arm's length by the scruff of the neck.

"Careful! Careful!" Sarah implored.

Reluctantly Zack cuddled the degrading dog against him. Promptly and silently she bared her teeth and bit him on the thumb. Zack yowled, and snatched his hand back. The motion flipped Rosie half across the room. She lit running, and crawled under the stove, whence she peered vindictively at Zack.

"I go an' buy you all these nice things, so's you'll winter good," protested Zack, between sucks at his injured thumb, "an' what do you do for me? Bring me a dog that bites me!" Abruptly Zack's chin stuck out, and he lowered his head, to stare accusingly at Sarah. "Is Rosie housebroke?" he asked, in a foreboding voice.

Sarah backed away, uncertainly. "Well—practically—you might say—maybe."

Temporarily, in the gladness of reunion and in the goodness of a chicken supper, the old people forgot that Rosie had come between them. They talked happily together, and there was warmth, and a sense in their hearts of homecoming.

"Did you miss me, Zack?"

"Honest to God, Sarah—I like to died. Nights I'd wake up in bed an' make a glom for you, an' you wa'nt there, an' I'd lay awake prayin' for mornin', so's I could cut wood, an' make myself forget you was away."

"You prayed, Zack? *You?*"

"Sure I did."

"What'd you say in the prayer?"

" 'God damn it to hell, I wisht the old woman was here beside of me.' "

"Well," sighed Sarah, blinking at the volcanic fervor of her man, "I—I guess you meant it, anyway."

It was the unexpected return of Buck and Slats that reopened the subject of Rosie, and established her as a lasting grudge. The two hounds announced themselves by snuffling in the crack under the cabin door with a sound like a cow drinking from a near-empty pail. Rosie emerged from under the stove, and cake-walked toward the door, every hackle perpendicular.

A look of passionate, anticipatory glee illumined Zack's eyes. But Sarah seemed suddenly to have recollected that ghouls were abroad in the land.

"Don't let 'em in, Zack! Let 'em lay out a few nights!"

"Why, they jest want to befriend little Rosie," wheedled Zack, in a sugary voice. "They'll jest love her. They figure to welcome her to their home."

Zack sidled to the door, lifted the latch, and braced his foot above the sill as the hounds hurled themselves against the outside. He grinned coyly at Rosie, saying: "Nice little Rosie— wants to meet her big brothers, old Buck an' Slats, don't she? Ye-e-e-es."

Rosie responded with a soprano snarl, and Zack flung wide the door. The inrushing torrent of hounds parted around Zack's knees, and converged beyond on the spot where Rosie had lately been standing. But Rosie, her eyes popping from her skull, had risen straight into the air, like a flushed mallard. It appeared that her frantic clawing might suspend her indefinitely, but at last she came down on Buck's back. With Buck for a take-off, Rosie next came to roost on the kitchen table in the platter of fricasseed chicken, lush with gravy. Buck was with her in an instant, but Slats hit the edge of the table coming up. Falling back, his front paws tangled in the red tablecloth, and the resulting avalanche of crockery set the lamp to jiggling on its chain.

The new congoleum saved Rosie. Lighter, and more accustomed to smooth surfaces than her pursuers, she was under the stove in a twinkling. Buck and Slats, their toenails vainly scrabbling for traction, got started late and couldn't stop in time. Back-pedaling, haunches down, they both cracked their noses on the stove. From her retreat, Rosie hurled insults in a shrill, pipsqueak voice.

"Zack!" Sarah screamed, trying to make herself heard above the furor. "You see to them hounds! They'll kill Rosie!"

Zack was no longer able to control his delight, or conceal his motive in bringing the trio together. "I was just fixin' it so's they'd meet sociable," he chortled. "May I drop dead in my tracks if—"

"Zachariah Bourne! You're lyin' to me! You wanted them to *kill* Rosie!"

"No sech thing," denied Zack, choking. "Say—did you see Buck make that grab for her? His neck stretched clear'n out till I thought his head would snap off."

Quailing at the memory, Sarah lifted her apron as though to blot the scene from mind: "You're just plain brutal," she moaned.

"Now, now, old lady. Quit carryin' on."

Zack's efforts to make peace were unsuccessful. He tried for an hour to regain the lost warmth of homecoming. He pointed again to the virtues of the new stove, traced with a hopeful toe the weeping willow patterns in the congoleum. Then he turned on the radio, and looked ingratiatingly toward his wife while the static, generated by the northern lights, crackled hideously in the cabin.

"I guess, now you got that thing up here," Sarah whimpered, "it ain't goin' to work good. Least you could do is try to get some hymns—it's Sunday—case you forget."

Zack's throat knotted with melancholy. He gulped, spun the dial, and, after ten minutes manipulating, isolated a dolorous voice, singing:

> "What a friend we have in Jesus,
> All our sins and griefs to bear—"

"Well, how's that suit you?" inquired Zack, in tones which

indicated faith that all his sins and griefs would be borne by himself.

Sarah's answer was to settle on her knees and commence the work of clearing up crockery and spattered gravy. While she worked, she sniffled damply, and Zack Bourne's heart was a pain in his breast.

"My—my first husband—" Sarah mumbled, "—Mr. O'Mahoney—never treated me like this."

"You couldn't remember if he did," grunted Zack. "He's been buried forty-six years—so forget him. An' I might as well say that my *first* wife never would of brought home a miserable whelp like that Rosie."

Sarah responded with a sobbing dissertation on the beauties of city life. Zack interrupted her just once to ask: "Then why for Chris' sake don't you go back there an' stay?"

Thereafter, whenever Sarah fondled Rosie, or Zack took a passing kick at her, the gulf widened. Christmas Day in the cabin was characterized by a kind of arctic courtesy, but Zack made one wavering attempt to straighten things out. There was a half-pint of brandy he had been saving for the occasion. With guarded overtures, he got out the bottle, uncorked it, poured Sarah a small drink, and blurted: "Here. Take a shot of this, old lady."

Sarah almost melted, but memory of the panic-stricken Rosie congealed her heart. She caught herself in the act of reaching for the brandy glass, and murmured: "It only makes me dizzy."

"Then I'll save it for someone that'd 'preciate it," said Zack, pouring it back into the bottle. "Like that widow woman over to Mopang—"

The widow of Mopang was fictitious, but Sarah didn't know it. She began to read the widow into Zack's previous trips to

Mopang. This was the last straw. Their estrangement was complete, and winter setting in.

Sometimes, in bed, forgetful of their feud in the sleepy need for companionship, the old couple would draw close, each gathering warmth and comfort from the other. In the loneliness of night, they could forget. But in the cruel cold of dawn, when Zack rose in his red merinos to build the fire, he often discovered evidence that Rosie was not even partially housebroken. Whittling his cedar fire-stick, and lighting the fire, he dreamed of tying Rosie in a sack and easing her through a hole in the ice. He yearned that his heart might harden to the deed.

It troubled Zack that Buck and Slats had made their peace with this insufferable creature, this focal point of hell on earth. True, the bold hounds gave Rosie an occasional work-out, but it was not real sport for them. Rosie couldn't run in snow. She simply bogged down. They had to retrieve her out of drifts and carry her squealing to safety. To Zack's further revulsion, Rosie seemed to have taken a fancy to *him*. Lately, she had scuttled from the stove mornings and licked his cringing, up-curling toes.

"God A'mighty," whispered Zack one morning, as, unthinking, he reached down to stroke Rosie's ears. "A man can learn to stand most anything." Then, hopeful that Sarah would be awake and listening, he had roared: "G-r-r outa here, you whelp!"

Always, when ridding Rosie's messes with dustpan and ashes, Zack would mutter: "I'll never do this again, so help me. I'll get my keyhole saw, an' I'll saw right 'round it, an' jest let it drop down through. Only in a month or so, we'd have to lay a whole new floor."

That winter there was almost no travel on the lakes. The

ice buckled, and reefed badly. The snow piled in drifts, melted, slushed, froze, and melted again. Dreading sickness or accident, Sarah prayed each night, fingered her beads, and remembered the faces of priests she had known. To keep himself busy, Zack got out some maple butts in March, quartered them, and made paddles and axe handles. He recanvased all Mr. Usher's canoes, and steamed out new ribs for them wherever a blemish showed. Sarah crocheted, and nursed her plants in the row of tomato cans on the window sill. She was starving, desperate for friends, for the sound of a new voice, for the look of open water instead of the deathly waste of snow and ice. One day she finished a sampler, into which she had stitched the words: THE ROAD TO A FRIEND'S HOUSE IS NEVER LONG.

The meaning she had made rose mocking her mind. There were no roads. There were no friends. There was no world but that of stillness and of cold. Desperate, she cried out: *"Zack—!"*

Her voice cut into him, and he looked up quickly, saying: "Yuh?"

She stood up, and started toward him, pleading: "Zack— can't we be friends again? I can't stand it any longer. We won't ever see anyone again. The ice—*the ice!*—it will never go out again."

"It'll go," Zack said.

"Zack—take me back to you, oh please, oh please."

"Damn right I will—if you jest say so." He wrapped his arms hungrily around her, and patted her head with his enormous hand. While she lay sobbing against him, he whispered to her: "Honey—jest you rest easy, now. Then you tell me what you want, and I'll get it for you, if I have to go to hell after it."

"I haven't been to mass in five months. I want to go to church. I want to go to confession. I want to see people, *people!*"

"I know, old lady," Zack said, his voice thick with tenderness. "But the way the lake is, we jest can't get out. Eighteen inches of slush." He stroked her head, touched her cheek with his lips, and added from the depths of his heart: "You're gettin' wrinkled, honey."

She clung to him, as if he were an anchor for her sanity. After a long time she said: "I can't get used to it, ever, Zack. Sixty years of my life was in the city, or near it. I—I could always go to church, an' 'specially Easter, an' Holy Week."

Over her shoulder, Zack peered at the calendar, and located Easter Sunday. "Say—here's what: we'll go to Easter service right here on the radio. We'll tie into some big church —maybe Boston, or New York—we'll hear the singin', choirs an' organs an' sech as that. An'—by God, say! We'll put on Sunday clothes, so's to make it more realer, too. Only ten days to wait."

That night Zack Bourne boiled an egg for Rosie and fed it to her with a spoon; and for the next ten days he and Sarah created for themselves a new world, inventing great things out of small. Sarah constructed three pots of paper lilies with green stems, and quit drinking tea. Zack took his broad axe and hewed a cross five feet high. Sarah thought it should be red, but there was no red paint, so Zack cut some underwear into strips and wound the cross in spirals. The effect on Sarah was worth it, tenfold. She told Zack it made God seem near, and she was no longer afraid.

The day before Easter, Zack spent nearly five hours tuning in the radio, checking times and stations for the holiest and most gratifying broadcasts, and lining things up so they'd run off without a hitch.

On Easter morning, they awoke early and lit candles. Outside it was snowing. On the lake were twenty inches of black ice. As yet there had been no geese, no ducks, no robins, no forerunner of spring.

In the gloom of the blizzard, the ghastly thought formed again on old Sarah's lips: "Maybe spring will never come. Zack—would that be possible? Maybe we'll never see leaves, or open water. Maybe we'll never get outside, never see anyone or talk to anyone again, and—"

"Hush, now, honey—it's always like this, waitin' for the ice to go. You get to thinkin' you can't wait no more, but you wait just the same, and then—bang—out she goes, an' we're in a canoe, an' paddlin' down to the church in the Injun Village."

"Church—church—," murmured Sarah, making the sign of the cross over her breast. "Mary, Mother—Jesus, Savior— I'm waiting—waiting. I am an old woman, and can't wait much longer."

Zack hugged her, and rested his cheek on her hair. "Come on—let's get ourselves dolled up fit to rise from the dead. If *He* done it, we can do it."

"Zack—don't talk like that, today."

"All right. Nor I won't smoke the whole day, neither, nor swear. But hell, seems though we'd ought to have some wine to drink."

"Don't talk about things we haven't got. There's too many."

"That brandy!" said Zack, emptying the moth balls from his black suit. "It's made out of grapes, same as wine. It'll do us all right. We'll drink the whole jeesely bottle. We'll get lit up, an' dance—"

"Zack, hush."

Sarah put on her aging Easter bonnet. She dressed with great care, and at last hung the silver crucifix against her breast. Together, in the cabin on the shore of the frozen lake, the old couple kneeled before their homemade altar. Zack turned on the radio switch. They bowed their heads to the yellow eye of the dial, waiting for the tubes to warm, waiting for the sacred chants to flow into the room.

Sarah's lips moved in prayer. She closed her eyes, waiting, waiting for the music to come. It came. It came so faintly she could scarcely hear it. It swelled, then faded away altogether. Zack turned the volume full on. There was no sound but a waning hum. The battery had gone dead.

Zack was frightened. Sarah kneeled, swaying a little, beside him. He stood up and lifted her to her feet. Numbly she removed her Easter bonnet and handed it to him. He hung it on a wall peg, and said: "Don't you care now, honey. Don't let it get you, see?"

The old lady's eyes were half glazed with disappointment. Zack led her into the kitchen, sat her gently in a chair near the stove, and put Rosie in her lap. Then he went back into the front room, and closed in on the radio, holding his vengeful fist close to the dial. Baring his teeth, he hissed softly to the dead instrument: "God damn your stricken spleen an' belly, you lissen to the Easter prayer of Zack Bourne! May you rot an' fry in hell, an' explode an' burn, an' die in convulsions with a maggot in every pore. May you—*no!* Wait a minute! Take it all back!"

Starting swiftly toward the kitchen, Zack cried: "Hey! *Sarah!* Steve Ireland's got a batt'ry recharger! Steve Ireland, down to Privilege. I'll charge this jeesely thing so's you'll have the Pope right here in the cabin—"

"Zack—please," the old lady called, weakly. "It'll take you four days to get to Privilege an' back, through the woods."

"Huh, that's so," said Zack, wilting. "I never give it a thought. They wouldn't hold over for us neither."

"We can just pray for strength to wait, Zack." She looked up, smiling into his eyes, and murmured: "You—you know, you been awful sweet to your old lady."

"Well, I'd *ought* to be." He had come close to her chair, and was resuming his gruffness with great effort. "Why wouldn't a man be good to the best damn cook in the county?"

Sarah's eyes lowered. "It ain't so, an' you know it."

"Well, it *is* so. Even Rosie—she's gettin' paunchy on your grub. Look at her."

Zack leaned over, prodded Rosie, and suddenly peered closer, his eyes puzzling: "Fat—*no* sir! 'Tain't that so much. Sarah! That dog's goin' to have *pups!*"

"You don't say!" Sarah clutched Rosie to her bosom, and murmured soothingly: "My sakes, I do believe—"

Zack drew himself up and scowled at Buck and Slats who lay snoring by the wood box.

Sarah stared at the slumbering hounds with a look of mingled approval and indignation.

On the second Sunday of May, two days after the ice left the lake in a northwest gale, Sarah Bourne kneeled in the slab church in the Indian Village.

Outside on a fence rail sat Zack Bourne, gloomily holding in his fingers a series of cords, odd bits of haywire and rawhide, to each of which was attached one or more puppies about three weeks old. In all there were seven puppies, some resembling hounds, some resembling Rosie, some resembling nothing at all.

"What in hell you got there?" inquired Uncle Jeff Coongate, ranging close, and inspecting the puppies from under a perplexed brow.

"There ain't a one amongst 'em won't run a buck to water," defended Zack.

"What'll you take for the spotted one?"

"He ain't for sale."

"How about the black one with the ears?"

"Same goes for him."

"Goin' to keep 'em all to your own self?"

"It ain't that, Jeff." Zack motioned as best he could toward the church door. "It's up to my old woman. She figures them pups are hern. You can talk to her when she gets done prayin' in there."

Inside the church, as she breathed a paean of gratitude, old Sarah kneeled, and her cheeks were wet with tears.

There were so many things to worship, so many blessings for which to be thankful, that God must surely listen to her with an unusually attentive ear.

"Holy Father, I thank Thee for the springtime, for the open water and the sun, for the salmon fishermen who will come, for the people we will talk to. Oh, Father in Heaven, I beg Thee to forgive my sins, which are many. I do not deserve Thy kindness in sending out the ice at last. I do not deserve a husband as kind as Zack; and even though he has no faith, please forgive him for his sins, and let him outlive me. Father, may Mr. Usher always be pleased with Zack, and hire him every year to care for his cabins on the lake, which has been our lovely home for seven years. Let us spend our last few years together there, Father in Heaven. I am grateful to You for bringing me at last to this beautiful land which I love so dearly. Amen. Zack shot a moose last August and I ate some of it on a Friday, but I thought it was a Thursday. Forgive me, I implore You. Amen."

Weather Prophet

ONCE I CAME UP in February because I had to see how the lake country looked under snow. Steve Ireland met me at Mopang, and we started for Privilege in the pung, with a northeaster building steadily behind us. Steve yelled into his turned-up collar: "Travel eight hundred miles to spend one day in a blizzard. Jesus!"

"Maybe it'll clear."

"Doc Musgrave says it'll hold northeast for two days. He don't often miss."

Whenever Steve mentioned Dr. Delirious Musgrave, there was a note in his voice of troubled fascination. I had always wanted to meet the doctor. His personality seemed to weigh on Steve's mind. I wanted to hear Steve talk about him now, but a quickened bitterness of the storm made talk an effort.

We were crossing the wake of an old burn where the blown snow towered around us, and the wind struck sharp. When at length we came into the shelter of the spruces, the wind seemed far away. You could hear it roaring in the branches, and the snow swept down like spilled veils, but the storm was at arm's length, momentarily.

Steve lifted his chin above his collar, and said:

"He claims the day he does he'll die."

"Does what?" I asked, my wits half numbed.

"Figures wrong on the weather."

"Oh, Doc Musgrave?"

"Yuh," said Steve, resettling his chin.

We put a blanket on old Chub in the Privilege stable, fed him his oats, and floundered up the hill above the lake to Steve's cabin. It was nice inside. You could smell peeled spruce, oakum chinking and wood smoke. The wind sent the fine snow hissing against the windows, reminding us of our comfort within.

"This time of year," Steve said, as he primed the pump, "there ain't much doin', only ice fishin'."

"I don't mind. I got to dreaming about winter on the lake, and had to come and see."

"You're seein' it, all right. You better stay over a few days."

"I can't do it. I'll have to go in the morning."

I opened the bottom draft of the stove, and the fire woke up and made the chimney roar. "Maybe if the storm holds, I'll be snowbound."

"He claimed it would," Steve said. A gust rattled the stove-pipe in its guy wires, and Steve added: "Listen to that."

We ate fried salt pork, pickerel and tea. Steve inquired for all my friends he had guided. I asked about Uncle Jeff Coon-gate, Neilly Winslow, the Iron Duke and Jim Scantling. Steve said they were all smart, and let it go at that, but when I mentioned Peter Deadwater, the Indian, he perked up.

"Say! Peter's wife's goin' to have a kid."

"Honest?"

"Fact, so help me. Talk about a happy Injun."

"I thought Peter and Sadie couldn't have any kids."

"Well," Steve said, "they thought there wa'nt no hope, an' so'd everyone. They been wantin' one twelve years."

"When's the baby due?"

"Peter figures apple-blossom time. He's been poundin' ash, an' got a cradle built, an' a basket, an' a doe-skin suit with pants to it, soft as silk. It's a caution, the way that Injun works. Changed his whole character. He ain't touched a drop of lemon extrac' nor essence of pep'mint, not for five-six months. Just works, an' tends Sadie, an' lays plans for that kid."

"That's wonderful, Steve."

"It's the Lord's mercy. Let's wash the dishes."

We cleaned up, and got out the ice-fishing equipment. We were ready to start for the lake, when Steve spotted a gap in the chinking. A fine spray of snow had blasted through, building a hard white mound on the floor. Steve got a mallet and caulking iron and closed the gap with a twist of oakum. "Some storm, to find a hole that small," he said.

"Steve, didn't you say you drove Doc Musgrave's buggy for him, when you were little?"

"Yuh. We was good friends in them days."

"Aren't you now?"

"It's mighty queer, but he don't care for me now, me nor anyone at all."

A moment later we were out in the blizzard, toting our fishing gear down to the lake. I was more than ever determined to meet the doctor some day; but now his prophecy of weather was of direct concern. We chiseled our holes in the lee of Genius Island, but shelter was scant. The snow gave visible shape to the turbulence in the sky, and my forehead ached with cold.

The tip-ups were active, but we couldn't hook a trout. "They're slapping it with their tails," Steve said. "You can watch 'em do it, if you lay still over a hole."

I tried it, shading my eyes with my hands. Down there in the deep clear water, you could see the togue swimming along slowly in single file. They would bump the bait with their noses, and, as they swam by, bat it with their tails.

"Can you see 'em?" Steve asked.

He was kneeling on the opposite side of the hole, facing me. I glanced toward him, but my answer froze. Just behind Steve, and to one side of him, stood Peter Deadwater, the Indian. He was wearing snowshoes—the long, narrow Cree model for open travel. Suspended from a thong in his left hand were two lake trout of about six pounds. Steve saw my astonished expression, and turned.

"You ghost," he said to the Indian.

"No." Peter made an up-and-down motion with his free hand.

"Heard us chiseling," Steve explained to me; and the Indian grunted.

I stood up and brushed off the snow. "Hear good news, Peter," I said. "Congratulations."

Peter grunted again.

"How things with Sadie?" Steve asked.

Peter shrugged. While we took up our sets, he stood perfectly still in the exact spot where we had first seen him. Steve kept glancing at him curiously, and, when we were ready to go, said:

"Peter. You come my cabin. Get warm. Tea. Pickerel chowder."

Peter declined with a headshake and held out one of the lake trout, saying: "Namaycush."

"Come help eat," Steve said, taking the trout.

"I go home. Sadie hot. Crazy talk."

Steve looked quickly at me. "He means Sadie's sick." Then he turned to Peter. "How long Sadie hot? How long talk crazy?"

"Morning."

"This morning?"

Peter Deadwater nodded, his eyes vacant.

"She got pain some place?"

Peter touched his forehead, then put his hand down over his stomach, groaned, and stared at Steve.

"You go home. Take trout to Sadie. I get doctor. See?"

Peter moved away a few steps, turned on his long webs, and came back. "Doctor cross lake to Injun Village in storm?"

"Yes."

"Tell him open water Leadmine Point. Spring-hole. Tell him very danger spring-hole."

"I know," Steve said. "I tell him."

Peter started off, the snow blowing shoulder high around him. Ten steps and he had vanished. It was six miles, due southwest across the lake to the Indian Village. In the falling dark, even with the northeast gale full on his back, it would be a bitter journey.

Steve and I hid our tackle on Genius Island and went straight in to Privilege. I had to stop behind a shed at the public landing to get out of the wind for a minute. I thought my forehead was frozen, but it wasn't. Steve drew off a mitten and blew on his knuckles. "You're goin' to get a hell of a start," he said. "Doc Musgrave talks like he wasn't there at all."

"What? How do you mean?"

The shed trembled in a gust. In the dark you could still see the snow-shapes racing. Steve said: "Well, he don't say 'I done this,' nor 'I done that.' You'll think he's talkin' about someone else that ain't anywheres around. Once, when I was a kid, he told me why. Thought I'd forget, p'raps, but I didn't. He told me it was his other self he is talkin' about—the man he might of been, he said. But all the time it's really him, because he ain't no one else. But you got to talk to him like he was."

"Are you going to drive him across the lake tonight?"

Steve put on his mitten. "You can't work a horse on the lake. Four bad reefs in the ice between Genius Island and Caribou Rock. He'll go on snowshoes."

In the back room of Sam Lurch's barbershop in Privilege, we found Dr. Musgrave. He was a man in his early fifties. He sat on the wood box, a bottle between his knees, apparently entranced by the gleaming nickel stove-rail. The air in the room was hot and foul, but Musgrave wore a heavy sheepskin coat. The lamplight showed the birthmark which spread from his right temple over his entire right cheek to his jaw. His upward glance was too swift for me to see his eyes. With no sign of recognition for Steve, whom he had known since boyhood, he resumed his staring at the nickel rail. Steve had told me what to expect, but no warning could have prepared me for talking face to face with a man who not only dreamed he wasn't there, but demanded that others honor his unreality.

"Well," Steve said to him, "he said it would hold northeast for two days."

"Yes," said Musgrave. "He is an authority on the weather, as well as on rum, axe wounds and obstetrics."

Outside, the wind rose shrieking. You could hear the hard snow batter the walls like shot. As if at this corroboration of his prophecy, Musgrave grinned and leaned closer to the stove.

When the gust had spent itself, Steve said: "Would he cross the lake tonight to tend a sick woman in the Injun Village?"

After a long silence, Musgrave said: "He would think hard during such a trip—think himself into a stupor."

To see the man actually sitting there, yet talking of himself as if he were absent, gave me the shivers.

"He would have his coat collar up," he went on, "and his face wrapped to the eyes. He would keep the wind dead fair on his back, and—"

Steve moved toward the doctor nervously. "He would want to keep the wind heavy on his right shoulder. That would bear him inside of the open spring-hole off Leadmine Point."

Dr. Musgrave took a small drink from the bottle, replaced it between his knees, and, as if Steve had not spoken, resumed:

"—his thoughts would keep him company, and he would hum. His humming, and the cadence of his steps, would make him forget the night."

"But," said Steve, his voice rising, "he would want to keep his mind on that spring-hole. If the wind backs into the north, it would veer the doctor off course. He would walk right into *open water* in the dark."

"He stated that the wind would hold northeast," said Musgrave, complacently. "And it will."

"Even so, he'll pass within two hundred yards of the spring-hole!" Steve took a radium-dialed compass from his pocket and held it out to Musgrave in his open palm. "The snow is blowing so he won't even see his feet," he went on, his voice growing unsteady. "Wouldn't he take this?"

"Does a prophet need a compass?"

The man on the wood box seemed to ignore our presence as well as his own, and, while we humored his strange conceit, the purpose of our visit had been obscured. When I could bear the suspense no longer, I began speaking to him, unnaturally, in the third person:

"Is he equipped to take a six-months baby from the wife of Peter Deadwater? While the men discuss the weather, the Indian's woman lies out of her head with fever."

"He has performed Caesareans in this country under strange conditions," Musgrave answered, "and with strange instruments. Once he cauterized an amputation with a heated abutment spike. And he did a transfusion with the quill of a goose."

"But the Indian woman has been delirious since morning," I said. "The man with Steve Ireland thinks it may be emergency."

"Ah, yes, no doubt," replied Musgrave, blandly, "but the doctor hates cold—cold and terror, they are the same." He picked up the rum bottle and held it to the light. As near as I could judge, he had drunk half the contents. He removed the cork, took another swallow, and said: "Northeast for two days."

"Maybe the Indian's woman will die," I said, "and they are all here, talking."

"Maybe," said Musgrave, rising.

In the act of buttoning his coat collar to the throat, he turned toward us, and I saw him full face in the light. I knew why Steve Ireland both feared and pitied him. Above the doctor's straight, merciless mouth, were the eyes of a child; and I saw in these features the evidence of a man divided. You looked into his wide child's eyes, and pitied. You remembered his mouth, and shrank from him.

Steve went to him, begging: "Would the doctor please take a friend for company tonight? The friend that used to drive the buggy for him?"

"No."

Musgrave jerked his snowshoes from a peg, and kneeled to tie their lampwick lashings. Whether Steve was driven by a superstition about putting on snowshoes indoors, or by his dread that the wind would shift, I do not know. But when Musgrave stood up, Steve clutched him by the shoulders, and shook him, saying:

"If he walks into that spring-hole, *both* of him will go under the ice together—the one he is, and that other one, too!"

For an instant, as Steve backed away, the child part dominated Musgrave's face. He seemed touched that anyone should go to such lengths to warn him away from danger; and, in the only natural sentence I heard him speak, he said: "That's all right, Stevie—I'll be there in two hours."

He put on the pack which I assumed contained his instrument bag, and we followed him out into the blizzard. At the lake shore, he said: "He will go on from here alone." He hesitated for just a moment, then turned away, and walked off in the dark.

For two or three minutes after he had vanished, we stood looking out over the howling blackness of the lake. Then we turned wearily up the hill to Steve's cabin.

The warmth, the smell of broiling trout, and the leaky kettle's hiss could not remove the spell of Dr. Musgrave. Steve kept glancing at the black windows. It was as if he thought he might actually see the wind's direction.

"Steve," I said, "how wide is that spring-hole?"

"Better than a quarter-mile, when I last saw it."

After we had eaten, I lay in my bunk; but, despite my snow-burned face and eyes, there was no drowsiness. And there was none for Steve. He looked at his watch, and said: "It's thirty-eight minutes, now."

"Where would he be, about?"

"Mouth of Hardwood Cove."

Presently, as if Musgrave were with us in the cabin, we began to talk his way. To Steve Ireland, whom I had known fourteen years, I said: "The men lay in comfort wondering if the wind would change."

Steve got up, opened the door, and looked out into the whirlpools of the sky. He had to use his strength to close it, and the cold wind drove in a spray of snow and tore the ammunition-company calendar from its hook. "One of the men knows the wind is changing," he said.

"Where would he be now?"

Steve answered so quickly that I knew he was with Musgrave almost step for step: "Forty-three minutes—off Bear Trap Landing."

"They thought of how, in summer, they had paddled often across the six miles to Peter Deadwater's shack."

Steve got out his compass and set it on the table. He looked again at his watch. "The men couldn't rest good."

"No," I said. "They were thinking of the other man, counting on the wind to hold him on course, and the wind veering him toward the open water, and the Indian waiting, and his wife hot and crazy talking."

"For Chris' sake!" Steve cried. "I'm goin' outside and see for certain."

When Steve came in again, his face looked numb. His hair, powdered white with snow, made him seem prematurely old.

He went to the stove and sat on the deacon seat, his back to the warmth. He kept looking at his watch, while the snow melted, glistening in his hair.

"Well?" I asked.

"The wind's due north—changed, with never a lull to warn him."

Steve got a lumberman's blueprint map of the lake, and spread it on the bench beside him. With a pencil he drew a straight line due southwest from Privilege six miles to the Indian Village on the far shore. Along that line he marked various points, and the times he estimated it would take Musgrave to pass them, at a speed of three miles per hour. Hardwood Cove, 38 mins. Bear Trap Landing, 43 mins.

At Caribou Rock, an hour and five mins., Steve drew a gradual curve on the map. The curve bore left—southward, as the wind veered into the north. A mile south of Caribou Rock, he drew in the spring-hole off Leadmine Point. Then he looked at his watch again, and said: "Munson Reef—an hour and twelve minutes."

"My God, Steve! How many, many times we fished that spring-hole in hot weather when the trout were deep."

Steve made a dot on the penciled line which curved and then straightened toward the open water. He sat tense, his watch under his eyes, his pencil poised.

"Sometimes," Steve said, "when we was makin' calls away out somewheres away from the villages, he was mighty nice. He was kind. He would tell me to stop the buggy by a field of daisies, or hockweed. Them things made him happy. If he saw a doe deer on the lake shore, that would make him happy, too, or a loon callin'. It was the same with insects, any livin' thing, or anything that was pretty to look at. He could explain them things. I thought the world was flat, till he told me why it

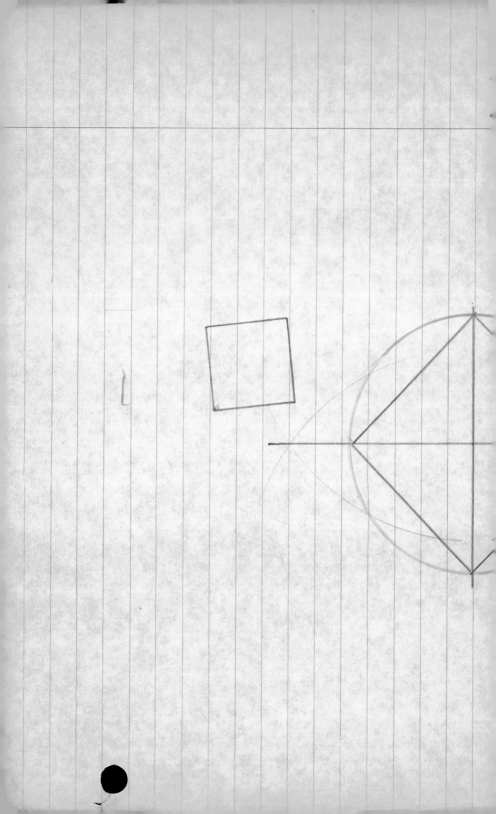

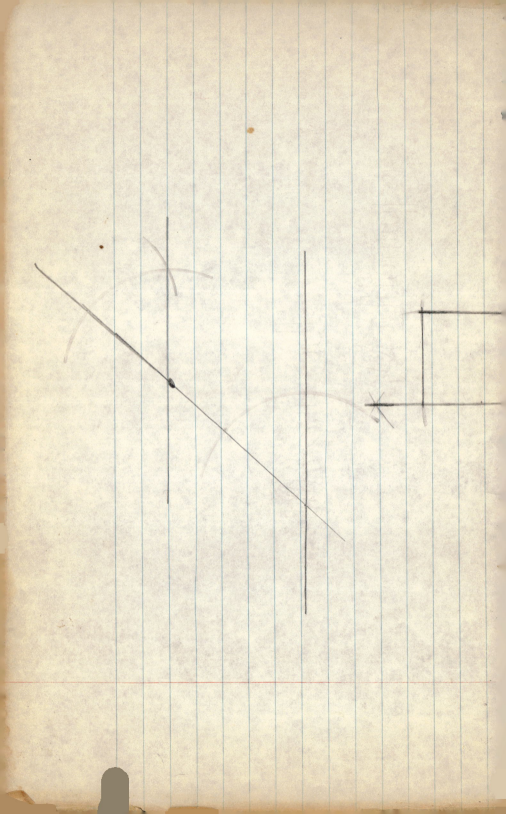

ain't. He said I was the only one he could talk to, or that could talk to him. I was eleven years old, then. . . ." Steve's pencil point touched the map, as he checked the time. "Little Mopang Bar—hour an' eighteen minutes."

"Steve! How close is he to it—now?"

"Seven minutes."

Steve brushed his hand over his damp hair, and wiped the wet palm on his thigh. "It was when I got older that he changed toward me. But I guess he thought 'twas me that changed. He wouldn't talk to me no more, nor he didn't want me 'round. He said people was no good after they stopped bein' children. But *he* was good, them times with me, when I was a boy. There wa'nt a thing he wouldn't do for people that was ailin'. But outside of for that, he wouldn't go near no one."

Steve got up from the bench, took off a stove lid and stirred the fire. A furious wind-blast drew back down the stovepipe, and the fine ash rose in the room.

"Big Mopang Bar," Steve said, "hour an' twenty-three minutes."

"That leaves him three minutes!"

"Two. . . . I wonder how Peter's woman's makin' out?"

"But he knows the lake, Steve. Maybe, when he got out there alone, with the storm, and the darkness—maybe he remembered what you said, and kept the wind heavy on his right shoulder. That would save him. He would pass Leadmine Point inside the spring-hole."

Steve looked intently at his watch. I saw his lips move, as he checked over the last minutes. Then he stopped counting. He was so quiet it was as if he had stopped breathing. After a long time he folded the map, put the watch back in his pocket, and stood up.

"Well," he said, "I liked him, just the same. It's like I was with him out there tonight, right beside him the whole way, till he drowned. Only nothin' I could do to help him, like watchin' a blind man walk off a cliff, an' your voice gone."

"Steve, I can't believe it!"

"That's 'cause you don't want to, an' I don't, neither."

Steve crossed to the table and turned down the lamp. He stood there with the dim light on his face, until I had stretched out under my blankets. "All set?" he said.

"Sure—maybe he made it all right."

"Maybe." Steve blew out the lamp and we lay in the dark, listening to the long-drawn fury of the storm.

Morning broke clear with a light north wind. Steve had the bacon frying. The cabin was warm, and bright sunlight streamed through the windows. I looked out, and saw the lake stretching white and lovely below us. That view, so peaceful now, so immaculate, made the night seem unreal.

"Steve, how do you feel this morning?"

"Frisky," he said. "That was bad last night."

Yet in Steve's voice there was uncertainty. I felt it, perhaps in his very cheerfulness. When we had eaten, and were on our way down to the stable, Steve said: "Would it trouble you if I got Jim Scantling to drive you to Mopang this mornin'? I want to cross the lake."

"No, Steve, of course not. I'd stay and go with you, if I could."

"Well, I just got an awful hankerin' to make it across," Steve explained.

Jim and Steve hooked up, and old Chub's breath blew white in the cold. We climbed to the seat, and I reached down to shake hands with Steve. "Let me know about things, will you?" I asked.

"Sure. I'll write you a letter. So-long."

I looked around once to see Steve striking off across the white-glaring lake toward the Indian Village.

Dere frend,

I seen from his drifted tracks right where it begun to change on him near Caribou Rock. I followed the curve of them until I dassent go no closer the open water, where his tracks run off I seen one of his mittens layin on the ice where he tried to claw back on but that is all so I swung back and went to the Peter Deadwater shack and the priest was there. Peter's woman was dead and the baby was dead.

Well my good frend I must close now as there is a diver comin from Eastport to dive for him and I am to lay a boom on the ice for him to work off of, but they will never find him as the currents will draw him under, as ever your frend Steve Ireland.

P.S. I told Peter how we tried to get the doctor to him and he said all right.

Owed to an Old Woodsman

NOT LONG AGO in Grand Central Station I ran into a man I used to know in the Maine woods. Neither of us had seen the other dressed in anything except moccasins, plaid shirts and dungarees, so there was a moment of mystification before we recognized each other, dropped our suitcases and shook hands.

"How's everything up around Princeton?" I asked my friend.

'Princeton' didn't refer to the university, but to the little town in Maine, where the St. Croix River flows under the town bridge below Big Lake, Lewy Lake and Long Lake.

"How's Roy Bailey?" I asked. Roy is a Maine guide.

"He's fine."

"How's Bill Sprague?"

"Bill's working at the fish hatchery in Grand Lake Stream."

"How's old Zeb Trunk?"

"Zeb? Didn't you hear? They buried old Zeb last Fall. Dammit. I've got to catch a train."

My friend looked at his watch, shook hands with me again, grabbed his suitcase and hurried away, disappearing through the gate to Track 20. That left me alone in the ghetto of Grand Central—with my thoughts hundreds of miles elsewhere, and my nostrils full of remembered woodsmoke.

So old Zeb Trunk was dead. It seemed hard to believe that his vast vitality was no more. The incomparable old woodsman with his wit and charm had been one of the joys of my life, and in memory still is. I owed Zeb Trunk a lot, and began to honor the debt by remembering. The great railroad terminal faded out and became Fifth Machias Lake, with its long scimitar of lonely beach. Zeb Trunk was with me . . . and wondrously alive . . .

The Second World War at that time was imminent, and on our Fifth Lake canoe trip, Zeb had been brooding over it for days. But as we beached our canoe and turned it over, he seemed suddenly elated, as if he had seen a sure and shining solution, or was about to write a matchless poem.

"These past days," he said, "I have been perfectin' an invention. I will prob'ly win the Nobel Prize for Peace."

Having hunted, fished and camped with Zeb for years, I considered myself immune to the bizarre surprises in his conversation. But this one caught me flat footed.

"What?" I said. "Nobel Prize? How come?"

"I would give the money to the deservin' poor," said Zeb. Although Zeb usually didn't have two dimes to his name, and had subsisted for most of his then sixty-odd years on salt pork, beans, venison and potatoes, his benevolence was in character and not to be discredited. Moreover, I had seen him one winter in the act of sharing his last spoonful of lard with two moose birds.

And now, in order to record the masterpiece that blazed within him, Zeb promptly went to work on the only canvas within forty miles. This consecrated fabric covered the bottom of our canoe, which rested on the wilderness shore of Fifth Machias Lake.

His medium, as he austerely called it, was white carpenter's chalk. He usually carried odd bits in his pockets, and a sliver of the stuff now dwindled in his nubbled and bony fingers while his old lips wrinkled in concentration.

When chalk and canoe canvas both played out, Zeb gestured onward and outward with his immense hands, thus extending his art across the beach and beyond into the forest.

"It's too great a thing," he remarked. "It can't be framed."

You could say the same about Zeb himself. In his instant of artistic glory there was grandeur about him. You forgot his frayed and stringless moccasins, his dilapidated, hand-rolled cigarette, the lame scarred knee poking through the hole in his blue jeans. In any role, in any attire, Zeb Trunk was a presence—especially now.

Standing over the canoe, he bowed his head in homage to his own handiwork.

"A masterpiece," he said. "You see before you the *Zeb Trunk World Peace Machine.*"

On the canoe bottom his scrawled design showed a vast platform mounted on tractor tires. Designed to stretch across an entire battle front, it portrayed three transverse rows of "fixtures." The first was a cocktail bar reaching for untotaled miles.

Alongside in the same row were platters labelled "moose meat," "venison," and "fried trout."

The second row consisted of league upon league of shapely maidens, each maiden fully dressed in no raiment whatever. The third row depicted nothing but beds, all invitingly turned down, and in number equal to the number of maidens in Row Two.

The basic idea was clear. Hunger and thirst are the first human drives, and love the second. Before the machine's enticements the enemy would fling aside his weapons and surge forward to partake of rum and provender. The enemy would then proceed to Row Two; and, ultimately, to Row Three, where everyone would go bye-low. The spirit of love would prevail, and wars would be nevermore.

By nature gentle and kindly, Zeb longed to believe in his engine of mercy, and almost did. But it had never been tried in battle, and, as he sensed it never would be, he was gradually crestfallen.

"It can't fail," he said, forlornly. "It jest *can't!*"

"You haven't got any motor in it," I said. "What are you going to use for power?"

Zeb looked at me as if I had spoiled his life, and said:

"Hot air. You can ride free."

The character, personality and supreme invention of this old woodsman brought merriment to innumerable wilderness journeys. He stood six feet and two inches tall, his knees and elbows both a little bent. His hands were as wide as a sleeper axe, the fingers curled as though stiffened around a peavey handle or canoe pole. He walked with a kind of wary ease, somehow resembling a heron stepping along a wet log, lifting his feet carefully and setting them down as lightly as if he suspected traps set all around under the leaves. He had gray eyes, sometimes sad, more often glad in their expression—and his brows were so bushy he claimed to be in constant fear that cranes would nest in them.

But Zeb's chief characteristic was his love of elaboration. He could, and did, invent fantastically devious ways of solving problems or overcoming obstacles. But far beyond that, this talented old man often invented the obstacles themselves for the sheer drama of overcoming them—by elaborate means.

For examples, there are The Killing of Rip Skillinger's Little Dog, The Great Whiskey Drinking Problem, and The Case of the Un-poached salmon.

At the time these incidents were conspired—or contrived —Zeb Trunk was employed by a small lumber company to maintain a remote depot camp on Scraggly Lake. He lived there with his wife, Effie, whom he adored and loved to plague —so that afterwards he could comfort her.

The story of the disposal of Rip Skillinger's injured dog really begins on a summer morning when Zeb was rigging up for the long trip out to town in the boat. He sat hunched over the table in the cabin kitchen making out his list of supplies to bring back, the stub of pencil a puny and contemptible instrument in his axeman's hand.

"Presint for Effie," he wrote. He licked the pencil and wrote painfully on, fretting out the words with his lips.

"bunk chain, allspice, files, lemon extrack, needles, dannamite, onions, presint for Effie, gasoline, buttons, whetstone, raisins, abutment spikes, fly dope, stove bolts, presint for Effie."

The one thing he would never forget he'd written three times on the list—and he headed uplake in the boat and had disappeared around Genius Island before I noticed the list still lying on the kitchen table.

"He forgot it!" I said to Effie.

"He often does," Effie said.

Zeb got back about four that afternoon. I went down to the dock to help him unload. I mentioned the forgotten list.

"Never mind," he said. "I got the essentials."

The essentials consisted of dry beans, salt pork, and a pair of nylons and a bottle of lilac perfume for Effie. Through the years, Zeb must have duplicated these items a dozen times. The back store room and Effie's bedroom closet were always supplied with dry beans, salt pork, nylons and lilac perfume, the thirty-cent size.

But this time there were two extra items—a fifth of rum, more than slightly used, and a little brown puppy with an injured leg. Effie, who had come down to the dock, looked anxiously at the bottle and the puppy.

"Zeb," she said, "you been drinkin' that rum. Don't drink any more."

"I *got* to," said Zeb.

"Why?"

" 'Cause I promised myself I would. I says: 'Zeb, I'll give you jest one more swallow.' Do you want me to be *dishonest,* honey? Want me to break my *promise?*"

He sat on the forward deck of the boat, the bottle in one hand, the little dog cradled in the other, while he gave a memorable address on man's obligation to keep his word. Poor Effie was so confused she didn't really notice the puppy till it uttered a whimper.

"Zeb Trunk! What you goin' to do with that dog?"

"I'm goin' to kill him."

As Zeb explained, you'd have thought his chief joy in life was assassinating small, defenseless creatures.

"Rip Skillinger," he said, "run over this here dog with a single hoss hay rack an' hurt its leg. Rip didn't have the courage to dispose of the pup himself, so I'm goin' to do it."

"How you goin' to do it?" Effie asked.

"I may decide to poison him."

We walked up to the cabin kitchen, Zeb whistling happily, the pup nested in the crook of his elbow.

"No," said Zeb, eyeing his Winchester on the wall pegs, "I guess I'll shoot him."

Then he bent his head and spoke directly to the brown, limp bit of fur.

"You'll never know what struck you, li'l feller. That .45-70 bullit'll tear your li'l head clear'n off your neck. Jest you wait an' see."

"*When* you goin' to do it?" cried Effie, twisting the hem of her apron in her hands.

"Right now," said Zeb. He took the big rifle off the pegs— and put it back again.

"Tomorrow," he said, "before breakfast."

True to his word, Zeb stalked off across the clearing into the woods in the early morning, the rifle and a shovel over his shoulder, and the little dog under his arm. He walked gaily, an eager tune on his lips.

Five minutes later Effie and I heard the blast of the rifle.

"It's all over," I said, and Effie began to cry.

While I was trying to soothe her, Zeb came in through the kitchen door, the dog still under his arm, alive and friendly.

"Missed him," said Zeb, and sat down to breakfast. "I've decided to drown him, anyway—soon's I finish eatin'."

"Drown him?" said Effie, horrified.

"Yes, honey. Pass the sugar, please."

Effie never touched her breakfast, and my stomach felt as if I'd swallowed a flat iron.

"Ed," said Zeb, pushing back his plate, "you get a paper carton an' put some rocks in it, so's it'll sink. I'll bring the dog —Zip, his name is. Come, Zippy, Zippy, Zippy."

I got a carton, put some stones in it and walked away. I didn't have enough heart left to see the pup into the box. Zeb did that, and then called merrily from the back shed.

"Come on, Ed—you paddle the canoe whilst I throw Zippy to the eels. You weighted the box good. He'll go right to bottom."

In the deeps off Loon Point, Zeb eased the carton into the dark waters. In the ripple of morning it rode high and dancey, and an eager yelp came from inside it. Not till moments later did I realize that Zeb had removed the stones and, in the back shed, substituted a kapok life preserver, or enough to float ten Zippys. Zeb had concluded his drama, and now—with tears in his eyes—he retrieved the carton and drew forth the puppy, and in deep emotion they sniffed each other's noses.

"Paddle me back, quick," he said. "I got to tell Effie I never intended to do away with Zippy. Why, him an' me loved each other from the first."

So there was rejoicing on Scraggly Lake, and we spent the rest of the morning making a cedar splint for Zip's leg. In a week he was as good as new. Zeb Trunk had acquired a dog, and it was for keeps in both their hearts.

"All that time you wasted," Effie said to Zeb, "you could of built me that ship's model you promised me."

"No, honey. You don't understand about them things. A man's got to be in the mood to create a work of art like a ship model."

"But it's been years! And the mood ain't come to you."

"It'll come," said Zeb, mysteriously.

The Great Whiskey Drinking Problem was solved by Zeb one winter I came up for the ice fishing. But the weather was so merciless we stuck pretty close to the cabin stove. Time dragged, till Zeb got interested in the bottle of whiskey in the medicine cabinet, and plans began forming in his illumined mind.

One morning he took down the bottle, set it on the kitchen table, and stared at it.

"Zeb," Effie said, "don't you touch that whiskey."

"I'm jest touchin' the bottle," said Zeb.

"Well—that's close enough."

"Honey," he said, "there may come a day when you'll *ask* Ed an' me to drink that whiskey. Why, doggonnit—you'll beg an' *beseech* us to!"

The idea was so outrageous I just laughed. Effie Trunk had never begged anyone to drink whiskey anywhere—especially her unruly husband.

But now that Zeb had stirred up anxiety in Effie and curiosity in both of us, he was happy. He spent hours reading a mail order catalog and humming mysteriously. At appropriately timed intervals, he would take the whiskey bottle out of the medicine cabinet, shake it, swallow with a dry, rustling sound like sand sliding off a shovel, and then replace the bottle.

The day the Fish & Game Commission airplane came in on skis, Zeb wrote out a mail order, placed it in the addressed envelope, and licked on a stamp. The pilot stayed for dinner, after which Zeb gave him the envelope, and he flew away to the land of Post Offices.

"Zeb," said the exasperated Effie. "What's goin' on?"

"Nothin'," said Zeb. "That's the trouble. Nothin' to do."

"Nothin' to do!" Effie said. "Then why don't you make me that ship model you said you'd make—if the mood come on you."

"Ship model?" said Zeb, as if he'd never heard of one. And then: "Oh, sure, I remember. But the mood ain't come yet."

He glanced forlornly at the medicine cabinet, and added: "Maybe, if I was to take jest a small taste of—"

"No, Zeb! No!"

There came a cold morning about a week later when Zeb announced that he was going out through the woods for mail.

"It's time my order is back from Sears Roebuck," he said.

He wound his gold watch with the fob as big as an anchor, buttoned his mackinaw, and kissed Effie. Outside the cabin door he tied on his snowshoes and swung off across the back clearing toward the woods, while Zip trotted behind in his snowshoe beat.

The roundtrip to the settlement, overland, was twenty-two miles. I marvelled at old Zeb's stamina and fortitude. Effie and I didn't begin to worry about him till a cold rain began falling in the afternoon. It turned into an ice storm, and a crust formed on the snow—tough conditions for snowshoes, especially without creepers.

"A tree might fall on him," Effie said.

"He'll be all right."

"He'll be so tired, an' his old face so long, an' sad. He's not as strong as he was. He jest thinks he is. Oh, dear."

It came dark, then black dark—and no Zeb. Effie kept watching the ancient clock, and it tick-tocked like footsteps in a haunted house. Outside, the wind was murder.

About eight o'clock we heard a scratching at the door, and I jumped and opened it. Zip was out there—alone! That's

when I got scared. I lit a lantern, put on my parka and
started out through the door—and then we heard Zeb's call.
A minute later he was in the kitchen, both cheeks frostbitten,
but a gleam of triumph shining through the exhaustion in his
eyes.

He had broken a snowshoe bow in from Hub Hall Cove
and had come from there—three miles—falling through the
crust, sometimes crawling on hands and knees. His huge, kind
hands were bleeding, his wrists raw. But he had made it home
through the wilderness—home, to comfort his Effie; and as he
sank down on the bench by the stove, he fumbled in his knapsack while Zip—old Zip, now—licked at his bloody hands.

"Here it is," he said, his voice far away and tired, "your
ship model, Effie. The kit come from the mail order people."

I bent close for a look. Sure enough, it was the three-master
number, complete with a delicate pair of tweezers for setting it
up.

"See, Effie?" Zeb said, his gaze wandering to the medicine
cabinet. "The directions calls for a quart bottle to set up the
model inside of. So we *got* to drink that whiskey. See?"

Effie was so happy and relieved to have him home alive
that she got the bottle down herself.

"Now," said Zeb, "I'm goin' to drink till my eyes look like
a dynamited salmon's."

But he didn't. He took one swallow, and the warmth from
the stove and the comfort of the kitchen stole through him. His
head nodded. His eyelids dropped, then lifted. Just before he
fell asleep, his hands groped once more in his knapsack, came
up with a small, familiar vial. He held it toward Effie, and
said:

"Jest you sniff this, honey—it's lilac perfume. The *fifty*
cent size. For you."

When, a few springs ago, Effie died, a great loneliness fell on Zeb. He told me how he used to pace the cabin floor, and go out around the clearing with Zip at his heels; how he couldn't sleep. He knew he couldn't bear to stay on at the remote depot camp much longer, but he liked his boss and didn't have the heart to quit. So, characteristically, he evolved an elaborate plan to get himself arrested by Jim Birch, the game warden, and thrown into jail.

"That way," Zeb said, "my boss would have to get a new man. And I'd be in jail thirty days in the cold time of spring. It would be warm, and I'd have nice meals, an' company to talk to."

So Zeb went out to the village and laid down a bunt rumor that he was going to catch salmon in a pool on Mink River that had been closed for years.

"Jim Birch would hear of my brag," Zeb said, "an' sooner or later he'd show up at Mink River, an' there I'd be—with a couple of them nice big salmon beside me on the ledges."

So that's exactly what happened—but with a strange result.

Zeb sat hunkered on the ledges over a little fire. He had two good salmon lying on some spruce boughs beside him, and a tea can warming over the fire, when young Jim Birch stepped out.

"Any luck, Zeb?" said Jim.

Zeb machined a look of surprise, guilt and consternation. He made as though to conceal the salmon. Then said:

"You got me, Jim—dead to rights. Them two salmon was caught, by me, in this pool. I'll come quiet, Jim. I'll go right down to jail with you."

"What for, Zeb?"

"Why, for poachin'. I can't pay the fine. It's a hundrid dollars."

"It *was*, Zeb—but no more. The commission opened this pool to fishing this spring. Just a few days ago, in fact."

"What?"

Jim repeated himself.

"But," said Zeb, "I got no fishin' license. You'll have to arrest me for that, Jim. It's your duty."

"Sorry, Zeb. You're a free man. You're over seventy. That means you don't need a license."

So old Zeb fought his loneliness till fall, when he was replaced at the depot camp by a younger couple. He spent his last years tending the schoolhouse in the village, and the kids worshipped him, so I heard. It couldn't have been otherwise. I heard he made them wonderful ship models. And that couldn't have been otherwise.

I think the story of old Zeb's death is also true. I heard it straight from the friend I met that day not long ago in Grand Central Station. Over the telephone my friend said that *he* had heard it straight from one of the cracker barrel bunch in Splinter Martin's store in the village down below Scraggly Lake. Maybe it's dressed up with legend, but if so, from the legend Zeb Trunk emerges as I knew him. Anyway, this is the way I heard it:

On the last hunting season of his life, Zeb had gone into an old wood chopping on Township Five. Johnny Harkness, a young guide was in there, too, with a sportsman from Bangor. They heard the roar of a heavy rifle.

"That sounds like a .45-70," Johnny said to his sport— and they went over slowly toward the place where the shot had come from.

Old Zeb was sitting on the ground with his back propped

against a big spruce blowdown. A few yards away, lying across a boulder, was the nine point buck he'd just shot.

Johnny Harkness, the young guide, looked from the buck back to Zeb, and he knew something was wrong. Zeb's rifle was sliding along slowly out of his lap onto the moss.

"Hello, Johnny," Zeb said, and his voice sounded far off. "Put my tag on that buck, will you, son?"

"Sure, Zeb," said Johnny.

And then Zeb said: "I ain't goin' to need that deer, Johnny. You take it, an' give it to the deservin' poor."

Those were the last words of the old woodsman whom I had once observed sharing his last spoonful of lard with a couple of moose birds.

Part Two

MEAT, FISH AND POTATOES

Jake's Rangers vs. Spring Fever

AS A SPRIGHTLY EPIC of Spring Fever, its contagion, witchery, horse power and high jinks, I offer herewith the case history of Jake's Rangers, of Damariscotta, Maine, and the handful of magic pine shavings which lured us, one and all, through the core of New England's last wilderness in quest of trout. The enchanted expedition took place during an unforgettable week in May, 1958. But before it ever got off the launching pad, many strange things came to pass.

At the outset, I must explain that Jake's Rangers are a group of seven, normally sane, business and professional men. Our roster includes Damariscotta's postmaster, its veterinary surgeon, a leading physician, grocer, artist, and insurance man. A non-military and non-belligerent organization, we are called "rangers" only because we range far and wide throughout our home state in search of trout and the blue horizon.

Dedicated to the outdoors, open water and fishing, I suspect we are representative of sportsmen groups in small towns all across our land. We have no bylaws, no regular meetings, no dues, and no headquarters unless you count Perley Waltz's drugstore on Main Street, or the Post Office next door. Our claim to distinction is our leader, the man for whom the Rangers are named. He is Maurice "Jake" Day, artist, naturalist, long-time explorer of Maine's wilderness region—and shrewd alchemist of the Rites of Spring.

In 1958, it seemed to us that Spring was deliberately avoiding Maine. Just when you were about to inventory your trout flies, or paint your canoe, another blizzard wrecked your dream. Six or seven of them pasted us in March. The most detested object in town was the snow shovel. Jokes about the weather wore out and fell flat, and by late March the morale of Jake's Rangers hit a deplorable, all-time low.

But, unbeknownst to the rest of us, Jake himself had taken on the task of reviving our hope of Spring and sun-warmed brook banks. Secretly and single-handedly, he had been at work on this problem through many consecutive snowstorms.

The first inkling I had that Jake was making Medicine came one dismal, ice-gray morning when I walked into Perley Waltz's drugstore for coffee. Three of the Rangers were already entrenched at the marble counter—Dr. Sam Belknap; Eddie Pierce, whose Yellow Front Grocery is a Damariscotta landmark; and Jack Glidden, our insurance man. They were talking with an animation long subdued. Dr. Sam and Eddie wore wide smiles, while Jack Glidden was laughing right out loud—a sound I hadn't heard since the Winter Solstice.

"What right have you guys got to be happy?" I asked. "Don't you know it's snowing again?"

They exchanged secretive glances, and immediately clammed up. After a moment, Dr. Sam said:

"Stop at Jake's on your way home."

"What gives?"

"Obey orders, and you'll find out," said Jack.

I left them and went into the Post Office, next door. Dr. McClure Day, our veterinary surgeon and Jake's son, was in the act of plucking his mail from his box. He held up a fishing tackle catalog he'd just received, waved it like a banner, and said:

"Hurray!"

"Hurray for what?" I asked. "Who do you think is going fishing?"

"You are," said Mac, mysteriously; and went out into the snow.

I stepped up to the mail window. Behind it showed the round, merry face of Bentley Glidden. Bentley, Jack's younger brother, is Damariscotta's postmaster. He seemed to be shining like a portly, human sun as he slid my mail under the wicket. My mail consisted solely of a seed catalog.

"That's a personal affront," I said. "I refuse to accept it."

"It's for your wife, not you," said Bent, gayly. "And there's two cents postage due. Drop in at Jake's on your way home."

Jake Day's house, up near the Baptist Church, is one of those solid, four-square, white colonials. Mellow with age, it was built by Jake's great-grandfather, and the door has seldom been locked in a hundred-and-sixty-one years.

I let myself in, scowled at the snowshoes stacked in the front entry, and went up the stairway to Jake's studio. It isn't the kind of artist's studio you read about. No skylights, plate glass or folderol. It's just a big, cluttered, upstairs, corner room. Nor does Jake himself resemble the standard concept of an artist. He doesn't wear sandals. He wears moccasins. His smock is an old flannel shirt, and instead of a beret his head is adorned with a vagabond felt hat, abused by countless rains and suns, its band a beat-up leather strap.

At sixty-seven, Jake is lean, wirey, and feather-light on his feet. On mountain fishing trips, he can walk the ankles off his Rangers, all of whom—except me—are his juniors by about thirty years. This gifted man has the spirit of youth, and the genius for embellishing life. Perhaps they are the same. Both seemed to beam from his deep-set, hazel eyes as he met me at the doorway of his studio, a corncob pipe between his teeth.

"There was an emergency meeting of the Rangers last night," he said, removing the corncob. "We tried to reach you."

"I was in Portland," I said. "What happened? The boys appear to be strolling in green pastures."

By way of answer, Jake stepped aside from his doorway; and—with a magician's gesture—waved me into the room. Suddenly, to all intents and purposes, I found myself in the wilds of Maine's immense, Baxter State Park in the green benediction of Spring. The impact, and the scene itself, in contrast with the bleak reality of the March day, are indescribable. But I'll try.

Flanking me on either side of the room were twenty or more of Jake's wonderfully realistic watercolors of the unpeopled Katahdin wilderness we loved and knew so well. Some were from his old portfolios and sketch books. Others he had painted for the occasion. They haunted me with ghosts of old campfires and inspired the promise of new ones. I saw Russell Pond under a blue sky, a pair of woodduck near shore. I saw

South Branch Pond, its fringe of birches misted with green. There was a lone canoeman on Wassataquoik Lake; and Traveller Mountain; and an old, black bear and her cub on Pinnacle Ridge. Trout were rising in Six Pond, a kingfisher riding on a cedar frond; and there was a tiny, flickering campfire with its smoke skeining through the spruces. You could smell it! The total effect was uncanny—as if Jake somehow had been working hand-in-glove with the Vernal Equinox.

I had seen many Springs in this wild country—but never a one without being there, till now. No one but Jake Day would ever have dreamed of such a mystic spread, let alone possess the talent to execute it.

"Jake," I said, "you've broken up a hard winter with a paint brush. I shall go home and burn my snow shovel."

"Wait!"

Jake stepped to an easel which stood between the two aisles of paintings. The easel was veiled—with the cover of an old sleeping bag. Sweeping this cogent shield to one side, Jake disclosed the Katahdin and Traveller Mountain quadrangles of the U.S. Geological Survey. He had mounted the maps on cardboard, and in red pencil scored the seventeen-mile foot trail which traverses the wildest part of Baxter State Park, from Roaring Brook Campground at the southern border, to South Branch Ponds Campground near the northern extremity. About midway of this trail, in the heart of the park, and accessible only on foot, is Russell Pond Campground. This mountain solitude, in Jake's lettering, was tagged:

"Base Camp, Jake's Rangers, Spring, 1958!"

"Does this mean we're going to fish those hidden ponds this year—at long last?"

"It does. Take-off day is May eighteenth."

"How are we going to sustain life, till then?"

From his shirt pocket, Jake ceremoniously removed a small cardboard box. He rubbed the box lovingly, which somehow made it resemble Pandora's—or maybe Aladdin's Lamp.

"I have here," he said, "life-giving medicine—the smelling salts of the wilderness."

He opened the box and held it under my nose, and the scent of clean, sun-dried pine pervaded me. Resinous, pungent, supreme. It seemed to put a kind of hex on me. I thought I heard the song of a White Throat Sparrow proclaiming life from a spruce top, a loon calling from a sequestered dead-water. Wind seemed to whisper in young leaves, and the full trance and heartache of Spring were upon me.

"Jake!" I said. "This is alchemy."

"No," he said, tapping his Pandora's box, "it's just a handful of pine shavings. I whittled them from that old stump above Trout Brook Crossing in the park last Fall. I've been sniffing them for weeks. I call them 'Old Doctor Jake's Golden Spring Medical Discovery.' "

What with his wilderness watercolors, his maps, and his siren pine shavings, Jake had deliberately created the worst case of Spring Fever since the Song of Solomon. The Rangers —including Jake himself—were smitten to the point of frenzy. And in April, when wild geese, green grass and lilac buds began to show, we had reached a state of euphoria. We could talk, think, or dream of nothing but May 18th and our expedition.

The rigors of the trail to Russell Pond were reduced to ashes in the fires of anticipation. The inner core of the park is a hundred square miles of jumbled peaks, ravines, glacial boulders, forests, ruffian watercourses—and isolated ponds, many of them rarely fished, a few of them *never!*

Only two of the Rangers had experienced this rugged terrain in Spring; but in our zeal for a try at the far-back ponds we forgot the facts of life on a hard trail and all fell into The Old Map Trap, or The Pitfall of the Contours. The trail looked easy—on paper. We simply levelled off the mountains. The congested contour lines were nice, artistic arrangements of brown curves. The streams we would have to cross were innocuous ribbons of blue. Trout seemed to be breaking up through the surface of the paper. We had breathed the giddy incense of Old Doctor Jake's Golden Spring Medical Discovery, and were all infected with invincibility and lightheadedness.

Whenever two Rangers met, even in the middle of Main Street, we would snap to attention and salute. On some occasions traffic was obstructed. Bob Turner, the town cop, threatened to lock a couple of us in the pokey as an example to the young. The saluting, prompted by Bentley Glidden, was but one manifestation of Spring Fever's lunacy and the perfume of the pine shavings.

On the back of his pack, as a challenge to the Russell Pond Trail, Bentley stencilled the words: U.S. DOMESTIC AIR MAIL. Jack, during his day's travels, stopped at any convenient field or bit of open water and practiced fly casting. Jake and Mac drew up the trip's supply list and submitted it one evening to the full roster of Rangers at Dr. Sam's house. This meeting was called a "Survival Seminar." The supply list was as lovely as a sonnet. Not a single item had been forgotten—except dry matches and salt. For this crucial oversight, we reduced Jake in rank. But we acclaimed him full Colonel the next morning, shortly after Bentley handed him a letter from Mr. Helon Taylor, who is Supervisor of Baxter State Park, and a long-time friend of Jake's.

Unbeknownst to the rest of us, Jake had written Mr. Taylor of our expedition. And Mr. Taylor was intensely interested. He was eager for a report on the park's remote trout fishing. There had never been one, a fact which would make our survey the first. The Supervisor concluded by saying that he had personally invoked Pamola, the legendary Indian god of the Katahdin wilderness, to watch over us. Our trip was now not only blessed by high authority, but by legend as well.

And all this was climaxed by a second letter. Addressed to Jake and me, this letter simply wished us godspeed, good fishing, and fine weather. It was signed by no other than the Honorable Percival P. Baxter, Mr. Maine himself—the man who, singlehanded, bought and gave Baxter State Park's two hundred thousand acres and fifty mountains peaks, to us and all men, "to be forever held . . . forever left in its natural, wild state."

The cheers, boasting and self-esteem inspired by these gilt-edged documents can't be imagined. It has to be endured; and it was endured by the citizens of Damariscotta, and by the seven, long-suffering wives of Jake's Rangers.

Perley Waltz, after threatening to bar us from his coffee counter, said:

"Why don't you characters buy something—or else pay rent?"

Skip Freeman, presiding behind the fishing tackle counter at Wickstrom & French's Hardware, was even more forthright. Skip said:

"Hurry up and get the hell out of town."

With equal vehemence—and in many cases verbatim— Skip's sentiment was echoed by the wives of the Rangers. The wives had had enough of palaver, of houses strewn with fishing gear and apparel, of forsaken children asking, "Why is Daddy going to another Rangers' meeting?"

In their homes, at night, some of the more earnest Rangers

had taken to sleeping in their sleeping bags for practice. This form of training was finally outlawed by their wives as being irrelevant, uncomfortable and unfriendly.

On May eighth, Jack Glidden started the count-down to our take-off day by yelling "TEN!" at the top of his lungs, right on the Main Street sidewalk. It startled the seagulls from their perch on the ridge pole of the Gay Block. Rangers within hearing took up the cry, as did many sympathetic bystanders. Thereafter, any morning at coffee time, you could hear the current count-down resounding anywhere from a point near the town library clear down to the Newcastle Bridge: "Nine!". . . . "Eight!". . . . "Seven!". . . .

Suspense mounted daily. Sleep, fitful at best, was disturbed by dreams of fishing the mysterious waters of our destination. The substance of these dreams was unwittingly, but publicly recorded by Eddie Pierce on the morning of the six-count. While chalking the day's offerings on the big front windows of his grocery store, Eddie somehow went adrift—and between a bargain in soap powders and another in ready-mix flour, he marked up this eye-catching, Special Sale item:

TROUT 59¢ a Peck

Eager purchasers filed into Eddie's store, and filed out again in disappointment when Eddie, re-orienting himself, explained that he had meant "potatoes."

Our revered and venerable leader, Jake, severely stricken by his own alchemy, went into Don & Bob's Barber Shop on the afternoon of count-down four, and, half-an-hour later, emerged —with a *crew cut!* His first hair-do of this dashing type since his army hitch at the Mexican border.

That same afternoon, Dr. Sam's charming wife, Lucy, sailed in to the drugstore and asked to buy some camera film.

Didn't she know, asked Perley, that her husband had already purchased a large supply? Lucy knew all about it. It was Sam's afternoon off, and the Belknap children were all scrubbed and dressed to be photographed by their father. But the films were packed for the Rangers' trip.

"Why don't you unpack them?" asked Perley.

"I can't. Sam's mowing the lawn."

"What's that got to do with it?"

"The pack is on his *back!*"

It was a fact. Dr. Sam, with his full pack—and a pedometer affixed to his belt—was mowing his spacious lawn as a kind of dry run for the Russell Pond Trail. At the conclusion of this training exercise, the pedometer registered slightly more than five miles. Sam, who had stood up well under the effort, was now confident and ready to face the real thing.

Count-down, "ONE!" Late Saturday afternoon, with take-off coming early Sunday morning, all seven Rangers gathered in the alley back of Eddie Pierce's store for the ceremony of loading the packed supplies into my station wagon.

Dr. Sam and Dr. Mac had arranged with colleagues to care for their patients, both human and animal, beginning tomorrow. Freedom was at hand, and the car-loading proceeding jubilantly, when a tall, sorrowful man appeared in the alley, and said:

"Is Dr. McClure Day here?"

Mac's face fell a mile. A serious emergency involving horse, cow, or dog, would scratch him from the trip. To judge by the sadness in the stranger's face, this was it.

"What can I do for you?" said Mac, balancing a carton of flour and bacon on the wagon's tail gate.

"My white cat, Snuggles," said the man, "has got mats in her fur—and she won't let me cut them out."

Mac looked at the man with infinite relief, gratitude and mercy. He said:

"You bring Snuggles to my office before eight o'clock tonight, because tomorrow, I'm going to be hard to find."

Next morning, in deceptively beautiful weather, we were on our way, rolling up the seacoast, then swinging northwestward, inland, to Maine's mountain region. That afternoon, with two hundred miles behind us, we entered Baxter State Park and halted for the night at the bunkhouse at Roaring Brook Campground. We stood fair in the shadow of the great, gaunt mountain, Katahdin—majestic, lonely, its ravines and higher elevations wearing the white scars of snow.

In the camp clearing, a sign said:

RUSSELL POND CAMPGROUND 7 MILES

"That means us," said Jake.

He pointed to the wilderness stretching to the north, then to the log bridge which spanned Roaring Brook.

"The trail," he said, "starts right there at the bridge."

There it was. The trail. We were looking at it. Anticipation was over. Realization was at hand. But "reality" is the truer word. On the bunkhouse roof that night, came the deafening drumfire of rain—an all-night, four-alarm downpour. In the morning, Roaring Brook was in flood, and our bridge had vanished. First baptism in ice water occurred right there and then. Soaked to the waist, chilled to the marrow, but with spirits never so high, we were feeling with the soles of our feet the trail we had been dreaming about for six weeks.

Some trail!

Less than a mile, and snowdrifts loomed. Blowdowns barred the way. Laughter and bright banter tapered away to silence. You heard only the tinkle of the tin cup suspended from Jack Glidden's belt; the scuff of boots on rock; a groan as someone made a misstep or sank to the hips in a ridge of snow; and always the pounding of your own heart.

Shoulders lunged into packstraps on a steep ascent. Sweat trickled. Breath steamed. The pace slowed, and steadied for the long pull. This was the shakedown of Jake's Rangers on the Russell Pond Trail. Not a Ranger will ever forget that seven-mile trek.

In August, it's an easy two hours or so. In an ordinary Spring, you'd make it in three. But in the Spring of '58, with three-foot drifts, blowdowns, bridges washed away and rivers in flood, it was seven-and-one-half hours of heartbreak and hazard.

Eddie Pierce went in all over fording the iced rapids of the South Branch of Wassataquoik Stream. On the Main Wassataquoik crossing, we thought Bentley was a goner. Bent stumbled, plunged through the last ten yards of whitewater, finally made land with helping hands yanking him ashore. Each crossing was a point of no return. You wouldn't dare cross back again. You couldn't. So you went on.

If the trek is unforgettable for its bone-wearying, all-out effort, it is even more so for the sweet, last turn in the trail, and the triumphant, heart-lifting moment of stepping into the clearing at the Russell Pond Campground. There were the log leantos; the log cabin bunkhouse; the encircling mountains; the blue, sunlit expanse of Russell Pond—and trout breaking the surface. And, above all, the solitude.

"I'm dreaming," said Jack Glidden, dropping his pack. "Don't wake me."

Merle Scott, the big, able, redheaded Park Ranger came from his cabin to greet us. Merle had been in there alone for two weeks. He said he was gladder to see us than we were to see him.

"We have just heard the misstatement of the year," said Mac Day.

It was Bentley Glidden who summed up both the trail's anguish and the sense of rest and achievement that now pervaded us. Bent had his boots and socks off and was gazing in open wonder at his bare feet. He wiggled his chubby toes. Admiration mounted in his eyes as he reckoned up what his pinkies had just been through. In an awed voice, he said:

"They ought to be buried in Westminster Abbey."

In the isolated ponds of Baxter Park, the best time for trout, if not for men, is mid-May, through June. In all ponds the limit is five fish per day. The trout are exclusively *salvelinus fontinalis,* variously called brook trout, speckled trout, natives, or squaretails. These inner waters have never been stocked. Neither the trout you catch, nor their ancestors, ever heard of a hatchery or rearing pool. Their color is sunset-brilliant, their flesh pink and firm, their flavor matchless.

The fishing began that afternoon right at Russell Pond after a rum ration and an hour's rest for all hands. We fished from canoes, which you can rent at Russell. No one carried those canoes over the trail. They were flown in on the pontoons of bush pilot Elmer Wilson's "Jet Cub" airplane.

Eddie Pierce scored first with a beautifully-colored fourteen-incher. In that first hour's fishing, the Rangers caught and released thirty-two trout. We kept a dozen more ranging in size from eight inches up to Eddie's fourteen-incher. They came to standard flies, and to gold-bodied spinning lures, and they were strong and jet-propelled.

A large moose wandered out of the forest and stepped into the pond to view proceedings. He seemed to take a special liking to Mac Day, wading in a leisurely manner toward the veterinarian's canoe.

"My office is closed, fellah," said Mac to the creature. "Snuggles was my last case. But I'll take your photograph."

Mac did. So did Eddie, Jake, and Dr. Sam.

At sunset we gathered in the bunkhouse and started a fire in the stove. When the cabin warmed up, the little spiders that had wintered there came creeping from their cracks in the wall logs to see what was cooking. The answer was native trout.

We were in our sleeping bags at dark, too tired for chatter or wisecracks. You could hear bone-limbering sighs of comfort, the "tap" and "hiss" as the drops from someone's wet socks on the line above the stove fell on the still-hot lids.

A whip-poor-will tuned up, and from 'way back in the forest an owl hooted. That was all—except for the distant roar of rapids re-echoing from the walled valley of Wassataquoik Stream. It couldn't touch us now.

There are miles of Wassataquoik Stream that are seldom, if ever, fished. They are too far and too hard to reach from either approach, upstream or down. We had "map-fished" these enticing reaches back home, but now unanimously abandoned the idea. The ponds were our real objective, and besides, we were on the outs with the Wassataquoik after what it had almost done to Bentley.

From the Russell Pond base camp, within a day's round-trip, you can fish approximately fifteen ponds—not all of them in a single day, by any means. Wassataquoik, Draper, Six Ponds (there are six of them), Deep, Long, Pogy, Weed, Bell, Russell itself, and a couple which are unnamed. We fished all but two or three of these ponds. Mac Day and the Glidden boys caught fifty-odd trout in Bell Pond. They were the first to fish it within the memory of man. The trout ran uniform in size— eight to ten inches.

The fastest fishing was at Deep and Six Ponds, where four of us landed and released over a hundred-and-fifty fish. The largest was Jack Glidden's fifteen-incher. Back at camp that evening, Dr. Sam Belknap treated Jack and Bent Glidden for an ailment he, or any of us, had never seen before. To wit, multiple, tiny lacerations on the patients' forefingers caused by the teeth of countless trout as the anglers released them to the waters of Deep and Six Ponds.

But no report—this first one, or any that may follow on the park's wilderness fishing—can pin itself to trout alone. Climb to the Lookout, a high crag two miles from Russell Pond, and you know why. The view from the Lookout, as described by an unidentified observer, is this:

"—from here you sense the full power and grandeur of the wilderness into which you have penetrated. You feel that right here is the place man has gone too far away from in his search for something he has never clearly defined. You feel that whatever you have longed for is here, around you, a full three-hundred-and-sixty degrees of mountains, streams, lakes and ponds, named, unnamed, solitary."

As you stand on the Lookout, you can see, near at hand, the spindles of the young spruces, silent and steady in the still air, aspiring to the sun, and aloof to the inquiry and presence of man. Then, lifting your eyes to the northward distance, you see the rolling, thoughtful peaks of the Traveller Range, and the valley where the Pogy Notch Trail leads to South Branch Ponds Campground. That was our trail out, and it was time to go. With hardened muscles and lightened packs, it was a lark compared to the Russell Pond Trail.

We had arranged to have our cars driven from Roaring Brook around the park's peripheral road to meet us at South Branch Ponds. This campground, with its two, clear-water ponds lying blue between the steep crags and faces of Traveller and South Branch Mountains, is one of the most beautiful on our continent. Here Jake's Rangers spent the last night of the expedition. And it was here we realized that something had happened to us, over and above our adventure. Our Spring Fever had been cured! But you don't actually cure it, like a disease. Recovery is a little like falling out of love. Suddenly it is there no more, and you can hardly remember its yearning and heartache.

But there was one among us who didn't treat it so lightly. On the start home, just after we left South Branch Ponds, a White Throat Sparrow sang. It sang as I had imagined I heard it in Jake's studio that bleak March day so long ago. It may be that Jake heard the White Throat, too. Because down near Trout Brook Crossing, just before you get to the main park road, Jake stopped his car and got out, and approached an old, pine stump, drawing his sheath knife as he went. He came back presently with a handful of rich, yellow, resinous shavings tied in his handkerchief.

"We'll be needing these next Spring." he said. "Now—home we go."

A Rifle Named "Sleigh Bells"

ANY RIFLE HAS A HISTORY—a story—and many rifles have strangely begotten names. This is the story of a rifle named "Sleigh Bells." It begins on a warm, still morning in May when Al Foster boated me across Grand Lake in Penobscot County, Maine, to my cabin on the wilderness shore. I had no inkling that I was on my way to discovering a secret concerning a buck deer I had shot almost thirty years before. There was something weird and haunting about it, because the secret was Henry Dennison's. "Pop" Dennison was my father-in-law—and he had been dead for more than four years!

I have no convictions about communication after death, one way or the other; but I hope Pop knows I have found him out, and perhaps he does. To me, it's a heartwarming thought. He was such a vital and dynamic personality that I don't have to listen very hard to hear the echo of his *basso profundo* chuckle over my discovery. You could call it leftover laughter.

Pop Dennison, more than anyone, got me interested in deer hunting, the Maine woods, and log cabins—including the one that loomed closer over the bow of Al Foster's boat that day in May, 1956. But when Al put me ashore, I wasn't thinking about Pop; and the buck I'd shot so long ago down on Second Chain Lake had been totally out of mind for years.

Presently, I was to do some intense thinking about both, but for the moment I was pre-occupied with the purpose of my trip to the cabin, which was to take an inventory of its contents with the idea of selling out—lock, stock, the works.

My wife and I had built this cabin, and many of the things in it, mostly with our own hands. We had lived in this remote and beautiful spot for ten incomparable years, and it was high in our hearts. The decision to sell had been tough to make, and hard to take. But it made sense. We had reached the age where a gale on the lake was a hazard, rather than a bright challenge; the toting and hauling a burden; and the twenty-nine miles to a telephone too far for peace of mind. But, as I waved goodby to Al Foster and walked alone up the path to the plank porch, I thought of the rich experience of our life here, and it pulled hard.

The wake of Al's boat followed along shore, and you could hear the little waves breaking. In the distance, the boat was a speck, and its motor sounded like a bee under a derby hat. I looked straight across at the long, dark peaks of The Traveller Range rising three thousand feet above the lake, saw the snow patch on Big Traveller, and the bald eagle doing a slow, superb lazy eight in a thermal above Birch Point. Then I turned, opened the cabin door and stepped inside. And the ghosts came stalking, one by one, with their sad whispering. They were nudging me toward Pop Dennison and his secret about that buck deer, but of course I didn't know it at the time.

Just inside the cabin door there was a loose floor board. It had been loose for years. I went in and stepped on it to see if it would make its familiar squeak. It did. Then I walked into the kitchen and looked at the wood stove. This spring there would be no ritual of lighting the first fire in this wonderfully familiar stove. What manner of man would succeed to the ritual? Would he love it, as we had? Whoever he might be, I said to him:

"Mister, you've inherited one hell of a good cook stove."

I had said it aloud, and the sound of my voice startled me. This was no good. If I didn't get going on the inventory, it would be but a matter of minutes before I'd be talking to myself—and *believing it!*

Al Foster had agreed to pick me up at noon for the trip back across the lake to my car. I had about two hours to finish my melancholy job. So I got out a pad and pencil, started by itemizing everything in the kitchen, and worked systematically through the cabin. I wound up in my den, where my deer rifle hung on the wall pegs.

This rifle is an old model .32 Special Winchester, half magazine. It has a sling ring on the receiver, and when I took the rifle down, the ring tinkled in the lonely stillness of the cabin, and the sound gave my memory a terrific clout.

It's ridiculous what an insignificant stimulus, like the "plink" of metal on metal, can do to a man's thoughts. On second consideration, it isn't ridiculous at all—because memory is one of the great marvels of life. For example, by a simple exercise of remembering, you can be in two places at the same instant. Actually, I was standing in my log cabin on Grand Lake. But the sound of the sling ring had given me such a yank that to all intents and purposes I was also a hundred-odd miles away, down in Hancock County. The time had changed, too. It was early in November, 1926—thirty years ago. And I was standing in Pop Dennison's deer hunting cabin that we had built the summer before. . . .

We had built the cabin at the head of Third Chain Lake in what was then virgin deer hunting country. It was twelve hard miles by canoe from Pop's permanent camp at the foot of

Dobsis Lake. Pop's annual hunting trip at the Dobsis camp had already been an institution for years. The select personnel, known as "The Old Bunch," consisted of Harry Wheeler, Bill Howell, and Pop. The guides were Harley Fitch, Harley Fenlayson, and Roy Bailey.

The 1926 hunting trip was extra special, extra exclusive, because it was Third Chain Cabin's christening. The trip's planning, which began weeks in advance, had a pioneer zest that was contagious. I had dropped heavy hints for an invitation, but Pop didn't field any of them.

"I haven't seen the big woods in fall yet, Pop. What are they like?"

"Wonderful," said Pop, and described them at length.

"I hope I cut enough firewood last summer," I said.

"If you didn't, we'll cut some more."

Just because I was a mere kid of twenty-six, with no deer hunting history to speak of, I was excluded from this all-important trip. And I had spent most of a treasured summer vacation helping Roy Bailey build the peeled spruce cabin where these over-privileged old characters would be sheltered. I had patched and painted the canoes they would use, toted in their cook stove, tar papered their roof. And they had cast me aside, depriving me of my rightful adventure.

The crowning misery was when Pop showed me his nonresident Maine hunting license with the deer tags. But no! The crowning misery was when, as though conferring an honor, he asked me if I'd like to drive "The Old Bunch" from Framingham, Mass., where they lived, to the night train at the North Station in Boston, where they would embark for Maine—and Third Chain Cabin.

If I wasn't green with envy and frustration, I felt that way. I helped them aboard the train with their duffel bags and rifles, and wished them luck, while inwardly hoping the cabin roof would leak and the stove would smoke. When the train pulled out, I stood glumly at the gate, reading the scheduled stops on the bulletin board: Portland, Bangor, Lincoln, Mattawamkeag, Forest Station, Vanceboro, St. John, Halifax, and all those wonderful places I couldn't go to. Then I drove home through the frosty night, bruised with self pity.

Three or four days later, I received a cock-eyed telegram from Lincoln, Maine. As near as I can remember, it read like this:

GALLOP THE SHALLOP AT FIRST CHAIN WEDNESDAY
(signed) POP

Some telegram! But what else could you expect from that artful, bald-headed, stumpy-built bundle of wisdom? It is a known fact—a matter of written record—that Pop Dennison wrote some of his annual reports to his stockholders in blank verse. If you don't believe this, and I don't blame you, check the reports prior to 1950 of the Dennison Mfg. Co., Framingham, Mass.

The whole shennanigan of the 1926 hunting trip is characteristic of Pop Dennison and the way he did things—always with careful staging, and elements of suspense, mystery and surprise. He'd probably been planning his stunt for weeks. Rather than say outright: "Ed, you join us at Third Chain Cabin after The Old Bunch has had a few days together," he had sweated me dry, just because he knew my ultimate delight would be magnified by ten.

Incidentally, it was no cinch in those days to get from Third Chain Lake to the town of Lincoln to send a telegram. And, just as Pop had intended, the telegram itself took some decoding. After about an hour's mystification and torment, I figured it out for what it was: a command invitation to take the Tuesday night train from Boston to Lincoln, get a ride from Lincoln to the head of Dobsis Lake Wednesday, find someone to boat me down Dobsis to First Chain Lake Carry, where, if I hunted in the right place, I would find a "shallop," which meant canoe. "Gallop" meant hurry. By means of the canoe, and several hours paddling and poling through the three Chain Lakes and their connecting streams, I would eventually arrive at Third Chain Cabin. . . .

Thirty years later, in the den of my Grand Lake cabin, I could feel myself smiling. I was smiling at the sound of Pop Dennison's voice. It was almost as if he were actually speaking, saying to The Old Bunch that fall at Third Chain:

"Wait till Ed gets that tellegram. His lid will fly off."

It had, too. The telegram reached me Tuesday afternoon, a few hours before train time. And I didn't even own a rifle, let alone a Maine hunting license or a ticket on the night train. I asked and got permission from my boss for a few days off, including that Tuesday afternoon. I telephoned my wife, and found she had been in on the scheme all along. Then I went down to Federal Street in Boston to the late Bob Smith's Sporting Goods Store and bought a hunting license and a second-hand rifle. The rifle was an old model .32 Special Winchester, half-magazine, with a sling ring on the receiver.

Because of my intense remembering of Pop, it seemed weird and spooky to be holding that same rifle, now, in my own cabin. Pop had spent a night in this cabin. His hands had held this rifle. Would I list the rifle on my inventory, leaving it to the unknown future owner of this beloved place? How would I describe it?

"One (1) .32 Special Winchester carbine, excellent condition."

No! The description was vastly over-simplified. It ought to tell how, after I found the "shallop," or canoe, on First Chain Lake, I laid the rifle along the gunwale, tossed my knapsack in the bow, and paddled up the lake; how the shod canoe pole sounded on the rocky bottom of Second Chain Stream; how the shell-iced puddles cracked under my moccasins on Third Chain Carry, and the middle thwart of the canoe bit into the back of my neck as I lugged across into Third Chain; and then the big moment when I hauled the canoe ashore under the leaning cedar at the cabin, and Pop Dennison opened the front door and waved both hands, and hollered:

"Hello, boy! Hello! Hello! I see you made it."

I couldn't remember when I'd been so happy.

"Where's the bunch, Pop?" I asked.

"Hunting. They'll be back."

"Do they like the cabin?"

"They're bats about it. What you got there? A new rifle?"

"Sure—new secondhand."

I handed it to him. He checked to see if it was loaded, and I awaited his distinguished approval of my pride and joy. No approval of any kind was forthcoming—nothing but a frown, and a stern look in Pop's steel-blue eyes.

"What's the matter with it, Pop?"

"The essential of still-hunting for deer is stillness."

"Okay, I'll be still."

"Not with this," he said, shaking the rifle so that the sling ring tinkled. "You might just as well go forth to the beech ridges with a bell dangling from your neck."

"What'll I do? Hunt with a slingshot?"

"No. I'll fix that confounded ring."

He got a piece of soft, white grocery string and wound the ring all around. When he had looped the end under the last two turns and cut it off, he shook the rifle again, and you couldn't hear a thing.

"There," said Pop, handing me the rifle, "from now on, it's up to you."

It was too late in the afternoon to hunt the long beech ridge back of the cabin, so we sat on the porch and watched the sun get low over Duck Lake Mountain; and, as the shadows lengthened, the hunters drifted in, and told their several tales. Bill Howell, with Roy Bailey guiding, had shot a buck where Killman Pond Stream came into the lake. Harry Wheeler and Harley Fenlayson had fallen asleep in the sun and dry beech leaves. When they woke up and stirred the leaves, three deer broke cover within a few yards of them.

"Just another 'caught napping' episode," said Harry.

Harley Fitch, hunting alone, brought in a fat, dry doe; and we had fresh liver for supper. Pop told about the noise my rifle made, and the Old Bunch promptly named the rifle "Sleigh Bells."

"Ever had buck fever, Ed?" Bill Howell asked.

"No. 'Course not."

"Old hand, hey?" Roy Bailey asked me.

"Sure."

"How many deer all told have you actually accounted for?" Harry Wheeler asked.

"Four—so far."

No one believed me—which was fair enough, because I had multiplied the truth by four.

"Wait till tomorrow," I said. "I'll bring one in. You'll see."

Pop Dennison said: "The steam that blows the whistle never turns the wheel."

"How many people at home did you promise venison to?" Bill Howell asked me.

"Just three or four guys in my office," I said.

"Poor, starvin' guys," said Harley Fitch.

As the kid member of the party, I was the target for all the jokes; and I had talked big. I had better produce. But, in two days hard hunting, my score was three porcupines, and Pop wrote in the cabin diary:

"Ed Smith and his rifle, Sleigh Bells, are doing well in Quill Pig circles.

The third afternoon I came in early, my moccasins soundless on the pine needles on the path to the kitchen door of the cabin. I heard voices in the cabin, and stopped, not intending to eavesdrop, but getting trapped into it. Pop Dennison was talking to Roy Bailey, and this is what he said:

"I'd dearly love to have that boy get a deer. Will you take him with you tomorrow?"

Roy said he would. He said he knew where there was a big buck working in the old burn over toward Second Lake. Then Pop said:

"Make it casual, Roy—so Ed won't suspect us."

I ducked back up the path, and started whistling, and they came to the kitchen door to greet me, none the wiser.

That night I couldn't sleep. Pop Dennison wanted me to get a deer even more than I wanted it myself. I had to make good—for Pop. I was suddenly weighed with responsibility to this devious and exciting old man, who was my father-in-law. I was no longer hunting for myself. I was hunting for Pop—and for the vicarious triumph he would derive from my success—if any.

The next morning at daylight breakfast, Bill Howell said his feet hurt.

"I think I'll take a day off," Bill said.

That left Roy Bailey free to guide me, and I knew that was the way Pop had rigged it. None of them had any idea I knew what was cooking; and so, just out of devilment, I said to Bill Howell:

"I'll stay in camp with you, Bill. We can play cribbage."

When I saw Pop Dennison's face, I could have bitten out my tongue. He was hurt, and shocked by my implication that I had quit cold, or—worse—didn't like deer hunting.

"It's your last day in camp!" he said. "Did you forget?"

I said: "For a second, I did. No cribbage for me—just the long, brown ridges."

"Good! Good for you. How'd you like to go with Roy?"

"Wonderful," I said. "I'll make some sandwiches, and we'll get going."

I made the sandwiches with thin slices of cold deer liver left over from breakfast. Pop followed us a little way up the trail back of the cabin. Then he slapped me on the shoulder, and said:

"Good luck to you," and turned back; and Roy and I were alone, cat-footing through the ghostly gray beeches.

I had already known Roy Bailey for several years. We had fished salmon together on spring trips, and been on canoe trips in summer, and worked together building Third Chain Cabin. But Roy was a hunter at heart, and still is, and I caught the fever from watching him work—three or four slow, careful steps, then a pause, and his head turning slowly, eyes searching, peering, listening. His rifle was an old favorite—a .45-70, the cartridges almost as big as your forefinger. Sometimes, when the angle was just right, I could read the number of his guide's license carved in the stock of his rifle. It was "8820."

We were traveling east toward Killman Pond swamp. We crossed the swamp and turned north toward the old burn, where a fire of years before had reached Second Chain Lake. We had entered the burn a distance of a hundred yards or so, when Roy stopped, tense. He moved his hand in a beckoning motion, and I knew my chance had come, and I started shaking like a twig in a current. Roy beckoned again, and as I moved up to him, I stepped on a dry stick—and a deer blew, blew again, and I heard the animal's hooves thud as he took off.

Roy looked around at me, a small, wry grin on his lips. I was sick. Anyone that would step on a dry stick at a time like that wasn't fit to be in the woods. What would Pop think, when he heard about it?

Roy pointed to a nearby spruce blowdown, and we went over quietly, and sat down on it.

"I'm some still-hunter," I whispered.

"Never mind," he whispered back. "Take it easy. Let's eat our sandwiches."

Roy took a big bite from his sandwich, and it bulged his cheek. I nibbled at mine. The new growth after the burn was dense, and black stumps loomed here and there. A jay screeched and a red squirrel chattered—and behind us we heard a crash, and the thud of hooves. Something caught the corner of my eye, to my left—beyond where Roy was sitting. It was the motion of a spruce branch, and I focused on it. The growth was so thick that it was like sighting through a pipe.

The branch moved again, and I saw the magnificent head and neck of a buck.

"I can see him!" I whispered.

"Go ahead and shoot," Roy whispered.

I reached down and picked up my rifle, and cocked it. The ivory bead front sight settled into the notch of the rear sight —and the shot broke open the silence, and Roy and I were standing up, our liver sandwiches lying on the green moss where we'd dropped them.

"Did you see the deer?" I asked.

"No. But it must have been the same one—circling to get us sized up. Did you hit him?"

"No. When I fired, he just disappeared."

"Where was he?"

I sat down on the log again, and sighted the spot with my rifle. Roy got the line, and walked slowly to the spot through the tangle.

"Come on over here," he called back, and I did—and the big buck lay on the green moss, dead from a clean neck shot, and Roy was shaking my hand, and laughing. I thought of Pop Dennison, and couldn't wait to tell him.

"Fire three shots," Roy said. "Pop'll hear them, an' come. I'll bet he ain't far."

Pop heard the shots, and came. He was all out of breath, and his head gleamed with sweat.

"Boy!" he said. "You're white as a sheet. Go and sit down. What a wonderful head—the buck's, not yours."

Now that it was all over, I felt weak as a starved kitten. I sat on a stump, while Roy and Pop bled the deer and dressed it, and skewered the heart and liver on a forked alder.

"Hey, Pop," I said. "You got here awful quick. Were you following us?"

"Oh–o–o–o——well, not exactly. Thought I'd like to be around."

What could you ever do to repay a guy like Pop? What he loved best, outside of home and family, was hunting. He had just given up a morning's hunting because of me. He had given up another day of it so he would be at Third Chain Cabin to greet me when I arrived from Boston. And he had made the long hard trip out to Lincoln, personally—to send me that crazy telegram. I would never catch up with him, and I would be a long time understanding his works and ways. But, sitting on that stump, looking down at my buck, I had what I then thought was a flash of pure inspiration. Much as I wanted that handsome trophy for myself, I would have it mounted by the best taxidermist I could find—and I would give it to Pop! It would surprise heil out of him. He'd think I was having the nine-point head mounted for myself, but all the while it would be just for him.

Now, after that inspired moment on Second Chain Burn, I know the secret of the deer head, and how Pop kept it locked for all the years in his eloquent skull. If it weren't for the tinkle of the sling ring on old "Sleigh Bells" that morning in my cabin, I'd never have found it out. The string that Pop had wound on the ring had been long since removed by a gunsmith who had re-glued the rifle, otherwise no tinkle.

I put the rifle back on the pegs on the wall of my den, and listened. I could hear Al Foster's boat coming, but I couldn't see it yet. I was thinking of the literally open-mouthed astonishment in Pop Dennison's face when, in the winter of 1927, I had presented him with the deer head, beautifully mounted.

"No!" he said. "Oh, Ed—no! You can't give me that."

"I could give you anything."

"But—this is *yours.*"

"No, Pop, it's yours—for keeps."

"Do you really mean it?"

"Sure. I want you to have it—and I really mean it."

My mother-in-law, Ma Dennison, was with us at the time of the presentation. She looked quizzically at the mounted head, and said to Pop:

"Where will we put it?"

"Over the fireplace in the dining room," said Pop, unhesitatingly—and, until Pop's death, the big buck of Second Chain Burn looked down for about twenty-five years on every meal that was served at the long, oak table in the house on Juniper Hill in Framingham; and sometimes Pop would interrupt his carving, turn and look up at the head, and say:

"That's Ed's buck—the one he shot on Second Chain Burn."

I looked from my den window out over Grand Lake and saw Al's boat rounding a distant point. My time was about up, and I thought of the last time I saw the deer head. Pop Dennison died in 1952, missing his seventy-fifth birthday by four days. He lived an unusual life, and died on an unusual day—a day which occurs just once every four years—February 29th, Leap Year.

Some months afterwards, Pop's widow gave the deer head to me. I was quite touched. But at the time I had no place to hang the head, and no place to store it, and I suspected that my wife didn't regard it too highly as a decoration for the cabin. So I gave the head to Pop's first cousin, Lew Bement. Lew gave it to a friend of his named Jack Wechter, who has a kind of club room, and at this writing it hangs in Jack's place near Greenfield, Massachusetts.

As Al's boat drew closer, I tried to visualize the deer head hanging in Jack's club room; but I could just see it where it hung originally, for all those years, over Pop's dining room fireplace.

"Harry," Ma Dennison must have said, innumerable times, "I don't like that deer head. We ought to have an oil painting of a ship."

"What? Don't like that head? Why, it *belongs* there. And we've got a ship painting in the living room."

There was something wrong with that dialogue, even though it was imaginary. Pop's secret was right on top of me. Why would anyone want a trophy that he hadn't shot himself, unless he was furnishing a museum or a club room? Pop Dennison never cared much for trophies anyway—except the white buck he shot on his last hunt, just a few years before his death.

"Pop," I said to him, "now I know! You thought I'd be hurt if you didn't accept that deer head. So you made a twenty-five year show of liking it and no one ever knew you didn't, least of all me."

Al's boat had landed, and I took old "Sleigh Bells" down to the shore with me, and Al saw me lugging it, and said:

"This isn't deer hunting season."

"The hell it isn't!" I said. "I was just on a hunt down on Second Chain Lake."

Al looked up at the cabin, then back at me.

"Say," he said, in a puzzled way, "did I hear someone laughing? Just a moment ago?"

I did a double take. Of course everyone will say that Al
heard me laughing at my discovery, but it might have been
Pop Dennison's leftover laughter that he heard, because I
think I heard it myself. . . .

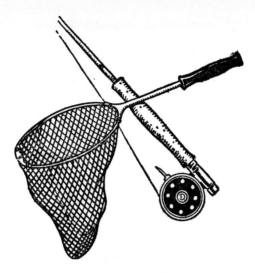

The Fish With a Sense of Humor

IN OPEN DEFIANCE of reason, I would like to assert that I know a fish with a sense of humor. I refer to the landlocked salmon, *salmo Sebago*. Since humor is an attribute seldom if ever ascribed to a fish, my assertion either puts the salmon in a class by itself—or it makes a screwball out of me. In the latter case, I ask forbearance on the grounds that in all fishermen a certain amount of screwballery is likely to crop out. In fact, once you take up the fly rod, lunacy is a calculated risk.

However, I am not so zany as to claim I have seen a landlocked salmon actually smiling. Nor have I seen one's eyes twinkle. The landlocked's eyes, as far as expression is concerned, resemble Buster Keaton's at best, and at worst Peter Lorre's during one of that accomplished actor's cozier knifing scenes. On the whole, the landlocked's sense of humor is of the deadpan, or macabre type. Nevertheless, he is clearly imbued with the spirit of fun. While it may not always be fun for the angler, it invariably seems to be fun for the fish. He gets the last laugh, as I shall presently demonstrate in this report.

But first, in order to establish my credentials as a student of the landlocked salmon, I must state that I have caught over four hundred of them. To remove the stigma of personal horn-blowing in reporting this score, I confess that in catching the quoted number I lost at least twice as many. This means that during my angling life I have been on more or less intimate terms with about twelve hundred landlocked salmon, and thus feel qualified to speak with authority.

I shall begin with the salmon that was responsible for the hitherto undisclosed incident of roller-skating in the austere corridors of Maine's all but sacrosanct Poland Spring House. Roller-skating on these premises is not only unthinkable, but virtually impossible. It is an act of Hoydonism comparable to riding a motor cycle in Widener Library, or appearing in church on Easter morning accompanied by a *nymph du pave.*

Yet I roller-skated. And it's time I put the blame squarely on the shoulders of a certain landlocked salmon which I caught in a late April blizzard on Sebago Lake near the mouth of the Songo River.

Undeterred by foul weather reports, Cy Flint and I had left Boston bound for Bangor, where we proposed to try our luck in the Bangor pool. Over the car radio, as we drove northward, we heard that the ice had cleared Sebago Lake. So we veered from our course, rented a boat on the shore of Songo Bay, and put forth into a gathering snowstorm.

With numbed fingers, Cy and I attached streamer flies to our leaders and began casting. The weather would have dismayed an arctic survival unit—but I was scarcely aware of it.

A salmon had taken a bat at my submerged fly. I struck too late. I cast again. He came to the surface, half-circled the Maribou I was offering, and appeared to nudge it with his body. This seemed odd, and it was.

I hooked the fish on the third or fourth rise. Cy Flint reeled in his line and handled the boat in one of the longest plays of my experience. The salmon wouldn't go three pounds, but he wouldn't tire. I was mystified by his endurance. When I finally brought him under Cy's net, over forty minutes had passed. We were lost in a blizzard on a barbarous-looking lake, and no shore was visible, in any direction.

"Look," said Cy, pointing to the salmon. "You hooked him through the dorsal fin."

It was true, and it accounted for the all but endless battle.

"I think the monster planned it that way," I said, remembering its strange behavior around the fly. "Which way is the boat dock?"

When at last we got ashore, eight inches of snow had fallen, and—according to Cy Flint—we had rowed twice around Sebago Lake. The driving was hazardous. It was still snowing, and we were beat out. So we abandoned our Bangor plan, and turned in, off the highway, at the Poland Spring House.

The famous old hotel wasn't officially open. But the skeleton staff took pity on us and invited us to stay. We contributed our salmon to the hotel larder, and the resident manager—noting that we were blue from exposure—brought out a bottle of bonded bourbon.

An air of fine friendliness soon prevailed. The memory of the slate-dark, snow-blown lake receded in the warmth of steam heat, and the bourbon brought about a deep understanding between guests and staff.

Along late in the evening, while searching the spacious, empty corridors for a door marked LAVATORY, I stumbled quite by accident into a storage closet containing a vast quantity of old roller skates. I backed out of the closet with an armload of skates, and called out joyously to Cy.

While we were harnessing the skates to our feet, someone put a spirited waltz record on an old, hand-winding Victrola, and we were off. The die was cast—and so were we. Not even the finest, most modern Roller Drome can compete with empty hotel corridors for roller-skating. In a really sedate hotel, you get accoustics, and triple echoes, that inspire you to fancy turns and spins, and you rebound from the walls—and floor—as though immune to the law of gravity, or the pain of contusions and abrasions.

When, at last exhausted, we turned in, Cy drowsily remarked how strange it was, that, having started off for Bangor, we had wound up in a roller-skating duel in the halls of Maine's most celebrated hotel.

"Nothing could have caused it but a landlocked salmon," I said. "If that fish hadn't deliberately hooked himself by the dorsal fin, we wouldn't have had this rich experience. I can hear that salmon laughing."

"It's your ears ringing," said Cy.

It was on Dobsis Stream, the dammed outlet of Dobsis Lake, in Maine's Washington County, that I first began to suspect the landlocked's latent sense of mirth, or drollery. Below the dam, as Dobsis discharged its clear waters into Pocumpus Lake and so on into Grand Lake, there is a hundred-yard stretch of quickwater. On the far bank of the stream, there was an abutment, or elongated wall, built of hemlock logs. With one gate in the dam full open, the lower end of the top log was just barely awash. You could walk, dry, down the top log, casting as you went, and so cover most of the fruitful water. In May and June, this stream is wonderful landlocked fishing, if you strike it right.

One memorable day, my old fishing friend, Arthur Clark, mounted the top abutment log, got his balance adjusted, and started casting. He was using a fanwing Greenwell's Glory, dry, and a nine-foot leader.

Clarkie, at the time, was Fish & Game Commissioner of Connecticut—subsequently of Missouri. He was an intense, consecrated fisherman—almost to the point of obsession, where landlockeds were concerned. He had been known to cut feathers from his wife's hats for fly-tying material that might— conceivably—please a landlocked's fancy. At the moment of this episode, the hackles of his Greenwell's Glory were from his wife's hat feathers. He was sentimental about it, and also very hopeful.

On one of his first few casts, a heavy salmon rose—just out of reach. I was watching the whole thing from the big, gray boulder directly across the stream from Clarkie. He took a step down the abutment log and cast a few more times. The salmon rose again, but had moved downstream—still just out of reach.

Right about then, I began to suspect that the salmon was laying plans to get Clarkie. As Fish & Game Commissioner of Connecticut, maybe Clarkie should have remained loyal to home waters. I don't say the landlocked was making a judgment on that. But I *do* say that it looked as though he were deliberately tolling and luring Clarkie down that log to the watery end.

And Clarkie was falling for it, irresistibly. The salmon kept backing downstream. Clarkie kept following down the

log, casting diagonally downstream, at an angle across the current, so he'd get a fair float on his fanwing before drag set in.

As reported, the lower end of Clarkie's catwalk log was just barely awash; and at this point the rough, outer bark of the log had peeled off. The only thing I can think of that's as slippery as wet, peeled hemlock is a fresh deer liver. I must add that Clarkie's moccasins, also wet, had been freshly oiled that very morning.

As the salmon, backing down, gave a final show, Clarkie's moccasins made contact with the juicy, peeled hemlock. You couldn't have got traction for a sparrow in this superlatively lubricated situation.

Clarkie uttered a cry, his feet churning as if on a "treadmill to oblivion." He flung his arms like a forlorn windmill, and straightway disappeared, rod and all, beneath the turbulent waters of Dobsis Stream, surfacing several yards below, and eventually fetching up against the bank, mad and gasping.

Right then, as if for a bit of gloating, the salmon poked its nose up slowly, appeared to stare Clarkie in the eye for a moment, and vanished permanently.

"That fish," reported the outraged Clarkie, later, "was *laughing* at me."

"Could be," I said.

"Was!" said Clarkie.

Within a year of Clarkie's experience, there occurred what Pappy Thornton calls "The Great Salmon Razzberry." Pappy was a witness, and will testify on behalf of my thesis that the landlocked has a gift for buffoonery.

Pappy and I were trout fishing on Oxbrook Stream Deadwater in spring. It was a bad day. The black flies were out early in mournful numbers, we were out of tobacco, and just after noon a violent thunderstorm drenched us to the hide. We decided to head for Harley Fitch's cabin on Upper Oxbrook Lake. While paddling across Lower Oxbrook Lake, in the still, flat calm after the storm, landlockeds—some of them looked like five pounders—began rising, leaping, flashing and splashing for a hundred yards in any direction from our canoe. I have seen similar phenomena two or three times since, but never a rise to match this one. There must have been fifty or sixty salmon joining in the display. We could see no hatch of flies, bugs, beetles, ants or insects of any kind, on or under the water.

It was a fisherman's dream. But as we frantically reassembled our rods, cast, changed flies, tangled lines in the air, cast and changed and re-changed flies again and again, it became a fisherman's nightmare. In the hour or so of the pandemonium on Lower Oxbrook, we became exhausted—not only from casting, but from frustration. You'd drop a Quill Gordon right on a salmon's nose. The salmon, in effect, gave your offering the horse laugh—while still another salmon took to the air five feet away.

"They're kidding us!" said Pappy, his pale blue eyes fierce with indignation.

Then, abruptly, the show stopped. The last ripple, the last swirl, leveled. The lake was calm again, and you could smell the damp, steaming spruce of the surrounding forest. We were wet, dejected, fly bitten, tobaccoless, and fishless.

"They *have* kidded us," I said.

It was over in the western part of Maine, on Rangeley Lake, that I saw a landlocked salmon make monkeys out of two, distinguished men. One was an Army General, the other a college professor. They had been friendly rivals since boyhood—for their first girls; for athletic prowess at school and college; for scholastic honors, and in later life for world achievement.

So, as members of a salmon fishing party, they immediately began competing for fishing honors. They made a five-dollar bet on who would catch the most fish over the full, ten-day trip. Trout didn't count. The scoring was on landlockeds only. That five-dollar bet took on the importance of a million-dollar deal.

The fishing party split into factions—one for the General, the other for the Professor. They couldn't legally kill all the fish they caught, but neither would trust the other for accuracy on the daily score. So each carried in his canoe a washtub half full of water. And their guides refilled the tubs as aeriation was needed. At night, they'd come to the camp dock, and count the salmon in the tubs, releasing them overside as each fish was tallied.

The score see-sawed for days. The contestants fished from daylight to dark. They and their guides were worn out. It was an altogether foolish performance—a fact which it took a landlocked salmon to point up.

On the final night of showdown, when they sided in to the camp dock, the Professor had four landlockeds swimming around in his tub, while the General had three. This evened the score for the full trip at thirty-eight fish each.

"No decision!" said a self-appointed judge.

No decision my eye! A landlocked in the General's tub— obviously having sized up the ridiculous situation—chose this instant to rise up out of the tub and flop overboard into the lake at dockside. The General made a frantic grab for the fish, and missed, of course.

"Hah!" said the Professor. "I've won. Where's my five bucks?"

"Right in my pocket—where it's going to stay," said the General. "That fish was counted."

"Yes—but *you* didn't put him back into the lake. He put himself back. So he doesn't count."

"He does."

"He does like hell!"

"The hell you say!"

"Do you count the ones that get away?"

"You're a quibbler."

"You're a welsher!"

"What did you call me?"

"I called you a—"

Cooler heads intervened before blows were struck, and the contestants and their supporters went their separate ways. It was a year before friendships were renewed.

Okay, I ask you: here were two intelligent, mature, and highly accomplished gentlemen fighting like two predatory cats over a single sardine. I am of the opinion that this idiocy was caused, deliberately, by a salmon with a certain type of funnybone. If there is any disagreement, I am now coming up with the clincher.

The fact that landlockeds have a sense of humor is finally proved and certified by the incident of the lunch hour that Roy Bailey and I were enjoying one tranquil June day on Grand Lake, Washington County. It is unquestionably the only case on record where a luncheon party was invaded by live fish. Only a landlocked salmon with a conniving buddy could dream up such a shenanigan.

Roy and I, in separate canoes, had trolled streamer flies and live minnows that morning for hours. Never a rise, never a slow roll. We were using separate canoes in order to cover more territory, but to no avail.

At noon we drew together, side by side, not far from Caribou Rock. Roy hooked his leg over the gunwale of my canoe, and I hooked my leg over the gunwale of his canoe. Thus, our legs acted as grapples, holding the canoes gunwale to gunwale.

We were facing each other, our rods lying along the gunwales of our respective canoes—the tip of mine adjacent to Roy's elbow, the tip of Roy's rod adjacent to my elbow, our leaders trailing in the water between the ends of the canoes.

We munched away at sandwiches, the canoes rocking gently in the tiny swells. Roy got out a big thermos of hot tea, balanced it on the flat of his paddle blade and reached the paddle toward me. I leaned forward, arm outstretched. I had my hand on the thermos bottle when, squarely between the canoes—at my end of them—the waters of Grand Lake exploded. A split-second later, the waters erupted at Roy's end of the canoes, and a heavy landlocked peeled through the surface and went straight on up about six feet in the air.

The thermos upset, and its contents landed in my lap—a poultice of scalding hot tea. It didn't matter at the moment. Simultaneously, Roy and I reached for our rods, an act which leaned us toward each other and tilted our canoes similarly. The canoes folded inward upon each other, like the closing of a huge, elongated clam—and Roy and I were within."

The canoes righted, but mine had filled. I jumped into Roy's, rod still in hand. I was so excited I didn't even feel the hot tea.

We each had a salmon on. Between the reel-whining runs, aerial acrobatics, and lightning-like direction changes of our respective luncheon guests, we found brief, odd moments to bail Roy's canoe with our hats and so stay afloat.

Both our dipnets had gone overboard in the early stages of the invasion. We were obliged to play the two salmon till they rolled sidewise on the surface and gave us the Peter Lorre eye. We got both fish into the canoe after twenty minutes of melodrama, and we sat there panting, laughing, and blaspheming for a while before salvaging my canoe.

We went ashore on a sand beach, built a fire and dried out, while reviewing our adventure. What absurd accident of timing and placement brought those two four-pounders directly under our canoes? What perverse devilment made them strike our trailing flies, almost simultaneously, at the precise instant when Roy was passing me the hot tea jug balanced on his paddle blade? And how come we had trolled in this vicinity all morning long without a single strike?

"You know what?" said Roy. "Those devils were following us all that time, waiting for their chance to catch us off base."

"That's funny," I said.

"You're damn right it's funny. And they knew it, too."

Of course, these two mischievous salmon had paid the supreme sacrifice for their lunch-hour prank. So you can say they didn't have fun, after all. But that night in camp, while we were eating one of them broiled, my lap began to burn. That hot tea! It had done its blistering subtly and well, and I went around for days afterwards wearing bandages over a most embarrassing and crucial portion of my anatomy. You think a landlocked hasn't got a sense of humor? Well, all right—but at least he has the last laugh.

The Vanishing Trout Pool

THE LONG, LONG DAY began on that June morning in 1958 when I met my old friend and guide, Roy Bailey, in front of Paul Hoar's store in Grand Lake Stream, Maine. I had arrived at the store ahead of our appointed time; and while waiting for Roy to show up, I took a look at the stream for which this famous sport-fishing village is named. I hadn't seen it for twenty years, but its green-white quickwater flashed exactly as I remembered it, and its song was wondrously familiar.

Over beyond the fish hatchery, in midstream, I recognized the gray rock below which I had once taken two handsome squaretails and a salmon.

"That's a sound old rock," I thought, "an old companion."

The rock, the stream and the village itself gave me a sharp nostalgic twinge. Untotalled fishing and canoe trips had begun and ended here at Grand Lake Dam with Harley Fitch, Bill Sprague, and, of course, Roy. I could hear the water rumbling in its sluiceways, plunging down into the pool below. It was only a step to the dam; and if I'd walked up there, and looked, I might have had a premonition that the day would be forty years long. But I didn't go, because Roy Bailey called to me from in front of the store.

A moment later we were shaking hands, searching each other's eyes, and trying to comprehend in two seconds all that had happened to us in the two decades since our last meeting.

This reunion with Roy was like no other in my experience, and there is a reason why. The first time I saw him was in 1918 at Dennison's Camp on Dobsis Lake Stream, two lakes or fifteen miles from where we now stood. I had been a teen-ager, green as grass, and full of eager dreams of woodsmanship. Roy, twelve years my senior, was everything I longed to be—a skilled canoeman, fly fisherman, hunter, and guide. His intense, pale blue eyes had reflected scenes I yearned to see: a hundred river bends; forests without footprints; deer in a glade; smoke lazing upward from campfires flickering in the wilderness; lynx tracks on a sand beach; canoes dancing in whitewater.

From that first meeting, and for long seasons afterward, I followed Roy everywhere, latching onto his canoe trips with the Dennison parties; lugging big loads on the portages to impress him; affecting a corncob pipe like his, even though it bit my tongue; wearing a blue flannel shirt and moccasins, as he did; patterning my paddlestroke after his effortless Indian style; and in general walking in his snowshoe beat.

A kid couldn't have had a finer model than Roy Bailey.

While he was caretaker of Dennison's Camp, I practically lived there; and when he left Dobsis for Grand Lake Stream, so his children could get proper schooling, I was heartbroken. After seventeen years of close companionship and woods adventure, our trails had parted. That year the lumber company swamped a road in to the head of Dobsis Lake. So instead of reaching Dennison's Camp from Grand Lake Stream, as always before, we came down Dobsis Lake by boat, and our tracks didn't merge any more.

But it was due to Roy's training and influence that I subsequently became a licensed Maine guide; and when my wife and I left Washington County to build a cabin home in Maine's remoter region north of Mt. Katahdin, we chose our site on another Grand Lake—in Penobscot County. Moreover, at the foot of this lake where our cabin stands, there's another Grand Lake Dam. Call it mere coincidence, or a nod from Fate. Or it could be a pattern sewn in boyhood with Roy Bailey breaking trail.

Now, meeting Roy after twenty years at the original Grand Lake Dam, you will understand why I felt a strange time-transposition. Today was yesterday, and yesterday today. Everything matched—even place names. I had come full circle. That's why this reunion was like no other.

They say you can't go home again. But I was close, especially when Roy said:

"Man! I've got something."

This was a kind of code-phrase from our past. "Man, I've got something," had as many meanings as an Indian word. It meant you had a good trout on; or you'd caught first sight of your destined lake at the end of a hard portage; or you had an urge for a canoe trip 'way to hell-an'-gone over to lonely Night Dam on Fifth Machias Stream. Come to think of it, Roy had used this phrase in his recent letter asking me to visit him. And to judge by the intensity of his expression, he had something really big.

"Of all the canoe trips we ever took," he said, "which would you choose?"

"Unknown Lake," I said. "You know that."

"Yes. I know. So let's go."

I had thought his question purely academic. He knew I had to leave for Bangor before dark. And the Unknown trip, starting and ending at Grand Lake Dam, would take about three days.

"Are you kidding, Oldtimer?" I asked.

"Would I ask you to come all this way just to kid you?"

He was giving me his lynx-eyed look. He had some kind of foreknowledge, and it was building up suspense.

"Do you want to go to Unknown Lake?" he persisted. "Or don't you?"

"Sure, but—"

"Then get in my car," he said, holding the door open. "Don't say any more. Just get in."

The road crossed Grand Lake Stream and climbed a ridge, winding through the forest. You could catch glimpses of Grand Lake—that long, blue, beckoning reach above Coal Kill Island.

"I don't remember this road," I said.

"It isn't old enough to be remembered," said Roy. "It was built just about day before yesterday."

It looked that way. The gravel was fresh, and loose, and you could see the marks of the bulldozers.

In the shadowy, twisting lane through the dense spruce and pine growth, I lost all sense of time and direction. Then Roy stopped the car beside the rotting timbers of an old logging dam. A stream flowed slowly among them, and a sunlit lake lay off above.

"Ever happen to have been here before?" said Roy.

Fragments of the past seemed to be knocking in my head like busted gears. I was positive I had once caught a pickerel here. Or had someone else caught it some other place? I knew where I was, but I didn't believe I was there. It was kind of like getting to a long lost home by some bewildering, new approach, such as through the roof.

Roy was studying my face as he pointed to the remains of the old dam.

"Name it!" he said.

"Wabassas Dam—and Wabassas Lake. This isn't possible."

"Your memory is all right."

It was not only all right, but it was giving me a severe jolting. Reaching Wabassas Dam, any way except by canoe, seemed like a strange, unclassified crime.

On the far shore of the lake itself I made out the familiar, low seawall, where you can lift your canoe over into the Getchell Ponds flowage, a matter of a few steps. This is an enchanting bit of Maine geography about ten feet wide. That mere ten feet of earth separates the St. Croix and Machias River watersheds. You just step from one to the other.

Roy and I—and later his sons and my son—had built countless noonday fires atop this little ridge of land. You had your choice of St. Croix or Machias water for your tea. While our trout were frying, and the tea water boiling, we'd look off one way toward the St. Croix, and in mind's eye follow the lakes and streams clear down below the town bridge at Princeton to the junction of Tomah Stream. Then we'd look the other way toward the wild Machias, remembering its rapids, the sequestered Machias Lakes, and the superb trout pools below and above its logging dams—Fifth Lake Dam, Sabio Dam, Rollerford Dam, and unforgettable Night Dam on Fifth Machias Stream.

"Don't tell me what you're thinking about," Roy said. "I can see it in your face."

I knew, now, what my old comrade was up to. Obviously, he'd been planning it for weeks. He was going to show me in a few hours, by car, half the haunts, campsites, cabins, lakes, streams and logging dam trout pools that had taken us days, or even weeks, to reach the old way, by canoe, from Dobsis or Grand Lake Dam.

Now and then, as Roy drove on through this lake and forest country, we'd see a pulpwood crew with chain saws; or we'd snug into a turnout to let a pulp truck pass. But mostly the road was silent, lonely, and sun-dappled.

"Where are you now?" Roy would say, stopping the car for a moment.

"Killman Pond Swamp," I'd say; or, "Third Chain Cabin is right down there."

We'd built the cabin in 1926. And the dark, magnificently-flavored trout we'd taken in isolated Killman Pond seemed to be alive again, and flopping in our baskets.

The road led us fair across a long, white sweep of sand-beach. This was unmistakably what we'd known as "the middleground" between the Unknown Lakes. The dark pine and spruce growth around the lakes was untouched, and the little waves danced in the sun. We stopped and boiled tea over a fire against a boulder, the face of which was first blackened by our pioneering fires of long ago.

"Unknown!" I said, remembering the trout pool below the dam at its outlet; and the deer I'd lugged across Unknown Carry to the head of Third Chain Lake; and the frozen moss crunching under my moccasins; and my breath blowing white in the cold.

"How many canoe poles do you figure we wore out getting back in here from Dobsis?" I asked Roy.

"And moccasins," Roy said, "and axe handles, and canoe canvases. Did you ever think you'd live to see a car parked on Unknown?"

"No—never."

"Well, what do you think of it?"

That's what I was trying to figure out, now that the first shock had passed. This road, and other new ones into our old, hard won, wilderness destinations, was both thrilling and appalling. It was exciting and numbing, depressing and inspiring, and a lot of other paradoxes. If you laughed, a lump came in your throat. It was big change, significant to all sportsmen and outdoorsmen. But I didn't catch up with the real story till after Roy had driven me clean to the foot of Dobsis Lake, and then across to the shore of Fourth Machias Lake.

"Oldtimer," I said, "this is my first trip across Fourth Lake Carry without a pain in the neck from the middle thwart of a canoe."

Standing on the curving gravel beach, here where the Fourth Lake Carry meets the lake, you look across by the Ledge Island to the mouth of Dead Stream. Beyond is the Bald Mountain fire tower. To your left, down lake less than a mile, is Fourth Lake Dam. To your right, up lake, is Finnegan Point, and the inlet of Unknown Stream. Still farther beyond is the mouth of Fifth Machias Stream, one of the best wilderness trout streams in Maine. In winter, I have dreamed of its dark, foam-flecked pools; the roar of Hell's Gate Rapids; and Smooth Ledge Falls, where your canoe pole was forever slipping and wrecking your balance. But the big, sustaining, winter dream was of Night Dam, the logging dam four miles up, with the vast, still pool above; and the deep, foaming, churning pool below, the sun flashing down through the branches of the leaning pine, and the mist veils drifting above the spillway. You smelled the dampness, the sweet mold and moss on the soaked timbers of the sluice. You beached your canoe at the tent site on the left bank; and you flung your canoe pole down beside your canoe, and you said to it:

"Lie there and rot, you instrument of torture!"

Then, in the eddy by the huge, fern-clad boulder, just below the apron of the dam, you'd see the brilliant, bronze flash of a trout; and as you set up your fly rod, your hands shook so you had trouble threading the line through the guides. . . .

Now, on the beach at Fourth Lake Carry, Roy and I stepped over to the cold spring and drank a cup of water.

"The spell of Night Dam is on me," I said.

"How many trout do you suppose we've caught there?" Roy asked.

"I don't know, Oldtimer. And what about Unknown Dam? Dobsis Dam? First Chain Dam?"

"Or Rollerford Dam, on Sabio Stream? Or Gassabeus? Or—?"

All at once, standing there by the spring at Fourth Lake, we seemed to be *collecting* dams. And right about then, I felt the big significance of the new roads in the wilderness.

"Man!" I said. "I've got something!"

"Name it," said Roy.

"The vanishing trout pool. And we've just named some good ones."

While we drove back toward Grand Lake Stream, with the shadows leaning out long in the forest, we discussed this haunting subject; specifically, the future of the trout pools favored, sought and remembered by at least three generations of trout fishermen. Those are the pools above and below old logging dams.

Built and maintained by lumber and paper companies, the dams were used for impounding water for the spring log drives and pulpwood drives. Millions upon millions of feet of logs and cords of pulpwood went through the scarred wooden sluices. The dams were used—some still are—for only a very few weeks each spring. After that, the pools and the dams belonged to us—the lumberman's legacy to the trout fisherman.

I never remember thanking any lumber company for the best fishing of my life, but I'd like to—now. Webster Dam! Telos! Millinocket! Dobsis! Sabio! And Night Dam—special thanks for that one. All of them, save those which may serve on as hydro dams, are going, slowly going back into the ground, decaying and flattening, till your beloved old pool is once again a mere stretch of river.

The reason for this is the dramatically swift change in lumbering method. River drives, and therefore logging dams, were doomed the day the first bulldozer was born. Transportation of lumber to mills via water has changed, almost overnight, to transportation by truck over bulldozed roads.

From my cabin on the shore of Grand Lake Penobscot, in June, 1952, I saw the last boom of logs go down lake, and so on through the big dam into the Penobscot East Branch. Louis Rowe, a River Boss for most of his life, got a job in a mill. Ed Travis, a teamster who could make horses talk, now drives a truck. Within six months, the seventy-five horses at remote Trout Brook Farm, became no horses at all. And the trout pools above and below K-P dam on Trout Brook are just about gone. This has happened in a matter of about six years.

But it would be asking quite a lot of the lumbermen to keep on maintaining our logging dams and trout pools. After all, they've been doing it, gratis, for approximately a hundred-and-fifty years. And they are now maintaining their bulldozed roads for us to use—for the same price. Many are marked: "Private —Open to the Public." They lead you to far places, and are rather more than strategic when it comes to fighting forest fire.

So you can be both sad and glad. The full defeatist attitude is no good. It never is. You trade in sails and clipper ships for steam and diesels. The railroads put the mark on the pony express. The auto retired the surrey with the fringe on top. And there are still a few good years before the logging dams vanish entirely. . . .

Roy had pulled the car into a turnout and stopped to load his corncob pipe. When it was giving off a proper turbulence, he asked me which dam was my favorite, and—just for fun—I said:

"Fourth Machias Dam—foot of Fourth Lake."

"I thought you'd say Dobsis Dam," he said, starting the car. "Or Night Dam—or maybe Webster Dam, on Webster Stream."

He had named my real prizes all right; but something had happened to me at Fourth Machias Dam when I was twenty years old, when Roy was my idol and mentor. I'd never told Roy about it, and this seemed like the perfect time.

"Digsy Jones and I had poled up Fourth Lake Stream to the dam," I said. "It was on our upriver Machias trip."

"I remember when you took that trip," Roy said. "It was 1921—the year of the big burn. What about it?"

"It was river driving time," I said, "and the boys were just about to h'ist the gates and start sluicing when they saw us poling up. They stood on the dam and watched us come, and when we made it to the wing of the dam, the River Boss walked over to me, and said:

" 'Young feller, the way you handled that canoe, I thought you was Roy Bailey!' "

What that River Boss had said was the biggest compliment ever paid me for canoemanship, and Roy knew I knew it. And it seemed to put an extra spice in our reunion.

We came along by Wabassas Dam again, and I thought how all the dams seem to take on a kind of beauty. They are hand hewn in all their timbers, with no concrete or metal except for drift pins or abutment spikes; and there is no falseness anywhere about them. You can see where the river-drivers' caulked boots have stippled the logs, and the gate posts and gates rise ghostly against the skyline on the upstream approach; and there is an air of mystery and loneliness, so that you think of a Stonehenge, made not of stone, but of ageless timbers hewn from an ageless forest.

Most certainly, if you have fished in Maine, you have come under the spell of the log dam trout pools. And if you have, you know how hard it is to name your favorite. You can't name one without feeling disloyal to the others.

But I have a soft spot for Webster Dam. It's a classic, mellowed by age, and by its history of lumbering and trout fishing, as it makes its slow way toward oblivion. The left wing has gone with the spring freshets. There's one gate post left; and you can always take trout in the sharp-angled bend above, and in the wide, sprawling pool below.

Webster seems to talk to me, because when the other gate post broke loose a few years ago, it sailed the nine, bouncey miles down Webster Stream in a spring pitch of water, picked up a fair wind on Second Grand Lake, made it on through the thoroughfare, and fetched up on shore right smack in front of my cabin on Grand Lake—a journey to my doorstep of about eighteen miles. A lot of good trout must have seen it drifting by over their heads.

Dobsis Dam is a favorite because it was the first one. That's where Pop Dennison taught me how to cast a fly, and Roy Bailey showed me just where to cast it. It's been ages since a log went through the Dobsis sluices. But it still stands in fine condition, because it's used now as part of the St. Croix Hydro system—and it has a concrete core, and a fishway.

It was in the still water above Dobsis Dam that you loaded your canoe for the trip across the foot of Dobsis Lake, then the Carry into Fourth Lake, and up Fouth Lake to Fifth Lake Stream—and Night Dam. That's the way you made it before the new roads. It's a matter of record in the faithfully kept Dobsis Camp diaries that I made this trip to Night Dam forty-five times. I mention it now as no boast, but as evidence of the spell and pull that Night Dam had for me—and still has. It's my favorite, Number One.

When you reached Night Dam, you had made a score. You had two lakes and a mile-and-a-half portage behind you. And you had four miles on a pole up Fifth Lake Stream. This stream is one hellish Baptism by canoe pole. The uneven bottom, the sudden, sharp drop-offs, are what make it a superior trout stream. The same unevenness is what makes you flip tail-over-bandbox out over the stern of your canoe when, with an all-out power thrust, your pole misses bottom by three feet, and there you are, sodden to the armpits, and your fishing license a mass of wet pulp.

Hell's Gate. High Rolling Tier. Smooth Ledge Falls. You round the last bend, and there, above a long, swift stretch, you see the Night Dam gates, and the crib work of the wings. You pitch your tent. You build up the stones of the fireplace. You cut a wood supply—and then go fishing.

At night, you sit around the fire, and the light flickers on the tent walls; and the sound of the water in the spillway seems almost like a part of you. You always felt the strange, lonely mood of the place; and some nights someone would start a song, and the others would move in close to make harmony.

There was one night when we hit a perfect chord—one of those wonderful ones you only hit once. There were five voices: Cy Stimson, the left-handed artist; Professor Paul Lieder of Smith College; Doctor (of philosophy) Otto Krauschaar, now President of Goucher College; and I. It was Otto who started the singing, and he couldn't have chosen a hymn more appropriate, and the rest of us joined. The words belong to everyone.

> Now the day is over, night is drawing nigh.
> Shadows of the evening, steal across the sky.

The fifth voice was the sad, sentient one of the dark water in the Night Dam spillway—the origin of the echo of solitude . . .

Now, in another twilight of a later June day, Roy Bailey stopped his car in front of Paul Hoar's store in Grand Lake Stream. I transferred to my own car for the drive to Bangor. Roy came over, and we shook hands.

"Night Dam is really it," I said.

"That's what I was hoping you'd say. Come back soon."

"I sure will—and thanks, Oldtimer. Thanks for the longest day of my life."

Potatoes: Maine vs. Idaho

I ONCE HAD a public debate with a friend from Idaho on the subject of potatoes. My opponent is ordinarily a righteous and talented man. But on the occasion of the debate, my friend came into the arena with a chip on his shoulder. To a person of my tastes and prejudices, the chip was inedible. It was an Idaho potato chip.

Gently knocking the above item from my opponent's shoulder, I proposed to substitute a Maine chip, or epaulet—sliced from that rarer and more luscious fruit, a potato grown on one of the Aroostook County farms up around Presque Isle, say Reid MacPherson's.

Of course "fruit," as used to describe potatoes, is a misnomer. It is intended to emphasize for the Maine brand the flavor of poetry. Actually, the potato is a vegetable. It is the most democratic vegetable in the world. Yet the finest potatoes on earth, I contend, are grown in the once most Re-

(146)

publican State—Maine. It thus becomes clear that certain inconsistencies crop up in the potato controversy.

For example, there's the one about the license plates. An Idaho tourist met a Maine tourist in Kansas. Both of them were hot, homesick and irritable.

"Your license plate says 'Vacation Land,' " accused the Idahoan. "So where you taking your vacation?"

"I was headed for Idaho," raged the Maine tourist, "But what do I read on your license plate? 'Famous For Potatoes!' And Maine is where potatoes were *born!*"

It is reported that the two tourists made peace by swapping cars. The Idahoan returned to vacationland in Idaho. The Maine man drove home to the potato state—which, to sober minds, is Maine.

Many of our Maine farms are generously sprinkled with rocks, a condition which imparts—perhaps—the firmness to our unequaled spuds. Good Maine potatoes run about the size and hardness of a heavyweight's fist.

This recalls my opponent's references to athletics in connection with Idaho potatoes. Dipping lightly into my files, I come up with an authentic retaliation, as follows: In 1947, the basketball team from one of Maine's small towns won the national schoolboy championship in its class. On the team were at least two sons of Maine potato farmers. All the team ate Maine potatoes regularly. They played and won the championship with but one two-minute substitution—an overtime game.

Maine raises its superlative spuds in the festive spirit. There is an annual potato blossom festival, and a queen is crowned, and the Governor usually speaks, and is unlikely to say anything at all about Idaho potatoes. At harvest time the school children are turned loose for potato picking, and you can hear their glad cries of freedom echoing over the October fields, and there is happiness throughout the land, and baked Maine potatoes for supper, dinner and breakfast.

What saith my esteemed opponent about calories? Only 100 in an Idaho potato? This is a sad discrepancy indeed. Maine potatoes have calories and lots of them. Brother, they've got fire-power. Here's a recipe:

Boil and mash six Maine potatoes, beating in butter and cream. Add salt and pepper. Place in large baking dish, and indent surface in six places with back of a large mixing spoon. Into each indentation, press a slice of ham. Over the ham, in each indentation, break a large fresh egg laid by a Maine hen. Over all sprinkle grated cheese liberally. Bake in a medium oven till eggs are shirred and cheese is golden brown.

There remains now but the one point of size. I admit that large Idaho potatoes are large. It hurts me, but I do. I can only fall back on a flash of brilliant Maine repartee which I overheard in a restaurant down Kittery way. Seeking to draw fire from the citizens of Maine, an Idahoan had brought some of his own potatoes with him. He had one baked for his lunch, and with a flourish drew a large hunting knife with which to carve the tuber.

"See that?" he crowed to the waiter. "Takes a ten-inch blade! By the way, brother, what do you slice your spuds with here in Maine?"

"For the small ones," said the waiter, "we generally use a scythe."

Part Three

RELIGION, RUM, AND RASCALITY

The Warden, the Rum,
and the Preacher

AFTER THEY PICKED UP the drowning game warden, Uncle Jeff Coongate and Zack Bourne had the whole lake to themselves. Considering the storm, they wanted the lake not at all. They wanted just once again to feel the stones under their feet, and sniff the smoke of a little fire on shore.

As for the game warden, they wanted him even less than the lake itself. They felt that he belonged not only with, but in the lake. Aside from the fact that the warden overloaded the canoe they had kept upright in the gale for two hours, there was a matter of six hundred pounds of illegal moose meat hanging in the shed back of Zack's cabin. However, it seemed that the waves would shortly solve the whole problem by swallowing them all, including the warden, who sat shivering amidships, bailing when he wasn't balancing.

Uncle Jeff Coongate had argued in the beginning against picking up the warden, whose canoe had swamped. The one-eyed poacher reasoned that word had got around about the moose, and that the warden had started uplake to investigate. Uncle Jeff did not believe in aiding an enemy, especially under these particular circumstances. Besides, the warden was a strange one.

Jeff and Zack had paddled down to Privilege to get a quart of rum with which to celebrate the killing of their winter's supply of meat. The gale had caught them on the way back. Their precious bottle of Hernando's Firey Dagger, untouched, lay tenderly swathed in a coat under the stern thwart. Its presence had cheered them on through the storm, giving them strength, and purpose.

"I'm brave jest from thinkin' about it," old Jeff had yelled from the bow.

"Let alone from really drinkin' it!" Zack had roared.

Shortly after this they had sighted the drowning warden. He was nearly exhausted, but his plight drew from the one-eyed poacher only the briefest sympathy. It was tough luck, but it was the warden's tough luck, Uncle Jeff believed. And to look at it squarely, you couldn't have a warden in the cabin where you aimed directly to celebrate the killing of a moose. This much was clear to anyone. The old poacher was for giving the warden a merciful push downward and holding him under till his misery was over.

But Zack Bourne would have none of it. To help a man drown, even a strange game warden who had come to spy on you, would weigh upon the conscience and dull the delights of wassail. Surely, in case they reached shore alive, they could figure out a way to keep the warden from snooping around the woodshed.

By a miracle of canoemanship, the two poachers worked their craft to a position where the warden could clutch the gunwale. Uncle Jeff's eye lighted balefully, but he gallantly refrained from banging the warden's knuckles with his paddle blade, and even helped him crawl over the side into the canoe.

"Take that tea can an' bail," ordered the one-eyed poacher, "or back you go a-swimmin'."

The warden numbly bailed, keeping about even with the waves which raked over the gunwales.

Quartering into the seas, Zack and Jeff stared straight ahead, watching the creeping approach of their destined shore. If they reached that shore, Zack realized that he must caution his wife, Sarah, about the warden. Sarah was a good cook, and mighty religious, and the loneliest times of Zack's life were when Sarah was away. But unless you talked firm to her, and drilled a notion into her good and hard, she'd forget where she was and who was around. It would be just like her to say to the warden: "My stars an' body! Did you see the lovely moose Zack an' Jeff Coongate jacklighted night before last?" Or she might just absent-mindedly slice off some of the loin and serve it to the warden for supper.

In the bow of the canoe, increasingly vigilant as they approached the narrows where the swells piled furiously, Uncle Jeff Coongate fought his weariness with dreams of rum and a safe arrival. And he, too, laid plans for thwarting the warden. The moment the canoe touched the landing at the cabin, Uncle Jeff decided he would leap out and go to warn Sarah Bourne, leaving Zack to stall the warden. After cautioning Sarah, Uncle Jeff would duck around to the woodshed, cut the moose meat down, and pile stove wood over it.

Steadying with his paddle, as a tremendous wave lifted the bow, Uncle Jeff kept on in his mind, elaborating his plan. When the warden came up to the cabin, he would be very considerate of him. He would suggest that he drink some hot tea and retire at once under five blankets. On second thought, he would offer the warden a big, double jolt of rum, because the warden would have to refuse it. It was strictly against orders for him to drink on duty.

After the warden turned in, Jeff dreamed, he and Zack would take the bottle and go down to the root cellar. They'd have the lamp turned low. They'd sit on the vinegar keg and lard tub amidst the winter's provisions. They'd drink till the rum was 'most gone, and sing a little, and lick their chops thinking of feeding off the moose meat through the cold weather. It would be mighty fine and cozy down there, celebrating a moose, and a warden asleep upstairs. It would tone things up just nice.

The canoe pitched crazily as it came into the cross-chop in the throat of the narrows. A wave poured in. The warden's face, except for the patches of purple veins over his cheek bones, went livid. Zack swung the canoe at right angles, and as they ran for shore, a ragged swell chased them into the gut, broke, and swamped them full length from the stern forward.

Taking to the water head first, Jeff Coongate came up gasping: "Save the rum, Zack!"

Zack got hold of the coat and held it up triumphantly as his feet touched bottom. They floundered to the beach, and dumped the canoe. Through the narrows, and sheltered by an island a quarter of a mile to windward, they were safe. Half a mile up the shore the cabin was visible. They saw the wind-ripped smoke scattering from its chimney.

Jeff took the rum bottle from Zack, unwrapped it, and read the label in an enticing voice: "Hernando's Firey Dagger, hundred an' ten proof."

"A whole damn quart." breathed Zack, wringing water from his mackinaw.

Jeff, his eye gleaming villainously, offered the bottle to the warden. "Care for a swallow?"

"Well—I—no." The warden gulped. He shuddered in the cold, his wet clothes clinging to him. "I'm on duty."

"What a pity," sighed Jeff, hugging the bottle. "What duty brings you clear up here?"

Jeff had re-wrapped the bottle and placed it back in the

stern of the canoe, but still the warden said nothing. He seemed entranced by the bottle neck which peeped brightly from the folds of the coat. Uncle Jeff repeated his question in a sharper voice.

"What?" asked the warden, vaguely.

"I was just wonderin' why in hell they'd send a warden clear up here."

"The department wants to find out if moose are workin' back in," said the warden.

"Oh. Moose?" Jeff casually wiped the water from his eye socket. "Hain't seen hardly any signs. Was they thinkin' of declarin' an open season?"

"No."

"That's fine. Moose had ought to be protected permanent. Mighty fine animal. Pratickly exstink, you might say, too. Shame to kill the few that's left. Let's get a-goin'."

"Yes," the warden said.

Zack's wife, Sarah, came out of the cabin and hurried down to the landing before they reached it. She had been watching for them anxiously. She was in a great state of excitement, and she was wearing her black dress. She began speaking the moment the canoe sided in to the log wharf. She kept looking over her shoulder toward the cabin, apparently fearful that someone there might overhear.

"Zack Bourne, did you get that rum? Where is it? May the Lord forgive you, riskin' life an' limb on the lake just for the evil purpose of—"

"We got the rum," said Zack. "An' we got a game warden, too."

Zack intended his remark to warn Sarah, but she went on unheedingly. "You give me that rum, Zack. I don't want it to appear in sight."

"Why not?" inquired Uncle Jeff, bristling. "We all seen it. Why hide it?"

"Because they's a preacher here, that's why! Right after the wind come up, he got blowed ashore. A lovely little preacher, too. Interested in rocks, and trees, and—"

"A preacher!" wailed Jeff, outraged that Fate in a single hand had dealt him the cloth and the law.

"Yes. A preacher. And mind your language before him."

"Honey," said Zack morosely, "where in hell is this preacher, now?"

"In the cabin washin' for supper."

Zack had turned the canoe over and was holding the rum under one arm. "Couldn't Jeff and me have a little snifter before we meet him?"

" 'Course not!" Sarah's eyes blazed indignantly. "Give me that rum. Not a drop till he's abed an' asleep. I'll just put it in the root cellar."

When Zack hesitated to relinquish the bottle, Sarah held out her hand. "Come on, hurry up! I got some of the meat fryin', an' I got to get right back to the stove."

Jeff Coongate stiffened, and the warden sniffed curiously.

"Oh, good thing we had some of the beef left," said Zack pointedly.

"I told the preacher that's what it was," said Sarah.

The warden watched narrowly as she tucked the rum under her arm, and he seemed attentive as she explained: "I told him 'twas western corn-fed beef."

"What else would he think it was?" croaked the one-eyed poacher.

The warden shrugged. They all followed Sarah to the cabin. Zack opened the bulkhead outside, and Sarah went down into the root cellar and came back without the rum. The

warden leaned over and peered into the dark interior of the
cellar. He wore a patient look when Zack let the bulkhead
doors down. Sarah faced them, a finger to her lips. "Mind, not
a drop till he's abed."

"Never you fear. Jest trust us," said Jeff, sidling toward
the woodshed out back. "I'll fetch in some wood for you,
Sarah."

"I'll help," said Zack.

"I'll help, too," said the warden.

Before closing the kitchen door, Sarah called: "The woodbox is full. The preacher filled it."

"May hell receive his stricken soul!" said Uncle Jeff.

"So it's in the woodshed," observed the warden. "Let's
take a look at it."

Quite clearly no one was fooling anyone any more. They
walked slowly to the woodshed, and in the dusk stood gazing
at the contraband.

"We got him plumb through the neck," said Jeff.
"Dropped where he stood."

The warden remained silent. Zack said to him: "Mind
we done you a little favor out on the lake this afternoon?"

In the dim light the warden's face showed pale. He
trembled a little. It was cold, and he was thinking of the lake.
"Yes," he said.

"Well, so now you got us. You'd pinch us, even if we
saved your life, wouldn't you?"

"I'd pinch my own mother."

"I know it. But jest 'cause she borned you, you would do
her a favor before you took her to the gallows, wouldn't you?"

"Maybe."

"Then for cryssake don't let on in front of the preacher

that you got us for poaching. It would jest about kill Sarah."

"All right," said the warden.

Filing through the back door into the kitchen, the three men stood blinking in the lamplight. At the table, a napkin tucked in his collar, the preacher sat before a platter of moose meat and a mound of hot biscuits. He was a small, happy man, as loquacious as the game warden was taciturn. No ill wind had ever blown so flattering a prize ashore at Sarah Bourne's lonely doorstep. Sarah hovered and fluttered, praying that her menfolk would make no glaring social blunders.

They didn't. The game warden was still as death. Zack and Jeff gloomily wondered where they could get five hundred dollars to pay their fine, and, if they couldn't, how it would be in jail. They sat down, silently wishing their clerical guest would finish his meal quickly and retire. Their rum, originally for celebration, was now essential to the cushioning of woe, but even for that purpose, it was denied them so long as the preacher remained awake.

When Uncle Jeff reached with his fork to spear a biscuit, Sarah rapped his knuckles with her knife. "Leave them be! There ain't only enough for our guest. Ain't bread good enough for you?"

"I always say," said the preacher, "that there's nothing like bread dipped in nice beef gravy. Do try some, Mr. Coongate."

"Thanks."

The preacher unselfishly passed the platter of moose meat to the game warden. The warden declined. The preacher then gave a brief discourse on the staying powers of red meat in the human system. Sarah listened worshipfully, as if his every word were gold. Zack and Jeff exchanged sad, thirsty glances, but the preacher showed no signs of drowsiness. In fact, he grew wider awake by the minute. He was enthusiastic over food, nature, people, and his own voice. Uncle Jeff tried mental telepathy and open yawning, but they didn't work.

Sarah kept prompting the parson. Zack feared that Sarah might take it into her head to tell him the story of the death of her brother Jonas. It was a long, harrowing story, but the preacher had a lot of stories of his own. While he was telling one, Zack dreamed of the first, cool feeling of rum in his mouth, then the shock and fire in his throat, then the strangling sensation, and at last the huge glow in his belly and the roaring in his brain.

The parson was off on a new tack. Uncle Jeff stood brooding by the woodbox. The game warden seemed lost in cold, black thought. But it was the game warden who first succumbed to weariness. "Guess I'll turn in," he said.

"Very wise decision," approved the preacher. "You have been through a terrible experience. Nothing like long and dreamless sleep to reknit the fibers sundered by terror, chill, and immersion."

The warden looked as though his fibers needed reknitting. Zack showed him to the front room of the cabin. There wasn't any bed. The spare bed was for the preacher. Zack spread some bearskins and got some blankets. The warden took off his boots and his pants and lay down, and Zack returned to the kitchen, closing the door gently behind him.

The preacher had opened up a new vein of conversational resource. He had arranged a peck or so of rocks on the table and was going nicely on geology and Indian relics. Sarah, her face ruddy in the lamplight, looked as if her soul were filling rapidly with wisdom. Uncle Jeff, now hunkered inside the woodbox, thought only of the sound of a cork squeaking out of a bottle neck.

"Should think," said Sarah, "that warden would of wanted to stay up and listen to these educational things."

"Guess he's beat out," said Zack, taking a chair. "He d— dang near drowned."

"I can readily understand his exhaustion," the preacher said.

"Ain't you a little mite tired yourself, Reverend?" graciously inquired Uncle Jeff. "We don't aim to keep you up. Any time you want to hit the hay, why—"

"I get along on very little sleep," replied the guest. "I attribute it to exercise in the great outdoors, and to the stimulus of exchanging ideas with people."

"Oh."

Zack ran his tongue along his lips. There was only one thing to be thankful for: Sarah had not started about her brother Jonas. She didn't seem to have much chance. The preacher had selected a fresh rock from his collection and was holding it up to the light.

"This," he said, "is a specimen of jasper, rather rare in these parts. Frankly, I was surprised to find it."

"My!" Sarah exclaimed. She looked around at Zack. "Ain't it interestin' to hear a man talk like this? It's very educational."

"Yuh."

Thus encouraged, the preacher dropped the jasper and picked up some other rocks. "Now here we have a very interesting quartz relationship. I—"

"Quartz?" said old Jeff, to whom the word had but one meaning. "Where?"

"Here. Now a crystalline schist, as you no doubt fully appreciate, is—"

"A rock is a rock," said Zack sullenly.

"Don't show your ignorance!" Sarah blurted. "Hold your tongue."

The preacher smiled tolerantly. "A rock, as your husband has pointed out, is, of course, a rock. But how was it formed? When was it formed? And under what conditions? These are the great questions."

The parson answered these questions at some length. He propounded others, and answered them. He spoke weightily of pyrites, lignites, chalcedony, fault scarps, moraines, stalactites, stalagmites, sedimentation, silica, and the great ice sheet. The two poachers suffered in silence. Not that they wanted to speak. Their throats were too parched. They were far less interested in rocks than in the cruel Fate which had first brought them a game warden who would jail them, and second a preacher who had kept them from their rum. Their mercy and hospitality had brought them misery tenfold.

Just as the preacher packed away his rocks and looked as if he might consider going to bed, Sarah's eyes lighted, and she began about her brother Jonas. Old Jeff settled deeper in the woodbox, too weak to sigh. Zack swallowed, and his throat made a dry creaking sound.

Sarah's brother Jonas had fought in the first war, and had died on the nineteenth anniversary of his shrapnel wound, just at sunset, when a neighbor's boy, a Scout bugler, happened to be playing taps. To Sarah the coincidence had a deep religious significance. Here was her great chance to get a clergyman's opinion.

Zack and Jeff had heard the story so many times that they could clock off the points accurately. Five minutes for Jonas's patriotism and character; seven for his *croix de guerre;* nine for his hospitalization; twenty-two for his operations; three for the neighbor's boy who had joined the Scouts at Jonas's suggestion;

two for Jonas's kindness in buying the boy the bugle; and from eight to twelve for the death scene. Sixty minutes might cover it for an ordinary guest, but Zack figured Sarah would take close to eighty for the preacher. He estimated that, with luck, he could live an hour and a half more without rum. But over in the woodbox, Uncle Jeff Coongate looked as if he couldn't hold out, that death by thirst would claim him before Sarah got Jonas out of the veterans' hospital.

Sarah had progressed as far as Jonas's second operation, and the preacher was listening in an attitude of deep thought, when they first heard the bumping noise. Sarah paused, annoyed. "That's your canoe blowin', Zack. Didn't you tie it?"

"The wind's died out," Zack said.

The preacher said: "Listen."

They listened for some moments, but the night was still. Sarah resumed her story: "Well, then Jonas says to the doctors: 'I'm willin' to undergo anything.' Jonas was brave, always brave. He says to them: 'You cut me open before, an' you can do it again.' So then they cut Jonas open, and——"

They heard the bumping sound again, this time much nearer against the outside wall of the cabin. Jeff Coongate looked up at the deer horns where his rifle hung. Zack had stood up and started toward the door, when a doleful, singing voice reached them:

> I'll go where you wan' me to go dear Lor',
> I'll travel o'er lan' an' sea.
> I'll do what you wan' me to do dear Lor',
> I'll be what you wan' me to be-e-e-e-e——

When Zack opened the door, the game warden almost fell into the kitchen. He caught himself with one hand. In the other he held the rum bottle, which was nearly empty. It was obvious to everyone that the warden had gone out through the front door of the cabin, and down into the root cellar to the bottle. Judging by the pittance of rum left, the warden had been in the cellar a long time. He was minus his pants and boots, and his long underwear lacked crucial buttons.

"Re-knitting fibersh," he said. "Fibersh fine now."

"Mrs. Bourne," said the preacher gallantly, "shall I show you to your room?"

"He got into our medicine that we keep in the root cellar," wailed Sarah, determined to explain the rum bottle on high moral grounds.

"It was for Mr. Coongate's cough," Zack softly added.

Jeff gulped out loud. "Zack sometimes coughed a mite, too."

The game warden reeled, aimed for a chair, and just made it, as his underwear opened all the way down the front. The preacher stepped between him and Sarah. Sarah fled to the bedroom, and the preacher turned to deal with the drunken warden. He placed a hand firmly on the warden's shoulder. "Listen to me," he said severely. "Are you able to understand me?"

"Shernly," said the warden, looking up gravely. "Shernly I understand."

"These men saved your life on the lake today. They brought you to their home."

"They had to," the warden mumbled. "Only place on the lake."

"They fed you. They gave you of their hospitality—their food and meat, their shelter."

"Didn't eat any meat," the warden said thickly.

"And in return, you steal their medicine, and get helplessly intoxicated."

"Unh," said the warden.

"I am therefore in duty bound," continued the preacher, "to report you to the authorities. An officer of the law, drunk. A serious offense."

At this moment, Uncle Jeff Coongate climbed from the woodbox and sidled forward. "Reverend," he said, "this man went through a mighty turrible time in the lake till we come along. He swum an hour in the cold water, with the fear of death on him."

"His poor wife an' children are dependent on him," said Zack Bourne.

"Lookin' at it one way, he wa'n't hardly responsible for what he done, Reverend," Uncle Jeff went on. " 'Course it's a turrible thing, jest the same. Shocked me awful. But I say he should be forgiven. On account of his wife, an' children, an'—"

"An' the work he does protectin' this country from the ravidges of lawless poachers," said Zack.

"Jest the very words I was goin' to use," said the one-eyed poacher. "So I say we forgive this poor man. But if we ever had cause to change our minds, we could always get you to witness what he done here tonight. Couldn't we, Reverend?"

"Indeed you could," said the preacher enthusiastically. "And I may say that you men have demonstrated remarkable forgiveness. I shall remember it as long as I live."

"Shame here," said the warden.

"You are a very fortunate man," the preacher told the warden.

"Shernly am," replied the warden.

He went carefully to the front room, closed the door, and sank down on the bearskins, knowing that he could sleep, for the cruelty of cold and the fear of death were no longer in him. "Everyone's very forshunit," he muttered, pulling the blankets around him.

The Diary of Death

ON A WINTER'S EVENING, in his apartment in Boston, Mr. Usher sat down to read the record of events which had transpired during the previous year at his camp in the wilderness on Mopang Lake. The record was kept in diary form, with daily entries by the resident caretaker. Mr. Usher opened the volume at hand with marked anxiety. He had been able to spend but two weeks at his camp during the previous year, and this diary, which he had just received, represented the first twelve months residence of a new and untried caretaker, Zachariah Bourne.

Mr. Usher had hired Zack Bourne with strong misgivings. There had been no doubt as to Zack's woodsmanship, or his qualifications to live happily in the wilderness. He was a mag-

(166)

nificent physical specimen, and he had lived in the wild lands most of his life, but he had a reputation for lawlessness, and a primordial sense of justice which both attracted Mr. Usher and frightened him. Moreover, in his desire to protect Mr. Usher's interests, Zack had seemed overzealous from the start.

"Jest you rest easy, Mr. Usher," Zack had said. "I'll shoot the feet from under anyone I see fishin' in our waters, or huntin' in our territory."

"But you can't do that, Zack."

"I'm the best rifle shot in Mopang."

"So I'm told. I simply mean that the lakes and the forests are free to anyone. Part of your duty would be to keep the peace, as I have always tried to keep it here."

"Sure, Mr. Usher. I'll jest fix it so things'll seem peacefuler to trespassers if they stay away from here."

Mr. Usher probably would not have engaged Zack if it hadn't been for Zack's wife, Sarah. Sarah was city bred, and Mr. Usher saw at once that she would have a gentling effect on her tall, tough-minded husband.

"Zack Bourne!" Sarah had reproached. "Hush that wild talk."

Turning to Mr. Usher, Sarah had then explained that Zack had lately returned from visiting a crony who was in jail down in Mopang. The crony's name was Thomas Jefferson Coongate, and he was an evil influence on Zack, and a menace in the community.

"Coongate?" Mr. Usher had inquired. "I seem to recall the name. Isn't he the one-eyed poacher of Privilege?"

He was indeed, said Sarah Bourne, and briskly sketched the Coongate character. Old Jeff Coongate, according to Sarah, was composed solely of vices. He was a chewer of tobacco, a drinker of bottled goods in any alcoholic form, and a kind of marathon blasphemer. He was a sworn breaker of game laws, and an enemy of the State. He was a jacklighter of deer, a gill-netter of salmon, a dynamiter of trout, and above all else a plotter against the lives of game wardens. In fact, he was currently in the clink for shooting the stern off a game warden's canoe with an automatic shotgun. Happily the warden was a good swimmer.

When Sarah paused to draw breath, Zack said: "But he's a good feller, jest the same."

"That's what you think," snapped Sarah, "because you an' him river-drove, an' poached together, when you was boys. Every time you been in trouble, 'twas him got you into it."

This conversation more than half convinced Mr. Usher that Sarah had Zack under control, and he had hired Zack on the spot.

"I want you both to regard this place as your home," Mr. Usher had said to Zack and Sarah Bourne. "The canoes, and all the equipment are for your use, as well as mine. I hope you will love this camp, as I do. I request that you do not leave the place alone for more than two or three days at a time, except of course in emergency. And there is only one thing on which I insist. That is the regular, and accurate keeping of the camp diary, day by day."

"You mean," said Zack, troubled, "that I'm to write somethin' down every day? Every single day?"

"Exactly."

"I'll tend to that myself, Mr. Usher," said Sarah.

Now, in his apartment, as he read Sarah's careful entries in the diary, Mr. Usher's mind gradually relaxed. Sarah had done an excellent job. From the simple facts she had recorded, Mr. Usher got a clear picture of the seasons, the work, the weather, and events. Mr. Usher read with absorption, and fascination.

The diary was vivid evidence of the reality of the place he loved beyond all others.

January and February told of blizzards, bitter cold, the crackle of northern lights, and the thunder of the ice at night. And always the loneliness:

"No one come by for seventeen days, too cold, 27 below today, mouse in back pantry, Zack has toothache, but hauled wood from choppin across dam."

March and April told of thaws and freezes which made travel on the lakes next to impossible. Then came May, and the last, deadly weeks of waiting for the ice to leave. And on the 23rd, the joyous entry:

"Ice went out overnight in northwest gale, flock geese landed in cove at sunset, Zack took me out in canoe, wonderful. Salmon fishermen be coming soon, and will have company here in this lonely place at last. Zack leaving daylight tomorrow for supplies."

So read Mr. Usher—on through June, and the fly season. He read of three deer feeding in the back clearing, a family of otter living briefly along the stream, and a moose sighted across the dam. Mr. Usher's satisfaction with his new caretaker was first clouded by an entry in late August.

"Game Warden Tom Corn stopped by today out of tobacco. Zack would not give him any, mean I call it. It was Tom Corn's canoe that Jeff Coongate shot stern of off. The warden reported Jeff Coongate gets out of jail October one. Oh dear. Hope he don't come to see Zack, we been so happy here, even through this long and terrible winter."

Mr. Usher began to read more rapidly. He had a feeling that the inevitable was about to happen, that the nefarious one-eyed poacher would soon arrive and lead Zack Bourne astray. On September 11th a swallow flew through the open kitchen window. Sarah wrote that this was a bad omen, that it meant that someone would be very sick, or get hurt. But the dramatic import of this was lost to Mr. Usher. It was completely overshadowed by Sarah's description of the turning of the leaves in early October—and by the following entry under date of November second:

"A most awful day. Thos. J. Coongate come up lake in night, arrived here crack of day. He had whiskey, and offered to Zack. I would not let Zack touch it. He tried to get Zack to go to Little Mopang Stream to trap beaver, this against law. I would not let Zack go, as I know Mr. Usher would not like it. Finely I told that one-eyed poacher to go away from this place, and he went after darkness fell as he don't want no one to see him. Zack mad at me, says am not cordial to his friends. Cannot be cordial to that outlaw man, for fear Zack will get himself in trouble."

On November third, fourth, fifth, and sixth, Sarah reported that Zack had not spoken to her. But then on the seventh:

"Zack made up today, kissed me, so sweet, said he knowed I was right, and if it hadn't been for me he would of done something foolish. Was so sweet, hugged and kissed me, till I am bruised and squoze, he don't know his strength. My!"

The entry of November 10th told of Zack's last trip out to Privilege for supplies before freeze-up. Zack returned two days later with a canoe-load of provisions, and the mail. November 13th:

"Unlucky day, Zack brought letter from my brother saying my sister very sick in Bangor. Must go to her, as if anything happened would feel awful, and shell ice on lake now in many places. Must go, hate to leave Zack alone, as don't know what will happen. Do hope and pray that one-eyed devil Jeff Coongate don't come back this way."

As he finished reading the above entry, Mr. Usher stiffened in his chair. He, too, hoped and prayed that the one-eyed poacher would not, or had not visited his camp when Zack was there without Sarah. November 14th, 15th and 16th were blank, indicating the time required for Zack to get Sarah out to Privilege en route to Bangor. On the 17th, Zack had returned to the job. The handwriting was no longer in Sarah's clear, even penmanship, but showed signs of tremendous effort. Mr. Usher remembered that Zack had seemed troubled when he learned that he was to write something every day. The first entry in the labored, masculine handwriting, was on the 17th.

"Hellish trip back uplake after leaving Sarah in Privilege, broke ice clear from Caribou Ledge and chewed canoe canvas plump to hell. Geese went South in night, big flock, wish was with them, lonesome for Sarah all ready, but brought plenty big supply medicine back with me, Hernando's Fiery Dagger rum an Old Blow-Torch gin, ha-ha!"

Mr. Usher's heart sank. This was the thing he had dreaded. But he had not realized that Zack would be so brazen as to write it down in his own handwriting. On second thought, he realized, Zack Bourne was exactly the kind of man who would do just that, and do it unblushingly.

From November 17th on to the end of the year, the diary of Mr. Usher's beloved camp was the plain, agonizing record of a bush-queer man going steadily and irretrievably to hell. It was both fascinating, and appalling. November 19th:

"Cold for two days, ice four inches caught pickerl through ice, will say anyone that can stand up on this black ice after drinkin pint of Fiery Dagger rum is sure good balancer. Fell flat a dozen times gettin ashore, found camp door open wide when got back, someone maybe comin. Wish Jeff Coongate would come, would have hell of time. Plenty rum and gin left."

This entry was enough to sicken Mr. Usher, but he didn't realize to what depths a lonely man would sink until, on December 4th, Zack Bourne became a squaw man.

"Down to Privilege over the ice with hand sled. Stopped at Injun Villige on way back, got a squaw here now to keep me warm nights, her name Elsie Brown Blanket. Found old cat, Daisy, had kittens in cloze basket, five. Elsie thinks kittens might be good to eat. Some squaw, all right. Big bull moose workin over in woods near cove."

December 5th to 10th, inclusive, were quite clearly given over solely to debauch. Mr. Usher, reading between the lines, saw the desecration of his camp, and his wilderness. The handwriting for this period had become an illegible, drunken scrawl. December 11th marked Zack's return to partial sobriety. Mr. Usher read this day's entry, his stomach revolting.

"Elsie been keepin diary for me past few days, but I can't read what she wrote, but I know what she wrote about, ha-ha, thats all we been doin anyway. Snowed last night an covered most all empty bottles an tincans in front dooryard of cabin."

Mr. Usher was but slightly relieved to note that, on December 14th, Zack Bourne had tired of Elsie Brown Blanket's aboriginal charms.

"Elsie wants to get marrid to me and raise famly, can you beat it? That's a squaw for you. I said did not plan to commit bigmy with her, but only a little adultery, ha-ha. She got mad an throwed hand axe at me, so am leavin today to take her back to Injun Villige. Good snow-shoein on lake, tempriture zero, wind north, clear."

There were only a few more entries. Zack's year, reflected Mr. Usher, his heart heavy within him, was almost over. So was Zack's job as caretaker of the camp on Mopang Lake. If the record of decay had so far sickened Mr. Usher, the last few entries did even more. They froze his blood.

"December 20th:

"My two dogs, Buck and Slats, been chasin moose in woods across dam. Will go after moose some day soon."

"December 25th:

"Merry Christmas, like hell. Buck an Slats dogged the moose out on ice. He dropped with first shot, I got the bastid right back of ear, some shot, as I had drunk 2 qts. rum yestdy an was shakin so couldn't hold rifle ver stiddy. Was dressin out moose when game warden Tom Corn stepped out of hidin in thick brush on shore, an got me for doggin moose. He drawed his service revolver and right before my very eyes shot both my dogs, Buck and Slats, best friends I ever had. Then he said for me to get ready to go to Mopang with him to jail, an I said would come peaceful, an told him I would get some things from cabin if he would wait. He waited all right, and will say that game warden will never shoot another dog in this world. How I know is my bisness, but wish Jeff Coongate seen it happen, as it would sure pleased Jeff, as this warden will never trail him nor anyone no more."

Mr. Usher shuddered, and closed the diary of death. He did not know whether to try and get in touch with Sarah Bourne, in Bangor, or to turn the diary over to the police. He finally decided to hire a plane equipped with skis for landing on the lake in front of his cabin door. His decision as to what to do about Zack would depend to some extent on what he discovered.

Taking with him the diary of death, Mr. Usher flew to Bangor the next morning on the regular transport plane. From Bangor he proceeded north by charter plane for Mopang Lake.

He had been fortunate in securing the services of a pilot who tended the wants of trappers throughout the north. The flier knew the country well. He set his ship down smoothly on the packed snow on the lake before the cabin. Mr. Usher noted that no smoke came from the chimney. Had Zack left the country? Had the game warden already been missed? Apparently not, for inside the cabin Mr. Usher found the stove warm.

The pilot, looking from the kitchen window over the lake, said: "I guess there comes your man now. Prob'ly been cutting wood over on the island."

Even at a great distance, Mr. Usher recognized Zack Bourne. He had harnessed himself to a handsled, and he was leaning forward, his great shoulders straining. The handsled was loaded with wood.

"I'll pick you up at three sharp this afternoon," said the pilot. "That is, if the weather holds."

"But won't you stay and eat something?" asked Mr. Usher. He felt strangely lonesome, now, and uneasy. He wished the pilot would stay, and told him so.

The pilot shook his head. "I've got to pick up beaver skins for six trappers over in the Golroy River district. There's a bulge in the market, and if I don't catch it, I lose their business. I won't be gone long, unless a storm comes up."

The plane took off, circled for altitude, cleared the big ridge, and was gone before Zack Bourne arrived with his load of wood. When he recognized Mr. Usher, Zack slipped out of the sled harness and strode forward, smiling as if his conscience were as clear as a child's.

"Say, if it ain't Mr. Usher! I'm sure glad you could come."

As they shook hands, Mr. Usher felt bewildered, and a little frightened. Now that he had arrived, he did not know exactly how to proceed. Moreover, every time he turned his head, Mr. Usher noted a new bit of evidence which added confirmation to his worst fears. Zack's deer dogs, Buck and Slats, were conspicuously absent.

"What happened to your hounds?" asked Mr. Usher, gently.

"Buck and Slats?" While he answered, Zack calmly went about building up the fire and preparing a meal. "Well, I was afeared they might get to chasin' deer on the snow, where the tracks would show too plain. So I left 'em down to Privilege when I took Sarah out."

The smell of frying pickerel brought forth corroboration of another item in the diary of death. The cat, Daisy, and her five kittens emerged single file from under the stove, and, with tails high and backs arched, rubbed against Zack's legs. Mr. Usher's stomach turned over, as he recalled the entry in which Elsie Brown Blanket had pondered the kittens' edibility.

"I—I—uh—suppose it must have been lonesome here without Sarah," essayed Mr. Usher, miserably.

"Turrible! I damn near perished nights," Zack answered.

Now, for the first time, Mr. Usher observed that Zack's left hand was bandaged. Doubtless this wound had resulted from Elsie Brown Blanket's throwing of the hand axe. Zack had apparently shielded himself with his left hand, and had been cut.

"How did you hurt your hand, Zack?" asked Mr. Usher, fearfully.

"Cut myself with the hand axe," came the brazen reply.

"How?"

"Splittin' kindlin' in the dark."

Zack set a plate of fried pickerel and potatoes in front of his employer. But Mr. Usher's appetite was completely missing. He somehow could not bring himself to break bread with a drunkard, adulterer and murderer. Zack himself ate with relish, and when he had finished, said: "I'd like to take you out 'round the place an' show you some things I done. Maybe you'd be pleased to see 'em."

Deciding to delay mentioning the diary until time for the return of the plane, Mr. Usher accompanied Zack on a tour of inspection. In between debauches, Zack had found opportunity for a prodigious amount of work. Mr. Usher smiled bitterly. Aside from the fact that his new caretaker broke all ten commandments, he was the perfect man for the job. He had built a cap-and-bunk fence around the garden, using dry cedar poles. He had cut the unsightly dead limbs from the great white pine which landmarked the place in Mr. Usher's mind and memory. He had shingled the shed roof with shingles he had split himself, with mallet and frow. He had re-canvassed three canoes as smoothly as a factory might have done it. But most pleasing to Mr. Usher was the magnificent axe work which had gone into the hewing of new sills for every building on the place.

"That's beautiful, Zack," Mr. Usher had remarked, momentarily forgetting that his man was virtually a self-confessed murderer.

" 'Tain't nothin' at all, hardly. You come in the workshop, an' see the paddles I made. Got six out of one big maple butt. An' I got the best one marked for you. It's got a spring, an' whip to it, an' the bird's eye in the wood makes it han'some."

Mr. Usher tested the spring of the blade, found it perfect, and set the paddle down with a sigh. "I am very sorry that your wife, Sarah, had to leave you alone so long, Zack."

"Me, too. But I think Sarah's sister'll die, an' that won't bother me a dang bit, neither, 'cause then Sarah can bury her an' come back."

As they left the workshop, walking toward the cabin on the

path Zack had shoveled in the deep snow, Mr. Usher decided to have his showdown and get it over with.

"Zack," he said, "I have read the diary. I have read it all. That is why I am here, as you may have guessed."

At mention of the diary, Zack Bourne showed his first signs of uneasiness. His eyes no longer met Mr. Usher's squarely, and he replied irrelevantly, plainly avoiding the subject. Pausing at the cabin door, he pointed to the windows, and said: "I puttied every dang pane of glass this side of the cabin."

"Zack, I want to talk to you about the diary."

But Zack's reluctance to discuss the subject continued. His guilt was palpable. He looked off across the lake, and, after a heavy silence, said: "There's someone comin'. There's two men comin'."

Mr. Usher glanced at his watch. Plane-time was but half an hour hence, and the two men, who were approaching rapidly across the lake, gave him extra confidence.

"Zack, I'd like to go over the diary with you and ask some questions. I brought it with me."

They entered the cabin. Mr. Usher sat down at the kitchen table, spreading the diary open before him. Zack put some beech chunks in the stove, and sat down opposite his employer.

"Ain't the diary all right?" he asked, avoiding Mr. Usher's eyes by staring from the window at the approaching men.

"No. I am sorry to say it is not all right."

"Well, dang it, that's Sarah's fault then. She kep' it."

"She kept it perfectly. I refer to the entries made by yourself, in Sarah's absence."

Zack swallowed. His forehead glistened, as the sweat began to come. He stared steadily at the two men, who were by now less than two hundred yards away.

Mr. Usher turned the diary toward Zack, and pointed to the entry for November 17th, the first following Sarah's departure: ". . . brought plenty big supply medicine back with me, Hernando's Fiery Dagger rum an Old Blow-Torch gin, ha-ha!"

"What do you suppose I thought when I read that, Zack? What opinion could you have thought I would have, about the new caretaker to whom I had entrusted my place here?"

Zack's huge hands clenched. The red of shame suffused his face. He averted his eyes, but made no reply.

"And this entry," continued Mr. Usher, turning to December 4th. "With your wife gone, you turned squaw man. You brought an Indian woman here—the one who threw the axe and cut your hand."

Zack guiltily thrust his bandaged hand out of sight under the table. Then, with a groan, he stood up and walked to the cabin window, his giant shoulders slumped abjectly.

"Zack," said Mr. Usher, "I am afraid I shall have to terminate my agreement with you. As for the entry about the shooting of—"

Zack had suddenly straightened and glued his face to the window pane. The two men were just entering the cabin dooryard. "Game warden!" said Zack. "A game warden with that—"

"The game warden," Mr. Usher asked gently, "couldn't be Tom Corn, could it, Zack?"

"Not unless it's his ghost," said Zack, turning fiercely. "He's been—transferred."

To Mr. Usher, the word "transferred," as it issued from Zack Bourne's livid lips, meant liquidated, purged, in short, murdered. But Zack's recent shame and guilt had suddenly dropped from him. He stood for a moment, tall, tense, savage.

Then, with the quickness of a huge cat, he reached for his rifle, snatched it from the wall pegs, jacked in a shell, and flung open the cabin door.

"Zack! Zack!" cried Mr. Usher. "You can't kill another warden, Zack!"

"I don't aim to kill no warden," Zack snarled, as Mr. Usher followed him from the cabin door. "I aim to kill the bastid that wrote that diary for me. Step to one side, warden—jest a foot to one side, till I get a shot at that one-eyed Jeff Coongate!"

Standing behind, and a little to one side of Zack, Mr. Usher observed that the warden's body shielded the second man. As he watched, spellbound, a face of splendid and grinning malevolence appeared briefly over the warden's shoulder. One eye was missing from the face. The color of the other eye was a kind of baleful blue. There was also a stringy, white mustache, from which icicles hung, giving the one-eyed poacher of Privilege the appearance of a sardonic Santa Claus.

"Warden," said Thomas Jefferson Coongate, "it's your duty to pertec' me. I'm your prisoner."

The warden moved a little, not especially liking his view of the hole in the end of Zack Bourne's rifle. The one-eyed poacher moved with him, and for a second or two the warden and his prisoner resembled a dance team, shifting feet in perfect synchrony, no mean performance on snowshoes.

"Zack," said Mr. Usher, almost happily, "I think you better let me take that rifle now."

"Go ahead an' give it to him, Zack," said the game warden.

When the rifle was safely in Mr. Usher's hands, the one-eyed poacher cautiously showed his head and part of his body. "Git me down to that jail quick, warden," he said. "I ain't safe, loose, while ole Zack's mad at me."

"You'll have time to cool off, Zack," the warden grinned.

"I think I can promise Jeff Coongate at least three months. He's been chloroformin' beaver over on Little Mopang Stream."

"An' to think," muttered Zack, leaning weakly back against the cabin wall, "that I dang near went with him, on'y for my wife, Sarah."

A few minutes after the game warden and his prisoner left for Privilege en route to the Mopang jail, Mr. Usher's plane landed. But Mr. Usher had decided to remain with his new caretaker for several days, so he paid the pilot off.

There were a few things that needed clearing up concerning the diary of death, but there was no longer any doubt about Zack Bourne. Zack's temper had cooled. Dark had fallen over the Mopang country, and in the light of the lamp in the kitchen, Zack read the one-eyed poacher's inimical work of art, and chuckled aloud.

"Why, that ole hellcat. There ain't a whisker of truth in him. What he wrote down, is jest what he wished was true, but knowed it never could be. It's a kind of a dream, like."

"Just how did it all get into the diary, Zack?"

Zack ruefully explained that Jeff Coongate had stopped at the camp for two nights, shortly after Christmas. To Zack, the writing of the diary had been an ordeal which he couldn't face. He had tried again and again, but in his fingers the pen had felt unnatural. As the days passed, and he had written nothing, the very sight of the pen had nauseated him, and he had continued his procrastination, brooding and ashamed. He had hoped that Sarah would return to fill in the empty days for him. But no. Instead came the one-eyed poacher of Privilege, who offered to take the whole thing out of Zack's hands and make a nice, interesting record. Zack hadn't even bothered to read what he wrote. Jeff Coongate had graciously wrapped the diary, sealed it and addressed it.

"Then you really did cut your hand splitting kindling," laughed Mr. Usher.

"Sure did. And Daisy sure had them five kittens, all right. 'Twas 'bout three weeks before Jeff showed up. He'd been clear out to Carterville to get chloroform for them beaver he'd located on Little Mopang Stream. An' I really took Buck an' Slats to Priv'lige, too, so's they wouldn't cause no trouble here. An' it's a fact about that warden, Tom Corn—he's transferred. An' that Jeff Coongate! Well, he's a good feller, just the same. But I figure he put that in about the squaw a-purpose to torment Sarah. He hoped Sarah might read about Elsie Brown Blanket."

"Zack," said Mr. Usher, "by way of apology, I'd like to renew my agreement with you for an indefinite number of years. Would you be willing?"

"Yes, sir, indeed I sure would. Me an' Sarah loves this place like it was our'n. But there's jest on'y one thing: don't you never tell her 'bout that diary, nor who wrote it. I wouldn't want Sarah to know that Jeff Coongae spent a couple nights here. He ain't a man that women understand."

The One-Eyed Poacher
Conquers Holiness

THE DOINGS around Zack Bourne's cabin, as viewed through Tom Corn's field glasses, were topheavy with innocence. The young Mopang County game warden was suspicious. For five days and nights he had spied in vain. He knew that Uncle Jeff Coongate, the one-eyed poacher, was visiting Zack Bourne; and he knew that when the two old woodsmen got together the violation of game laws was practically certain. But Zack's deer dogs, Buck and Slats, were chained in the back shed. There hadn't been a rifle shot to break the stillness, nor had the dreary nights been cheered by a single ray from a jacklight.

On the sixth afternoon of his vigil, Tom Corn cased his field glasses. Certain that his quarry had scented him, and was parading its saintliness for his benefit, he realized he must resort to trickery. On a letterhead bearing the State seal, he wrote himself the following note:

Warden Corn: Proceed to Mopang Corners on the seventeenth November to receive illegal fur confiscated by agent. Imperative.

After forging the commissioner's signature to the letter, Tom stepped into the clearing and walked briskly toward Zack's cabin.

His scheme was so simple that he felt a twinge of shame.

He would spend the night fraternizing with Zack and the one-eyed poacher. Tomorrow, the seventeenth of November, he would depart early, leaving behind him his wallet containing the forged letter. Zack and Jeff Coongate would find the wallet, open it, read the letter, and assume him to be well on the trail to Mopang Corners. Thus assured that the coast was clear, they would promptly get about the business of killing a winter's supply of moose meat. Returning that night after dark, ostensibly to recover his wallet, Tom would catch his men red to the elbows.

"Damn it to hell," reflected Tom, as he crossed the clearing, "a fellow owes his conscience a decent excuse for snooping, even if he's a game warden!"

With the wallet to come back for, he wouldn't look quite so treacherous, either to the poachers or himself. He would even leave his money in the wallet. A man's pride required him to take at least a sporting risk, and it would make things look genuine, too.

By the time he had reached the cabin dooryard, Tom Corn had begun to dislike himself heartily. He had orders to catch his men, but what good would it do? He could fine them, and imprison them, as he had done in the past. But he knew he could never change them. They were of the breed which still believed the fish of the waters and the creatures of the forest theirs for the killing.

Tom cat-footed across the dooryard and peeked through the nearest window. The scene which greeted his eyes caused him to groan with exasperation. The two old rogues had set a record in the elaborate staging of their innocence. Uncle Jeff Coongate held an open Bible in his hands. His head was tipped back, his one eye half-closed, as if in prayer. Zack Bourne sat jackknifed in the woodbox by the stove, his hand to his forehead in an attitude of reverence. Not for an instant was Tom Corn taken in by the show. It was too incredibly remote from precedent. But what the young warden didn't know, and couldn't believe even if he did, was that love had come to the one-eyed poacher of Privilege—and along with it paroxysms of moral uplift which for a week had been driving Zack Bourne nearer the brink of lunacy.

Through a magazine conducting a brokerage in lonely hearts, the one-eyed poacher had located Mrs. Edna Buckle, a blonde widow of New Wampum, Idaho. Uncle Jeff had never seen his beloved. She had reformed him by air mail. Edna Buckle's long range evangelism was a spectacular, if not enduring success. After a whole week without meat, rum, or blasphemy, the one-eyed poacher's holiness oozed from his every pore, and he had journeyed up lake to Zack's cabin in order to bring Zack into the fold.

How eagerly the unsuspecting Zack had rushed to the canoe landing to greet his old comrade! Zack hadn't seen a living soul in three weeks, much less a salvaged one.

"Jeez!" he cried, helping Jeff with his canoe. "But ain't I glad to see you. I got a quart of Old Sabre Tooth rum—just had one little snifter out of it—and I got a last year's lamb deer hangin', an' gawd a'mighty, Jeff, I been so lonesome—"

Drawing himself to his full, towering height, Uncle Jeff had held up his hand, and intoned: "Sinner, repent! And take not the name of the Lord thy God in vain, lest His wrath smite you in thy tracks."

Zack sniffed. His old comrade's breath, while not exactly perfumed, was innocent of rum, gin, rye, or Hand Brand alcohol. So Zack honored his visitor's unique utterances as being an experiment in humor. Thumping him on the back, he said: "Come up to the cabin an' we'll have us a couple snorts. Then

we'll eat a feed off that lamb, lay 'round till dark, an' tonight
we'll go out an' kill us a moose to winter off of."

"Thou shalt not kill!" Jeff said sepulchrally.

"Then thou is slated straight for hell!" said Zack emphati-
cally, but growing vaguely uneasy.

"Where is the bottle of Old Sabre Tooth?" asked the one-
eyed poacher.

"Now you're talkin'."

But Zack's relief was momentary. In the cabin he produced
the bottle, graciously offering it to his guest. Uncle Jeff took
the bottle, stepped out of the cabin door, and smashed it against
a boulder.

"Where is the lamb deer that you slaughtered?" he asked,
while Zack, stunned and speechless, leaned limply in the doorway. Zack was so slow in recovering from shock that Jeff was
obliged to find the deer carcass by himself. Zack watched,
quaking, as Uncle Jeff dug a pit, tossed in the precious meat,
covered it with chloride of lime, and filled in the hole.

"There," said the erstwhile poacher, as he mounded the
little grave. "Henceforth we shall eat of the berry, the yerb,
and the fruits which growith in the earth, but roamith not upon
its surface. Amen!"

"In the name of Aunt Becky, what's got into you, Jeff?"

"The Holy Spirit—in the name of Mrs. Edna Buckle, which
shall be my bride-to-be! Where is them dirty magazines, Zack?
I got to burn 'em to the ash!"

"Roscoe Carrion took 'em with him trappin'," said Zack
numbly.

"Then fork over all your patint medicines, thet I may dis-
troy same. The only remedy is prayer!"

"Who—uh—who's this Edna Buckle? Where in hell'd
you run afoul of her?"

"We have corresponded each day for a month. Sit down. I'll read you the messige."

Zack wilted into a chair. Clumping his elbows on the table, he hid his face while, for an hour-and-a-half, Uncle Jeff read letter after sanctimonious letter from Edna Buckle. At the conclusion of each, the one-eyed poacher asked: "Do you feel better? Do you feel the spirit borin' into you?" Zack answered variously. He began by saying he felt as if someone had lammed him in the midriff with a post maul, but his responses gradually weakened until, after the twentieth letter, he answered lislissly: "I—jest—feel—sick, Jeff."

As the days passed, Zack Bourne felt even sicker. If he ate meat of any kind, including salt pork or bacon, Uncle Jeff immediately launched into prayers for him. So after the fourth day Zack resigned himself to a diet of turnips, beans, and potatoes. On the sixth day Zack's stomach began to make dismal rumblings. Uncle Jeff promptly informed him that it was the voice of the Lord within him. And by the seventh day, at about the time young Tom Corn abandoned his vigil and stepped into the clearing, Zack was so corroded that he half believed anything his friend said.

The one-eyed poacher was going nicely on the tortures of hell-fire as the penalty of poaching, meat-eating, rum-drinking and profanity, when Tom Corn rapped on the cabin door.

Zack squirmed out of the woodbox where he sat wedged, opened the door, and stepped back blinking in surprise.

"Game warden!" he yelped.

"Howdy, boys," said the warden, smiling. "Camp meetin'?"

Uncle Jeff Coongate's guilty leap at the appearance of the warden was mere habit. He composed himself, and smiled beatifically, realizing in a stronger light than ever that God's word was good, and virtue its own reward. For he held in his hands not a jacklight, a salmon spear, or a crimson skinning knife—but the Holy Bible.

"Tom, my son," said the one-eyed poacher, almost sweating with righteousness, "you were never more welcome. Here shall the weary find rest. His feet shall be laved in sweet oil. He shall be fed, and given fine raimint, and jewils, and—"

"Leave out everything but the grub, old-timer," said Tom. "What's the menu?"

"Turnip hash, beans without pork, prune sauce."

Tom grinned wryly. "No venison, or moose meat perhaps?"

"My boy, before God we have foreswore the eatin' of flesh," said the one-eyed poacher.

"Sure, sure. I bet." ironically replied young Tom.

The holy light, hitherto so elusive to Zack Bourne, now struck him a dazzling blow. Zack saw that his old comrade had been right all along. In fact, had it not been for the sacred influence of Edna Buckle, Tom Corn would have found the deer carcass hanging in the shed. And Zack didn't even have a hunting license. Zack winced at the narrowness of his escape. Supposing they had shot a moose? Five hundred dollars fine, or six months in jail at Mopang.

"Praised be the Lord!" Zack blurted, awed.

"Hallelujah!" said Uncle Jeff. "Put on the skillet. What brings you here, warden?"

"You old hellions ought to know," said Tom.

Zack stared numbly at the warden. Holiness, he began to feel, was mighty fillin' stuff. "You been layin' in the cedars with your glasses, Tom? Your clothes is wrinkled considerable."

"You know the answer to that one, too, judgin' by your behavior the past five-six days."

Zack looked at Uncle Jeff, his eyes bleary with salvation.

The one-eyed poacher himself had reached a new summit of blessedness, and looked it.

"We never suspicioned you was near," he told the warden.

"So help me, it's the truth." said Zack.

The warden, grinning from one to the other, said: "Uhuh."

While Zack heated the detested turnip hash, Uncle Jeff and young Tom Corn reminisced.

"Mind that time," said Jeff, "when you nailed me an' Zack with eleven beaver skins?"

"Sure, I mind it all right."

"Who's the turnkey down to the jail now, Tom?" asked Zack, churning the hash with a spoon.

"Ed Post."

"Good old Ed," said Uncle Jeff. "Kind of makes me sorry me an' Zack's reformed. Best we ever wintered was with Ed. That's a mighty comf'table jail."

"Now that you fellows turned a new leaf, I suppose I'll get some peace," said Tom suavely.

"Yessir, boy. Your troubles is over." They nodded in agreement.

"Thanks," said Tom, more than ever suspicious that his troubles were just beginning.

Zack scooped out three helpings of hash and said: "Come git her."

"Warden," said the one-eyed poacher unctuously, "will you ask the blessin'?"

The hash, having been blessed by young Tom, was eaten in silence. After the meal, Uncle Jeff gushed about the benefits of a strictly vegetable diet. Tom Corn said it must be a drastic change for one who was accustomed to venison, moose meat, or broiled poached salmon twelve months in the year. Uncle

Jeff admitted that the change had a purging effect, both to the bowels and the soul.

Zack Bourne, silent except for the rumbling in his harassed stomach, wrestled with his new-found faith.

They turned in early, young Tom Corn in the spare room, and Zack and Uncle Jeff in the double bed in the room just off the kitchen.

"Jeff," whispered Zack, when the lamp had been put out and the November dark enfolded them, "you was right. Think if we'd of done like always, and killed a moose. Or if Tom had found that deer carcass, and me without no license."

" 'Who knowith not in all these,' " intoned the one-eyed poacher, " 'that the hand of the Lord hath wrought this?' "

"Dear Lord, have mercy on my soul!" whispered Zack, now fully saved.

"May He drive the holiness clear'n through us both."

"An' clinch it!"

"Praised be His name, an' may He bless Edna Buckle, 'way out in Idyho."

"You bet."

"Amen! An' move over a little, Zack, will you? I'm crowded."

Tom Corn left the cabin at the crack of day. But Zack and Uncle Jeff didn't find the planted pocketbook till along toward noon. They might not have found it at all, if it hadn't been for the mouse in the spare bedroom. They heard a skittering and went to investigate. It was then that Zack spied the warden's wallet lying in plain sight on the chair beside the bed.

"Look! Left his wallit!"

"A gift from the Lord!" said the one-eyed poacher.

"We'll split her up, fifty-fifty!"

Zack picked up the wallet and started to open it, when

Uncle Jeff caught his hands and held them. "No, Zack. It's the devil temptin' us. We got to fight him."

"But lookit," said Zack, crestfallen. "We could take out maybe five dollars apiece. Lemme jest open her up, an' we'll have a look."

"Wait!" Uncle Jeff bowed his head in thought, and after a time rendered his decision. "Nope. We can't even open a man's pocketbook. It ain't moril."

Though he secretly felt this was carrying things too far, Zack was obliged to give in. "Well, what'll we do with the darn thing, anyways?"

"We shall return it. I shall take this wallit down to Privilege, and deliver it intac' into the hands of its rightful owner."

"It's twelve mile through the woods—six each way! He'll come back after it, his own self."

"No—not till duty calls him this way again. 'Cause if he was comin' back, he'd be here now." Uncle Jeff sighed religiously. "Fact is, young Tom trusts us. An' I say puny is the soul of him who breakith trust. Give me that wallit, Zack. I aim to give the stren'th of my body in a good deed."

Zack accepted the decision, and glumly resigned himself. For a lifetime he had supported the credo of finders keepers, yet his new-born purity had quite clearly saved him from jail. There must be something to it.

Before Uncle Jeff departed on his errand of honesty, he ate a prodigious platter of turnip hash. Then he picked up his rifle, stuffed a cold pancake into his hip pocket, and stepped to the cabin door. "If I ain't back by dark, you set out down the Priv'lige trail with a lantern," he said.

Zack nodded, and the one-eyed poacher was on his way, the warden's wallet bulking heavy in his shirt pocket. Where the trail touched Leadmine Cove, on the lake shore, Uncle Jeff fought a battle with sin and won. He was becoming curious about the wallet's contents. One little peek couldn't do any harm, said the voice of the devil. But the voice of the Lord and Edna Buckle prevailed. Four miles out, at Caribou Ledge, the one-eyed poacher fought a second battle. He took the wallet out and turned it over and over in his hands. "Jest a lettle mite of a teeny look inside," said Satan. "NO!" said Edna Buckle. Back went the wallet into Uncle Jeff's pocket—still unopened. But the forces of virtue had suffered heavy losses. At Mopang Bar, but a quarter mile beyond Caribou Ledge, Uncle Jeff stepped off the trail and leaned behind a giant spruce. "Now's your chance," whispered the boys from hell. And Edna did not answer!

"Holy Mother save us!" muttered Uncle Jeff, examining the inside of the wallet. "Thirty-seven dollars, an' a letter! That'd be eighteen for Zack, an' nineteen for me. What's this letter about, anyways?"

A second later, Uncle Jeff was reading:

Warden Corn: Proceed to Mopang Corners on the seventeenth November to receive illegal fur confiscated by agent. Imperative.

The old poacher was chagrined. Since today was the seventeenth, Tom Corn must by now be well on his way to Mopang Corners. The town was in the opposite direction to Privilege. If young Tom wasn't in Privilege, there wasn't any point in lugging his wallet down there anyway.

The old woodsman had decided to return to Zack's cabin, when the rustle of dry beech leaves froze him. He crouched, peered around the trunk of the big spruce, and saw Tom Corn approaching. The warden was not over thirty yards away.

The one-eyed poacher saw what was up in a flash. The letter was a plant! Sure enough! Else why was Tom Corn on the

Privilege trail, and heading back toward the cabin? Uncle Jeff craftily tucked money and letter in the wallet, quieted the detonation of oaths within him, and with a facial expression so sanctified that a halo was all but visible, he stepped out into the trail in front of Tom Corn.

Oh, holy day! For when Tom Corn saw him carrying the pocketbook to Privilege, then would Tom be positive that neither he nor Zack had peeped inside. And this would convince him beyond all doubt that the reformation of Zack Bourne and Thomas Jefferson Coongate was genuine!

"My, Tom!" said Uncle Jeff. "But you sure give me a turn. I got your wallet with me, son. Aimed to bring it down to your home. Wanted to save you comin' all the way back."

Young Tom Corn went crimson to his hatbrim. Clearly enough, the two oldtimers hadn't looked in the wallet—or Jeff Coongate wouldn't be on the trail to Privilege. Then they hadn't been putting on a show. They hadn't known that he had been watching them for days from the cedar thickets. For once, they were playing straight.

"Why—uh—thanks, Jeff. You needn't of put yourself to all that trouble."

"Boy, the good deeds is fodder for my spirit. Here's your wallet."

"Well," stammered young Tom. "You saved me four miles."

"Eight, countin' roundtrip. But it ain't nothin', son. Mighty glad to have this chance to favor you. Shake."

The warden shook. True enough, there was a holy light in Uncle Jeff's eye. A miracle had happened. You just couldn't get around it.

"Guess I better be gettin' back to Zack's, Tom. Gits dark early, these days."

Young Tom stuffed his wallet in his back pocket. He smiled at his erstwhile enemy. "Good luck, old-timer. Here's hopin' you winter good."

"The Lord will 'tend to that. So-long, son. Come see us."

"Guess there's no need to see you fellows any more—uh—after this, Jeff. I'm darn' glad, too. I don't like snoopin', not even a little. So-long."

They separated. Tom went long-striding toward Privilege. And the one-eyed poacher, his holy expression slowly changing to his more becoming grin, legged it for Zack's cabin, his trigger finger itching unbearably, and his mouth watering for the taste of red meat.

"So the son-of-a-bitch thought he could trap us, did he?" said Uncle Jeff.

The sound of the epithet, so long suppressed, was music to his ears.

He repeated it several times with relish. He ran through his splendid vocabulary of profanity, and as he quickened his pace, the virtue fell from him in chunks as large as anvils. Thus lightened, he made splendid time.

And in the popple growth, not over a half mile from Zack's clearing, he came in the dusk upon a bull moose, wounding it in the fore-shoulder with his first shot. Reckless of the rough going and of the falling dark, the oldtimer half-circled the animal, crept close, and jumped it again.

"The nearer you run to Zack's cabin," Jeff growled, "the less we'll have to lug you. Go it again, you bastid."

When the moose had staggered to within two hundred yards of the cabin, Uncle Jeff killed it. Hearing the shot, Zack came out roaring.

"Bring that lantern!" yelled the one-eyed poacher. "I got one down. Size of a goddam truck hoss!"

"Comin'!" called Zack, whose backsliding was practically instantaneous.

Uncle Jeff drew his skinning knife. The game was properly bled by the time Zack arrived. A few minutes later, they had the hide half off, and were rolling out the paunch.

"Jeez!" said Zack fervently. "This is what I call heaven! Meat! Oh, my God, ain't he fat?"

Blithely feeling for the moose's liver, the one-eyed poacher said: "Shove that lantern nearer. 'The tabernacles of robbers prospers, an' them as pervokes God is secure.'"

"Hell!" said Zack, his knife poised. "What you goin' to do about Edna Buckle?"

"Nothin'. On'y just thet you're goin' to write her a letter. When Roscoe Carrion comes by on his trapline, he can mail it down to Priv'lige."

About three weeks later, Mrs. Edna Buckle, in New Wampum, Idaho, received the following news:

Dere madam, I have the honor to inform you that mr. Thos. J. Coongate past away yestdy a.m. as he hung hiself in jail sell at Mopang. mr. coongate ast me in his wil to inform you this news and say he did not have the ten thousan dollars as he lied about same to you.

I am yrs trly, Zachariah Bourne, Sherif Mopang Co.

Man Hunt in Mopang

EMERGING FROM A DREAM of pursuit by game wardens—a figment too often duplicated in the reality of his life—Thomas Jefferson Coongate, the one-eyed poacher of Mopang Forest, sat upright under a dripping cedar. He fought his way through layers of sleep which hung upon him like the folds of a collapsed parachute dipped in alcohol. He knew at a glance exactly where he was, but as yet, not how he had got there. From where he sat, Zack Bourne's cabin was less than a mile up the shore of Mopang Lake, and that, then, must have been his destination. There were signs that the object of his excursion had been the illegal slaying of game.

Old Jeff's rifle lay beside him on the wet moss. In the

pocket of his mackinaw rested a bottle of rum which went by the brand name of Dark Hazard. From the song in his temples and the savor of his mustaches, the one-eyed poacher concluded that he had been drinking. Moreover, he became aware suddenly of a unique and startling hang-over symptom—the sensation of someone kissing the back of his neck. At first, Jeff did not dare look around. The kissing was rhythmic, damp and musical, and he believed it to be an illusion which would pass, along with the brown mists of rum. Yet, while in memory he retraced the steps which had brought him low, the kissing lavishly persisted.

Earlier that spring day, Jeff recalled, he had strolled into Sim Pease's store in the hamlet of Privilege to see if his Spanish War pension check had arrived. Sim Pease, storekeeper and postmaster, said, "Nothing doing, old-timer. You're about three days previous."

"They might've made a mistake an' sent it early."

"The treasurer," Sim said, turning up the radio on the counter, "has never been known to make a mistake of that kind."

Over the radio, a horticulturist was giving an address on the treatment of potato seed prior to planting. Jeff recalled being bored by the subject matter.

"Who cares about potatoes," he asked Sim, "without venison gravy to pour over 'em? Turn that dang thing off—no, wait! Hold her steady, jest as she is."

An announcer had broken in with the latest news on a man hunt which was then in progress in the wilderness areas to the north and west of Mopang Lake. Until then, Jeff Coongate had been scornful of efforts to trace the fugitive, an escaped murderer named Creeper Conway. To Jeff, who could track a bug across a dry ledge, the efforts of the law had seemed shameful. But the current newscast brought incidental tidings of the sweetest kind.

Two bloodhounds, the newscaster said, had been on the trail of Creeper Conway for several hours. And the entire game-warden personnel, including young Tom Corn of Mopang County, had been called into the hunt. It was this last item which had claimed the interest of the one-eyed poacher, moving him deeply. A forest from which game wardens had been amputated was a blueprint of paradise. Such luck seemed like compensation for a life of poverty and hardship. Scarcely able to believe his ears, he checked with the storekeeper.

"So they ain't overtook this Creeper Conway yet?"

"That's what the fellow just said," Sim said. "Maybe them two bloodhounds'll help."

"Too much water in this country to work a bloodhound good—except on deer an' moose."

"There's a law against that."

Ignoring the storekeeper's reproof, the one-eyed poacher proceeded to his final point. "Did the radio say thet the game wardens—includin' Tom Corn—was huntin', too?"

"You heard the man," Sim said. "I saw Tom Corn go by at daylight, this mornin'. Jumbo Tethergood said Tom was goin' to the Junction for the bloodhounds."

It was true! For once in his persecuted life, thought Jeff, he and Zack Bourne, comrades of the jack light, the demijohn and the jailhouse, would have a free field, and already the small bucks were fat on the spring meadow grass along the deadwaters.

The one-eyed poacher's future lay clear. He would proceed at once to Zack's cabin up the lake, lure Zack away from his devout and law-abiding wife, Sarah, and together they would set forth into the forest to feast upon wild meat, as the Lord had intended they should.

Jeff could not depart without a word of sympathy for the fugitive, who, unwittingly, had done him such a splendid turn. "That poor Creeper Conway," he said to the storekeeper. "All them state policers, an' mounties from over the border, an' bloodhounds, and now game wardens, too, after him. I feel sorry for him."

"How do you feel," Sim asked, "about the man he killed in the car on the highway, two weeks ago?"

"Don't feel nothin' about him. I never knew him. Now, Sim, if you'll jest sell me a few supplies, I'll be on my way."

"Your credit's a mighty skimpy thing, old-timer."

Glowering, the one-eyed poacher drew himself tall. "You can charge 'em against my check," he said, "when it comes."

The storekeeper sighed, and gave in. The Coongate financial dealings were as erratic and uncertain as a beetle on a hot stove. Jeff concluded his list of supplies. "An', yes, I might's well take them two bottles of Dark Hazard rum. I'm goin' up to visit Zack Bourne, an' Zack likes to take a swallow before meals, or after."

"What'll Sarah have to say about it?"

"I ain't come to that, yet."

Jeff stowed his provisions in his frayed knapsack, picked up his rifle, and departed. At seventy, he was tall, erect, and long-striding—a magnificent figure of a man, nimble of wit and foot. . . .

Now, under the dripping cedar, he recollected that at several points along the trail toward Zack's cabin he had sampled the Dark Hazard. He had enjoyed solitary high tea at Lead-mine Cove, and an exclusive party at Caribou Rock. Opposite

Genius Island, the cold spring rain had overtaken him. He had warded off the chill to the extent of four bobs of his Adam's apple, and had advanced through the storm, singing in fine voice, and kicking the puddles dry, till drowsiness fell upon him, and he had crawled under the cedar to rest.

Having brought himself up to date, Jeff cautiously turned his mind to the kissing sensation. The businesslike approach of the kisser, whether real or imaginary, caused the back of Jeff's neck to tingle. Warily, Jeff turned around. He was not alone.

On similar awakenings in the past, the one-eyed poacher had seen a variety of horrid hallucinations, such as large reproachful trout, and falcons perching on his wrists, but never had he seen anything beautiful, lonely and lovable, like the hound which was now laving his cheek with a tongue as limp and slippery as a wet moccasin.

"It ain't possible," Jeff muttered. "It'll disappear."

But the hound, far from disappearing, turned his massive head, and sniffed. Jeff gasped in astonished sympathy and affection. It couldn't be true. It was just a trick, like those other times. The hound, like Thomas Jefferson Coongate, had but one eye!

Jeff clasped the hound. "Sweetheart," he said, "we're made for each other. I'm goin' to name you Zibe, after my first deer dog that a warden shot forty year ago in cold blood for runnin' a moose to water."

The hound snuffled moistly against Jeff's shirt collar, and sighed like a seal blowing. The one-eyed poacher had never seen such wonderful ears. They were over a foot long, and velvet to the touch. Jeff shook his own head violently. This rendezvous in the forest could not be real, he thought. But while it lasted, he intended to make the most of it.

"You pertected me in my sleep," he said to Zibe. "We will hunt together, long's we live. You want to smell a buck track, Zibe? You come along with me."

On the last, rainy mile to Zack Bourne's cabin, Jeff conducted small experiments to determine Zibe's reality. At the Chancery Portage trail, he held a doughnut in his hand, and called Zibe. The doughnut vanished, but Zibe remained, his tail batting the brush. Several times, Jeff stopped short in the trail, and whirled suddenly. Always Zibe stood there, his one eye watery with trust and adoration. But the acid test came at Zack Bourne's cabin door.

Jeff entered without knocking, took off his dripping hat, and shut the door squarely in Zibe's face. Sarah Bourne had just lighted the lamp, and, at sight of Jeff, her face clouded. No good would come of this marauder's visit. To Sarah, Jeff Coongate was an ill omen, bringing only catastrophe. Even now, he and Zack were greeting each other with loud roars, and an exchange of welcoming blows.

"Jeff! It's you. My, I been lonesome to see your ole face," said Zack.

"Why, dang your empty soul, Zack. It's been months since we had a feed of venison. You know what's happened? All the wardens—"

"I knowed it!" said Zack. "Knowed you'd come, if you heard what me an' Sarah heard over our radio about Tom Corn, an' all of 'em, up here huntin' the murderer. I says so to Sarah, didn't I, Sarah?"

Blinking unhappily, Sarah said, "You told me Jeff Coongate would be here."

Sarah was interrupted by a sound, which, through the bottom crack of the cabin door, sounded like a giant clearing his throat. This was followed by the raking of toenails on wood.

Zack jumped for the deer horns where his rifle hung. Sarah blanched.

"The murderer!" she said.

Jeff Coongate's one eye rolled in grateful relief. Zibe, beyond all doubt, was real.

"That ain't no murderer, Sarah," he said, soothingly. "That's my hound, Zibe. I ain't had him long." He flung open the door, and Zibe solemnly trotted in.

"Ain't he a lovely animal?" Jeff said proudly. "He come to me, whilst I lay sick with indigestion under a tree. He tended me, an' guarded me. We took to each other right away."

It seemed to Jeff that he was not getting a proper response from Zack and Sarah. They exchanged anxious looks.

"Jeff Coongate!" Sarah said. "There is a brutal murderer at large, and you have deliberately stolen the state's bloodhound."

Jeff's one eye narrowed. The state's bloodhound! This was the trick, which, all along, he had suspected would be sprung on him. You build up a pure love, he thought, and they take it away from you, and you are lonesomer than ever.

"You can't steal a dog that ain't got no collar," he said defiantly. "That dog's a maverick, like. Belongs to the first man as claims him."

"But he's a bloodhound!" Sarah said. "And the radio said not half an hour ago, that one of the hounds slipped his collar and got loose in this section."

"Zibe come to me his own self, cold an' miserable in the rain," said Jeff. "I don't allow that he's the missin' hound, an' I got plans for him, my own self. The state's got another hound, an' beyond that, you can't work a hound good in all this rain—except maybe on a good fresh deer track. Hey, Zack?"

Zack remained glumly silent. Sarah didn't. "Jeff Coongate," she said, "people are out searching for that dog."

"It's a fact," said Zack. "It come over the radio."

"Searchin' for Zibe, are they? Searchin' for my hound? In that case," said Jeff, "I'll jest tuck him away in the spare bedroom. I'll need a dry blanket to cover him, Sarah. Zibe's had a hard day."

With Zibe concealed in the spare room, a pall of anxious waiting hung over the cabin. To ease things, Jeff brought out his remaining bottle of Dark Hazard rum, and Sarah resigned herself to prospects of a dangerous evening.

Presently, her husband and her uninvited guest began relating past experiences in law-defiance, some true, some fanciful. They spoke of illegal moose hunts, of venison gravy in May, of salmon speared in posted waters by torchlight. As the Dark Hazard loosed its havoc, their heads drew close in friendship, conspiracy, and the vast confidence of rum. They devised imaginary tortures for imaginary game wardens.

Sarah had listened before to these fantastic plots, none of which had ever seen fruition. But against the possible day, she offered silent prayer: "Dear Lord, forgive Zack for coming under the evil spell of Mr. Coongate. And please, Lord, remove Mr. Coongate from my midst, and his stolen hound, too, and bring the murderer in these parts to justice, so that we may sleep again."

Now, through the roar of the rain on the cabin roof, Jeff Coongate heard footsteps in the mud outside, and a hail from the darkness.

"The law has arrived," he said casually to Zack.

Zack opened the door to admit two game wardens and a

gentleman from the Northwest Mounted. As always, in the presence of game wardens, the one-eyed poacher was at his histrionic best. It was simply by way of maintaining the dignity of his caste.

The leader of the wardens was young Tom Corn. Even though soaked to the nether parts of his clothes, Tom seemed crisp, quick, and canny. He was blond, and nicely knit to a compact one hundred and ninety pounds. But the old woodsman stood a head taller, as, in distantly mutual respect, they gazed at each other.

"We're looking primarily for the murderer," said Tom, moving toward the comforting warmth of the stove, "but we've also lost a bloodhound."

"Your busy day," said Jeff, with seamy solicitude. "Have a swallow of Dark Hazard, an' forget your troubles."

Warden Corn disdained so much as a glance at the bottle. "This hound," he said, "comes to the name of Jep. He might have wandered up here."

Jeff managed to look meekly co-operative. "Don't remember a hound by that name," he said, "but I never forget a face."

"Jep's got only one eye," Tom said.

"Poor feller. How'd he lose it?"

Sarah Bourne appeared on the verge of collapse and revelation. Zack stared hard at the empty woodbox.

"I didn't hear how he lost the eye," said the warden, holding his hands to the stove.

"I should think," said Jeff, "that the other bloodhound would be enough."

"He got caught in a bear trap."

"Then why can't you fellers track this Creeper Conway by your own selves? If you could track a moose in wet sand, you'd've had him a week ago."

Tom turned. "Jeff," he said cannily, "there aren't many left that can track like you. If we had you, it might be a lot easier."

Gazing haughtily at the three visitors, Jeff said, "I am otherwise occupied."

"Sure, Jeff," said Tom. "I know. We're intent on catching a killer. That leaves you and Zack a free field. I'll be seeing you around. And if you happen across that bloodhound, just get in touch."

"Glad to be of any small service," said Jeff, his voice like pure syrup.

Suddenly seeing a way out, Sarah said to the visitors: "Won't you stay the night with us? We have vittles—an' a spare room."

Irresistibly reveling in the suspense, and relishing the dread in Zack's eyes, Jeff joined with Sarah for a hair-raising moment. "Nice, comfortable room Sarah's got here," he said. "Two could sleep in the bed, an' one on the rug. Warm, an' dry."

"Thanks," said Tom, "but we're on our way."

When they had departed, Sarah took up her knitting, too frightened for speech.

The latest newscast merely corroborated what they already knew. One of the bloodhounds had slipped his collar and got lost; the other had been caught in a trap; the rain had impeded the search; and the murderer was still at large in the district northwest of Mopang Lake.

"I know every brook an' branch in that country," said Jeff.

"You ought to," said Zack. "You spent your whole, dismal life there."

"Shame to you both!" said Sarah.

"I think," said Jeff, "that I'll jest give Zibe a bite to eat. Any of that canned venison left, Zack? I want him to have the best."

During the next two days of rain, Jeff's conscience grew as slowly, but as resplendently, as a pearl in an oyster. He had trouble sleeping, and sought comfort in nocturnal confidences with Zibe, who lay upon the bed beside him.

"Sweetheart," Jeff said one night, "I got to leave you for a day or two. I got to go an' search out that murderer."

At this threat of parting, Zibe moaned and thrust his slippery nose against the old woodsman's cheek.

"The radio said last night," Jeff patiently explained to Zibe, "that two wardens and a mounty hadn't been heard from in two days. I ought to let 'em suffer, but I got to go, Zibe. You stay true, an' don't wag at ole Zack. I don't trust him."

The next morning Jeff stalked restlessly about the house. Zack thought he recognized the signs.

"Goin' to let Zibe loose on a deer track?" he asked.

Jeff turned, glaring. "Turn my dog out in this rain? You think I'm cruel to animals? I'm goin' out there, my own self."

"What?"

"I'm goin' to find them wardens, an' maybe Creeper Conway, too."

"If you let Zibe loose, he might jest happen to pick up a scent an' lead you right to 'em."

"No," said Jeff. "If I find 'em myself, it lets Zibe out of the whole deal. I love Zibe, an' aim to keep him. If I, personal, find the wardens an' this murderer, too, what use they got for Zibe any more? It follows that Zibe will then be mine."

The old outlaw of Mopang Forest said goodby to Zibe, took his rifle, and his knapsack, and struck out into the rain.

From the radio reports, he knew that in a general way, his destination was the Golroy River district, rugged, densely forested, remote. The storm had obliterated most of the signs, but he picked up a few: drenched, blackened coals of a fire, broken twigs showing fresh, white ends, and finally, when he was sixteen miles from Zack's cabin, the paper covering of a roll of bandage.

"One of 'em must've got hurt," he muttered, and, as a matter of policy, hoped that it was one of the wardens.

It turned out to be the mounty, however, when Jeff stepped around a boulder an hour later and saw the posse's fire. The mounty lay half asleep against a log, his right leg in a crude splint and bandaged to the knee. Tom Corn sat in the shadows beyond the fire, the light gleaming restlessly on his rifle barrel.

"Howdy, Tom," said Jeff. "Campin' out?"

The warden was on his feet like a shot, his rifle leveled. When he recognized his visitor, he lowered the gun, and said, "Howdy, Jeff."

"Where's the other warden? Git homesick?"

"I sent him away this noon, to try to get out, and get some grub to us. We ran out day before yesterday."

"Oh," said the one-eyed poacher, elaborately taking a cold pork sandwich from his knapsack. "Hungry?"

The mounty and Tom Corn stared longingly at the sandwich. Jeff sat on a cold stone and munched delicately.

"What happened to you?" he asked the mounty.

"Fell. Broke my ankle, I think."

Jeff flipped crumbs from his mustache. "Too bad. Seen anything of Creeper Conway? I come to help you boys out."

"Yes," said Tom. "Right here is his last sign. Our fire is on top of the last one he built—maybe yesterday. By the way, you heard or seen anything of that lost bloodhound?"

"Nope, Tom. Not a thing. You won't need him, not with me along to do your tracking."

"That . . . just . . . might . . . be," said Tom, swallowing as he saw the last crust of sandwich disappear into Jeff's mouth. "We found one of Conway's moccasins here, worn out. One foot will be bare."

"Well, Tom, if you'll jest be quiet now, so I can get a wink of sleep, I'll catch your man in the morning."

The young warden smiled. The old-timer's boast, superior as it sounded, might just come true. Tom watched Jeff settle his huge, catlike form around a root. The old poacher was instantly asleep. He was at home, thought Tom, anywhere in the woods. Root for a pillow. Rain meant nothing, cold less. And that tantalizing trick of his with the pork sandwich was just like him; he was an actor beyond everything.

The thought of the sandwich made the warden's throat contract. He glanced in the dying firelight at Jeff's knapsack. It bulged attractively. And even as he watched, old Jeff's hand fell lovingly, and protectively, across the sack.

A soft footfall broke the stillness. Tom dropped a hand on his rifle. Jeff was instantly alert. Both men turned their faces toward the black forest at the moment a sad-faced but seemingly happy bloodhound trotted toward the fire.

The mounty, too, had awakened. "There's our hound," he said.

"Here, Jep! Here!" said Tom Corn. Tom couldn't believe such luck. With Conway's castoff moccasin, and the rain stopping, Jep would surely run Creeper Conway to earth. "Here, Jep! Here, boy!"

It was just as well that in the dim light neither the warden nor the mounty could see the look of righteous malevolence in Jeff's eye. Zack and Sarah had double-crossed him! Zack, softened and corroded by marriage, had been prevailed upon to let Zibe loose. Together, you might say, they had robbed him of his one friend.

"Well, Jeff," said Tom, "it looks as though Jep had made your acquaintance."

The one-eyed poacher cringed and glowered, as Zibe cavorted about him.

"Go away, dog! I'm sleepin'."

Zibe stopped, perplexed. "Warden Corn," said Jeff. "Call off this monster. He's lappin' my face."

"He does seem extra friendly," said Tom, exchanging a wink with the mounty. The answer to the missing bloodhound was now clear to both men.

"Pat him, Jeff. Just be kind to him," Tom said. "He might not stray any more."

"He trusts you, Jeff," said the mounty.

Zibe playfully caressed the embarrassed poacher with a muddy paw.

"He wants to play," said Tom.

"Then let him play with you fellers. I don't aim to sleep with no strange dog."

But it was obvious that the dog and the old man were not strangers. Jeff gave up all pretense.

In the first light of day, Tom Corn's stomach was a vacuum, and he awoke to find Jeff and Zibe sound asleep in each other's arms. It was a sight which, under ordinary circumstances would have been touching.

"I could eat a photograph of a load of hay," groaned the mounty.

Tom said, "I could do with an old skull stuffed with bugs. Let's wake up Jeff an' see if he'll give us a sandwich."

They woke the one-eyed poacher and pleaded that they had been three days without food, and that it was unnatural of him not to share with them. In fact, it was criminally unmerciful.

Jeff Coongate yawned and stretched. He smiled in a manner commensurate with high sacrifice and self-esteem.

"I have shared," he said. "I have given all. I have fed your danged old bloodhound till he's all podded out."

Zibe leaned worshipfully against Jeff Coongate's leg. There was a moment of silence, and then the one-eyed poacher played the sweetest revenge card of his career. "Boys," he said, "how would you like a loin steak of venison, salted an' peppered, an' broiled right over this fire? I might be able to find a little water cress to go with it, though it's early for cress. I got a junk of pork—Zibe couldn't quite finish it—to make a little gravy out of . . ."

"Shut up!" the mounty croaked.

" 'Course," said Jeff, "I realize it's only late May, an' the law's on deer, but still an' all . . . There ain't a trout brook within ten mile of here, even if we had a fishline, or a bit of dynamite an' fuse."

The mounty looked pleadingly at the warden. The warden scratched his head. Jeff Coongate had him backed to the wall; Tom swallowed painfully. His stomach now seemed full of old tennis balls. But then he thought of Creeper Conway's moccasin.

"Go ahead, Jeff," Tom said. "Get a deer."

"I have your permission, Warden? An' can I take Jep, an' dog this deer? It would be quicker."

Tom played beaten. He hung his head. "Take the dog," he

said meekly. "Get the deer back here soon. We can't hold out much longer."

"Very well," said Jeff. "I shall obey your orders, Warden Corn. An' I hate to think of what people will say."

Jeff went down to a spring to drink, and while he was gone, Tom Corn rubbed the bloodhound's nose with the escaped murderer's moccasin. He rubbed it deeply, and thoroughly. "There, you mutt!" he said. "You've been in bad company, and you're going to be in worse, if you can remember the smell of that moccasin."

Jeff returned cheerfully from the spring. He caught up his rifle, and examined the breech. "Come, Jep," he said. "Come along with ole Jeff Coongate, an' see life in the woods."

Jep went slowly. He whimpered in a strange way. "Did I feed you too much?" asked Jeff, as they went along in the forest. "Here, here, Jep. Here's a buck track made after the rain. It's hot, Jep. A little buck. Jest right for us to feed off of. Drive him to water, an' I'll do the rest."

But Jep, it seemed, had other ideas. He bore away from the deer track, snuffling and rapt in the mysterious obsession of a strong scent. He began to run, and Jeff had difficulty in keeping pace.

It was nearly noon, when both Jep and his master were sweat-drenched and tired, that Jep began to sound the call of a chase near end. "A-roop, a-roop" he went.

A short time later, the one-eyed poacher saw the track of a bare foot. That moccasin! Tom Corn had tricked him! Ahead of him the fugitive came into view, climbing a tree. Below the tree, Jep danced and loudly and triumphantly a-rooped. Jeff saw the man draw an automatic from his pocket, and level it at Jep.

But the old woodsman's rifle was too fast. His shot ripped

loose the echoes, and Creeper Conway dropped from the tree, holding his right wrist.

"You don't want to shoot at dogs, young feller," the old woodsman said. "They's plenty deer an' moose around here. Shoot at them. But not dogs."

By way of emphasis, Jeff closed his hand on Creeper Conway's arm, and Creeper thought he had been clutched in a steel trap. "Leggo, you big lug!" said Creeper.

"I'll jest have to take that little gun of yours, Creeper, an' we'll go along back."

"You know the way?"

"Know the way? Why, son, this is my home. You take the lead; me an' Jep'll be right behind you."

"Does the pooch bite?"

"Nope—he jest swallows whole."

Thus escorted, the Creeper made no further attempts at escape. The lonely forest had whittled him down, and he thought he might prefer hanging to being lost in the wilderness.

The party was welcomed by the mounty, young Tom Corn, and several others, who, during Jeff's absence, had arrived to rescue the missing searchers.

Among the newcomers were several newspaper reporters and photographers. They took pictures of Jeff Coongate and the Creeper, Jeff Coongate and the mounty, Jeff Coongate and Jep. They also asked to take a picture of Jeff Coongate and Warden Tom Corn, of Mopang County. Jeff declined.

"He tricked me. He sent me out to dog a deer, but he filled Jep's nose full of old moccasin, an' all we got was this Creeper Conway. Spoiled a whole mornin's hunt. I ain't goin' to appear in no photograph with him."

On the trip out to the settlement of Privilege, the one-eyed poacher craftily reminded Warden Corn of his order for venison—in May. "That order ought to hold, Tom," he said. "I give all my food to the state's hound."

"It doesn't hold, old-timer. There is no longer an emergency."

"How do you know anything about the emergency in my stomach—an' Zack Bourne's, too—for the taste of venison?"

"You'll have to wait till fall. It's the law."

Jeff's one eye lowered demurely. He bowed his head. "I understand, Tom. An' there's no hard feelin's. I reco'nize the position of the state."

"What?" Tom Corn blinked suspiciously. He would have been willing to bet that the old poacher's humility was about as genuine as a plastic nickel, and that even now he was planning a meal of fresh liver. "So you've reformed, hey, Jeff?" he asked.

Jeff sighed. "Yes," he said, "when I seen you men out there, pertectin' us from crim'nals, an' the privations an' hardships you went through, to uphold the peace, it jest come over me, at last."

"Uh-huh," said Tom.

"But, Tom—they's jest one favor I want to beg of you."

"Yes?" said Tom, warily.

"I want a few moments alone with Jep, before we part."

"All right, old-timer."

Jeff drew Jep apart from the others. It was a tender farewell. It seemed to Tom that in the two faces there was a singular and moving likeness—each with one eye, each with vast folds of wrinkles, each with a great and uncompromising heart.

"So long, sweetheart," murmured the one-eyed poacher.

Jep ran out his tongue a foot or more and caressed Jeff's forehead eloquently, and a lagging photographer got a nice, heart-rending shot of the scene. A moment later, Jeff turned and stalked off into the forest, where he doubled back, half circled, and came out on the trail to Zack Bourne's, making excellent time.

Some days later—Jeff and Zack decided to let things quiet down a little—the pair strolled innocently into Sim Pease's store. They were planning a well-rounded expedition into the Little Mopang country. They dreamed of speared salmon, dynamited trout, and a hind quarter of poached moose.

"Your check's come," said Sim, as the two woodsmen entered. "You got about twelve dollars of it left over, from what you owe me."

"Twelve dollars is ample, Sim," said Jeff. "Give us that slab of bacon, some tea, four sticks of dynamite—we got to blast some stumps out of Zack's back clearin'—an' fuse an' caps. An' four bottles of Dark Hazard rum, an' . . ."

"You've run over already," said Sim.

"Lay it against my next pension check, then."

"All right," said Sim, "but what'll I do about the dog?"

"Dog?"

"I been holdin' a dog for you for two days—some kind of a hound. He's out back."

"Holdin' a dog for me?" Jeff was perplexed.

"Sure," Sim said. "Seems all the newspapers run a lot of pictures an' stories about you, an' Creeper Conway, an' this old hound-dog. Jep, his name is."

The one-eyed poacher mopped his forehead. "You mean to say Jep's here? Where is he? Lead me right to him! How did—?"

"It seems," said Sim, determined to conclude his explanation, "that some ladies downstate read all them newspaper stories, an' got to fussin' an' grievin', an' finally took up a collection. They bought the dog, an' sent him to you. He come by express Tuesday, an' he's got a bad cold."

"You let my dog catch a cold?" said Jeff, edging toward the storekeeper.

"No. I never done it. He had the cold when he come off the express car. 'Twas drafty."

Jeff paused no longer. He charged across the store and into the back room. He ripped the crate apart, and Jep leaped forth, alive and beautiful, but ill.

"Honey," moaned Jeff. He spread his arms wide. "You've come back to me!"

"A-roop," went Jep, twitching his fevered nose.

Jeff gathered the hound in his arms, and, with great dignity, re-entered the store.

"Leave that hound with Sim," said Zack, "an' let's get on our way. I got the rum an' stuff all packed."

"Take it all out again," said Jeff. Gazing imperiously first at Zack, then at Sim Pease, he said, "Cancel the whole order, an' charge it to five pounds fresh ground hamburg, one dog collar, best grade with brass studdin' an' name plate, an'—"

"Cancel the rum, too?" said Zack hoarsely.

"Cancel the rum, too. An' instead put in three bottles Dr. Waldo's Cough an' Cold Elixir, that little woolly blanket on the top shelf, an' one of them little cynical thermometers for takin' the temperature of the sick."

Zack wilted, bewildered by his unpredictable comrade. "What about our trip that we been plannin' an' dreamin' of, all these last days?"

"Ain't goin' to be no trip. I'm a fam'ly man, now. I'm

savin' my money, these days. I got two to care for, an' pervide for. You can have my jack light, Zack, an' my salmon spear an' gill nets, an' snares. Come, Jep. Come along with me, honey. See you sometime, Zack—maybe."

Breath in the Afternoon

ONE HUNDRED AND SEVEN MEMBERS of the Bourne family were assembled in the pine grove on the lake shore near the hamlet of Privilege. From the surrounding wilderness, from isolated farms and lumber camps, they had come afoot, by buckboard, canoe and pulp truck to eat one another's pastry, bread and beans, to compare one another's failures and successes, to see how the children had grown, and who was married, pregnant, dead, or in jail.

If old Sarah Bourne had suspected there was to be a keg of whiskey at the reunion, she would not have coaxed her husband into attending. Here against his will, Zack Bourne was in a position to make the most of the whiskey and blame Sarah

(216)

for the consequences. The arrival of Uncle Jeff Coongate, the one-eyed poacher of Privilege, doubly darkened the day for Sarah. Zack and Jeff were inseparable cronies. In combination with a full keg of whiskey, their limit was unknown.

Though the reunion was strictly for members of the Bourne family, Uncle Jeff, hearing news of free whiskey, had appeared in the pine grove at the appointed hour, claiming relationship through some fictitious cousins, and inquiring the location of the refreshment. He found it near Zack.

"You Zack!" hissed Sarah, as her husband and the one-eyed poacher made their seventh journey to the keg, "and you Jeff Coongate! Do you keep away from that!"

"Didn't want to come down here in the first place," said Zack. "You drug me right into it, honey."

"We ain't had only a little," said Uncle Jeff, his eye rolling damply.

"Seven times!" said Sarah. "Seven times I seen you two hoverin' at that keg. Shame to you, Zack Bourne. Supposin' Mr. Usher was to come up unexpected, an' you smellin' this way. What would he think?"

Mr. Usher was Zack Bourne's revered employer. He owned the remote cabins on Mopang Lake where Zack and Sarah lived as caretakers. Two or three times a year Mr. Usher came up from Boston for the hunting and fishing.

"What would he think?" said Zack, glowering at Sarah. "Why, only las' night you told me 'twas all right to leave for two-three days, 'cause it's August, an' there ain't no chance of his comin'. Now, by God, you turn right 'round an' threaten me off the whiskey keg, claimin' he might appear at me like a dang ghost."

"Woman's way," sighed the one-eyed poacher darkly.

"Won't you jest eat a little somethin'?" begged Sarah, thinking that food might check the onslaughts on the keg. "Can't I fetch you both a dish of beans, an' some pie?"

"Eat now? An' spoil my good feelin'?"

"But you'll both feel desprit tomorrow. You know you will."

The Bourne hangovers were the criterion of torture in the lake country, but Zack, patting Sarah's shoulder tenderly, said: "There, now, honey. Don't fret. Jeff's comin' up lake with us tomorrow to stay a while, an' he's got a new hangover cure. A fisherman told him 'bout it. Drink by the name of—of—"

"Thomas Collins," supplied Uncle Jeff. "You take an' mash the juice out of a lemon, an' you put in sugar, an' about a half-pint dipper of Old Blow-Torch gin, an' you ram the glass full of ice, if you got any, an' then you charge her to the nozzil with fizzin' water. In hot weather, they claim it'll—"

Zack, who had sighted another of the drinking Bournes, cried: "If there ain't old Doug! Come on, Doug. Step right up. Let's you an' me an' Jeff have one together."

No match for the masculine spirit of rum and reunion, Sarah went off to seek sympathy from her own sex. Sarah was proud of her husband, and anxious that he conduct himself with dignity. Zack's job as caretaker for Mr. Usher was the envy of all the Bournes. Mr. Usher was gentle, kind and fair. He gave steady work and steady pay, and everyone respected him. Sarah grew tearfully apprehensive as she talked to her sister-in-law, Jennie, who had married Zack Bourne's brother, Amos.

"Why do they drink whiskey?" Sarah wailed.

"There, there, dear," said Jennie. "No one knows, least of all them that drinks it. Only a month ago, my Amos come home slanted like a billygoat. Fell into the kitchen, an' kicked the door to with his foot. Laid there lookin' up into my eyes, an' says: 'Jen, here I am—an' damn' if you understan' it, an' damn' if I do, either.' "

"But what if Mr. Usher *did* jest happen to come," said Sarah, imagining the worst, as she saw Zack steering toward the keg again. "He's so refined, an' nice. An' him an' Zack so fond of each other. Zack couldn't never get another job at his age."

Someone beat on an iron washtub, announcing supper. Tables and benches of rough-sawn planks were piled with layer cakes, pies, pots of beans, preserves and sweets. All rushed for places—all, that is, save the handful of drinking Bournes, who, rocking and swaying, remained faithful to the keg.

Sarah noted that the end was near. Zack and the one-eyed poacher had begun to peer at each other in the vast, dim understanding of whiskey. She didn't know whether they would burst into song, blasphemy or battle. They shook hands lingeringly and often. They thumped shoulders, and congratulated one another without cause.

There was a grandness in their gestures, a vision in their words, and a general effect of horizons. At times they put out their hands in order to brace themselves against trees which were non-existent, or far out of reach.

"Zack," stated the one-eyed poacher, trembling with sincerity, "I want to say right now, for all to hear, that you're the best goddam friend any man ever had in the whole world."

Zack, in perfect accord with Uncle Jeff's opinion, said: "Any little thing you wanted, if I had it, or if I could steal it some place, I'd give it to you. So help me!"

They were preparing to drink a series of toasts to the beauty and durability of their friendship, when Sarah came over with two plates of green apple pie. If she could only get some food into them, they would wander off under the trees and fall asleep. But they declined the apple pie with stupendous courtesy.

"Then ain't it time you quit, Zack?" Sarah wheedled.

"Not qui' shet, honey. Stay right here beside us. Me an' Jeff want you with us. Don't we Jeff? All have a drink together—drink to Mr. Usher. Won'ful man."

"Won'ful man," echoed the one-eyed poacher.

Sarah shook her head in despair, as Zack and Uncle Jeff drank to Mr. Usher, and to several of his friends, individually. "Go through hell for Mist-Usha," said Zack, dragging the back of his wrist across his lips. "Cut my throat for him, if he jest ast me to, an' I had a knife handy—cut her ear-a-ear, by God!"

"Won'ful man," mumbled Uncle Jeff, leaning against an imaginary tree, and settling gently into the soft moss.

"I wish he could see you both right now!" snapped Sarah.

"Can't see us now, swee'art," muttered Zack. "Ain't here," he added, enlighteningly.

"Oh, Zack! You're gettin' that fish-eyed look!"

"Perf'ly all right, swee'art," said Zack, resting both elbows on an absentee fence rail, and easing forward on his face.

Zack's last thought, prior to oblivion, was of preparedness for the fires of morning. Laboriously shoving his hand across the moss, he prodded his prostrate friend. "Jeff, you sure you got that hangover stuff hid good? That Thomas Collinstuff?"

Uncle Jeff Coongate moved like something not quite dead. He brushed dreamily at a detachment of black ants which crawled to and fro in the wrinkles of his neck. "I got her all safe—in my knapsack. All safe." Lifting his head a little, the old man's eye was attracted by the bright colors of the costumes of some of the younger girls over at the tables. "Silk shorts," he muttered disapprovingly. "Girls in silk shorts. Immorill! Don' know what the younger generation's comin' to!"

In the cool of the evening, when folks were packing their baskets to depart, a volunteer crew put Zack Bourne and the one-eyed poacher to bed in the haymow in Jumbo Tethergood's barn beside the lake. . . .

The awakening began about eight in the morning, and as the minutes passed, it grew more and more abrasive. Dreaming of a spring from which flowed unending Tom Collinses, the one-eyed poacher merged into the first stages of consciousness. He was under the impression it was raining; but, on opening his one eye, he discovered that he had rolled some little distance during the night and fetched up under a beam where chickens had been roosting. The one remaining bird eyed him reproachfully.

Zack Bourne, hearing a metallic clinking sound, thought he was a boy again down on the coast. It was a foggy morning, and the can-buoys were tinkling in the tide rip. He next attributed the tinkling to ice in a tall glass. Then, fully and frightfully awake, he looked from the hayloft window to the shore of the lake. The tinkling, he saw, was caused by empty beer cans knocking against shore in the tiny waves of morning.

"How you feel, Zack?" croaked Jeff.

Comrades in hell as in happiness, the two old-timers compared their symptoms.

"There's a dozen little red men filin' my eyeballs," said Zack, "with a rusty file."

"I got the cutter bar of a mowin' machine stuck in my

throat," the one-eyed poacher announced. "She's red hot, an'
half way down. Can't swallow her, nor can't spit her up."

"Is she mowin', Jeff?"

"Jest commencin'. The blades is jest chatterin' a mite.
How's your belly feel, Zack?"

Zack moaned, rolled over, and stood up. "Did I eat an
anvil any time yesterday?" he asked, fearfully.

"No."

"Well, I got one in my paunch, somehow. Where's that
hangover stuff, Jeff?"

Uncle Jeff crawled across the hay to his knapsack. He un-
strapped the flap, started to open the pack, and stopped short.
"I don't dast look," he said, shakenly. "Someone might of
stole it. I couldn't stand the shock."

At the mere thought of the precious materials being stolen,
the anvil in Zack's stomach multiplied into a small but active
drop-forging plant. "Shut your eye," he said huskily, "an' jest
feel inside with your hands."

"She's here!" exulted Uncle Jeff. "All here—lemons, sugar,
gin, fizzin' water—all but the ice. I got a couple empty tin
cans for us to drink out of."

The prospect brought life to Zack. He climbed down the
haymow ladder to the floor of the barn. He sneaked out back
to Tethergood's ice house, got a small piece of ice, washed the
sawdust from it in the lake, and returned. He found Uncle
Jeff, sitting dejectedly on a crate, the Tom Collins materials
around him.

"Git that gin poured," said Zack impatiently.

Uncle Jeff's eye was watering with misery. "I can't pour it.
Hand shakes like a chicken's foot in the mud."

Zack attempted to do the pouring, but the sound of the
bottle, rattling against the edge of the tin can, was too hard on

his nerves. They finally made it by holding the bottle against the wall, and turning it downward over the cans.

"Does a man get relief right away from this here medicine?" inquired Zack, adding lemon juice and sugar.

"This salmon fisherman told me it's pratickly instantaneous, if you use enough gin," said the one-eyed poacher.

The addition of ice made the rime gather on the cans. They stirred cautiously with splinters pulled from the crate. Their lips twitched, and their throats worked in anticipation of the first, long, cooling swallows. They had used nearly a half-pint of gin for each can.

"She's ready!" croaked Uncle Jeff, sucking his splinter and tossing it away.

Each sufferer grasped his can in both hands for steadiness. They looked at one another over the rims, each frightened by the woe in the other's face. And they had barely made contact between cup and lip, when they heard a quick step on the barn floor.

"Wait! Zack! Don't you tech that!"

The voice was Sarah Bourne's. She stood in a patch of sunlight just inside the barn doorway, holding a paper in her hand. Zack and Jeff were so startled that they almost spilled their priceless nectar.

"Honey," said Zack piteously, "we'll die if we don't drink this one little drink."

"You'll die if you do!" declared Sarah. Approaching, she removed the dewy can from Zack's hands, did the same for Uncle Jeff, emptied the contents of both down a crack in the barn floor, handed Zack the bit of paper she had brought, and said: "Read that!"

"I can't," said Zack. "Can't hold her steady enough, honey. You read it."

Sarah knew the message by heart. Standing with her hands on her hips, and looking from one invalid to the other, she quoted:

ARRIVING AT TEN BRINGING ONE GUEST PLEASE HIRE JEFF COONGATE FOR EXTRA GUIDE AND MEET US IN PRIVILEGE

(Signed) REUBEN USHER

Zack told Uncle Jeff later that each word was like a horse shoe striking him in the back of the neck. The silence following Sarah's quotation of the message was broken by two dismal groans. Ten o'clock was a little over an hour hence. If they drank their medicine—two full doses remained in the gin bottle—they would both reek of juniper when Mr. Usher and his guest arrived. But if they didn't drink it, they felt certain they would go up in flames.

"Yest'dy afternoon," said Sarah, eyeing her shaking husband, "you declared you'd go through hell for Mr. Usher."

"He's doin' it," moaned the one-eyed poacher. "So'm I."

"I said I'd cut my throat for him," gasped Zack, with a desperate glance at the half-full bottle of Old Blow-Torch, "and by God, I've done it."

"Shame!" said Sarah. "Come in an' eat a morsil. I fixed you up a platter of pork chops an' sweet potatoes in Effie Tethergood's kitchen."

At the mention of food, both culprits went gray to the gums and nearly keeled over. Their suffering melted Sarah's heart, but she was determined that Mr. Usher would not find Zack and Jeff with gin in every pore at ten in the morning. Zack and Jeff were equally determined, and their misery thus intensified.

"Come outside, Zack," Sarah said. "It's hot in here. But there's a little breeze comin' in off the lake."

"I felt that breeze when I went out to get the ice," shuddered Zack, "and it scraped me."

There was work to be done before the arrival of Mr. Usher and his guest. Zack engaged Jumbo Tethergood's motor boat for the trip uplake, changed a spark plug, and filled her with gas. The one-eyed poacher bought a list of supplies at Sim Pease's store. As ten o'clock drew near, the two comrades discovered new and more terrible pains. Fear of dying and fear of living were about equal. Uncle Jeff's neck took to twitching, and Zack's tongue was an open flame searing his lips.

"When we get to the cabin," Zack said, his voice rustling like stirred gravel, "we'll go down in the root cellar, and we'll make our medicine. No one'll be the wiser, then."

"That will be about three o'clock this afternoon," rasped Jeff.

"Nearly ten now," Zack nodded. "That's five hours."

"Jesus! Don't know's I can hold out."

"If we jest kind of fasten ahead to three o'clock, we might last," said Zack. "Here comes Mr. Usher now. Got the gin an' stuff hid safe?"

"In that bulkhead in the stern of the boat," said the one-eyed poacher.

For Zack and Uncle Jeff, the trip uplake was an ordeal. Dearly though Zack loved Mr. Usher, respected him, and depended on him, he wished the kindly old man wouldn't talk. Invariably in the past, these trips up-lake, full of reminiscence and happiness at seeing one another, had been a delight. But not now.

"There's Genius Island, where we caught the trout, remember Zack?" cried Mr. Usher.

To Zack, Genius Island appeared to heave and totter. Fantastic trout, the size of mako sharks, seemed to bulge beneath the adjacent waters. "Yes, sir," replied Zack, through his parched throat, "that was the day we struck 'em good."

Mr. Usher's guest was a man about his own age. His name was Henderson, and he was tall and dignified, with a white mustache, and graying hair. Mr. Usher joyfully pointed out objects of interest to Mr. Henderson—Caribou Rock, Mopang Bar, and the white cross on the church on the far shore at the Indian Village. Sometimes Henderson and Mr. Usher came astern to talk hunting and fishing, and doings of other years.

"Beautiful country!" exclaimed Mr. Henderson to the one-eyed poacher. "Beautiful! I'm already indebted to Mr. Usher for bringing me. The heat in Boston was terrific. It drove us up here for relief."

"Well, sir," said Uncle Jeff, to whom the local, or internal heat was 212 degrees, "me and Zack'll see you have an enjoyable stay. Too bad there ain't any huntin', legal huntin', that is."

"We brought some sandwiches," said Mr. Usher, offering them to Sarah.

Sarah beamed, and accepted one. "My, that's good!"

"Pass them on to Zack and Uncle Jeff," urged Mr. Usher. "There's tuna fish, and sardine, and cheese, I think."

With a sick glance in the direction of Mopang Ridge, Uncle Jeff muttered: "Jest et a big charge of beans."

"Me, too," said Zack, gulping hard, and stooping to turn a grease cup on the engine.

Mr. Usher and Mr. Henderson went forward out of earshot. Sarah gave both Zack and Jeff a distressed-mother look. But they were beyond her help. Zack pulled out his watch, and held up two fingers to his companion in pain. "Leadmine Cove," he said. "An hour to go." Uncle Jeff sighed, crouched lower in the stern, and tapped the bulkhead where the gin lay hidden.

After the fearful trip was done, there remained but a few chores before the quenching in the root cellar. The cellar was under the cabin where Zack and Sarah lived. Mr. Usher and his guests used the larger cabin, thirty yards away among the spruces on the point. Zack aired out the cabin, and helped Mr. Usher and Mr. Henderson with their bags. The one-eyed poacher got some ice, washed it, cached one piece in the root cellar, and put the other in a pail of fresh water, which he carried to the main cabin. Sarah made the beds, and went over to fuss about supper.

"Is they anything else we can do for you, sir?" said Zack.

"Can't think of anything," said Mr. Usher. He had been showing his guest some of Zack's beautiful axe-work, which had gone into the building of the cabin. Mr. Henderson was enthusiastic.

"Would you an' Mr. Henderson like us to get the canoes an' take you out on the lake?" Zack asked.

Uncle Jeff Coongate, standing in the cabin doorway, held his breath till the answer came.

"I don't believe so, now, Zack. It's pretty hot. I think we'll just unpack our bags, and sit on the porch. That suit you, Henderson?"

"To perfection," said the guest.

Two minutes later, Zack and the one-eyed poacher were lighting a lantern in the root cellar. There was the cool odor of earth, vegetables, and stone. The two sufferers spoke in eager whispers.

"Gawd A'mighty, Zack—hurry an' git that ice busted up."

"I am hurryin'! Hurried so I closed my jacknife on my fingers. Put in plenty gin."

"I put her all in, half an' half, every jeesely drop."

In the lantern glow, the dew glistened on the cans. There was a sweet scraping sound, as they stirred the nectar with a couple of rusty abutment spikes. Overhead came Sarah's footsteps, as she worked in the kitchen.

"Ready?"

"Sure!"

"Never thought we could stan' it! I damn' near had a convulsion, when Mr. Usher offered me that tuna fish sandwich."

"Don't mention it!" whispered Zack. "I seen trout forty foot long in the water 'round Genius Island. You got yours stirred good?"

"Yuh. Well, here's to——"

A knock on the bulkhead door paralyzed them. They pushed their cans back out of sight. They heard the creaking, as someone lifted the bulkhead. A gray patch of daylight reached into the cellar, and Sarah's voice came to them, whispering:

"You Zack! You down there with Jeff?"

"God, I thought it was maybe Mr. Usher showin' Mr. Henderson around!" groaned Zack. Then he hollered to Sarah. "Sure, honey—we're down here. Got our medicine all fixed to take."

They heard Sarah's firm and hurried steps descending into the dungeon. "Don't you tech a drop!" she hissed. "Where's them gin cans?"

"Right here, honey—why?"

Sarah caught the gleam of lantern light on tin, and with a single swipe of the broom she was carrying, knocked the cans over. As the contents darkened the earth of the cellar floor, Zack let his head fall forward into his hands, and moaned: "You've killed us, Sarah—killed us both."

"I can feel myself dyin'," said the one-eyed poacher, his hands to his throat. "That's all the gin we had."

"Well, you can both come right straight to life!" said Sarah Bourne. "Mr. Usher come over here jest a minute ago. Said he wanted both of you right away over to his cabin."

"I couldn't get that far," said Zack. "I'm a goner."

"You'll go! Both of you. If you have to crawl. You're indebted to that man, an' you'll do your job for him, like he says."

"Prob'ly wants us to take 'em canoein'," wailed Uncle Jeff. "Oh, Lord—I couldn't hold a paddle."

"Up with you! Out of here! Get them cobwebs off your heads!"

They dragged themselves from the cellar, and swayed across to Mr. Usher's cabin. Their moccasins were soundless on the porch, as they stood before the cabin door. "You knock, Zack," said Jeff. "I ain't got the stren'th left."

"Don't need to knock," quaked Zack. "They'll hear my teeth chatterin'. He'll think it's the dead caperin', and come."

But they managed to knock, and presently Mr. Usher came to the door, smiling a welcome through his warm, blue eyes. He opened the door and beckoned them in.

"You wanted us, sir?" said Zack, bracing himself against the wall.

"Why, yes—if you weren't too busy. But it was nothing important, really."

From the rear of the cabin, Zack and Uncle Jeff caught a motion. They turned their heads slightly, the effort exploding rockets in their eyes. Mr. Henderson was coming toward them carrying a tray on which stood four of the tallest glasses the two woodsmen had ever seen. Zack passed his hand across his eyes. Uncle Jeff Coongate blinked. Both were wary, suspecting a mirage.

"This what you wanted us for?" Zack managed to ask.

"Why, yes—it was."

"Just try these, boys," said Mr. Henderson.

As in a dream, the two old-timers reached for their glasses. The rich, aromatic smell of juniper smote their nostrils delectably.

"Well," said Mr. Usher, "it was so hot, we thought these were indicated. Here's luck."

Speechlessly, Zack and Uncle Jeff brought their glasses to their lips. There was a long, cool, gurgling sound, as of horses watering in a shallow trough. At last Zack took his glass down.

"Mighty good—mighty quenchin', sir. What is it?"

"It's called a Tom Collins," said Mr. Usher. "You take plenty of gin, and sugar, and ice, and the juice of—"

Part Four

PINE TREE TOWNS

Dahlonega, Georgia

NOTE: Reasons for including this sketch of a Georgia town in a book about Maine are as follows: First, there is that phrase "from Maine to Georgia." Second, this town is near the southern terminus of the Appalachian Trail, which begins on Mt. Katahdin. Third, it reminded us of Shin Pond, Maine, and thus brought on an all but fatal case of homesickness for the Pine Tree State. EWS

A ROOSTER CROWS. A hound barks last refrain to conquered night. In his cabin by the creek old Bill Jenkins, lifelong gold miner and prospector, dreams of busheled nuggets as big as persimmons. Just then the bugler at North Georgia Military College puts the hot brass to *reveille.* The notes pierce the paling dawn like the cry of conscience. The sleep of seven hundred students is asunder, and Bill Jenkins wakes to deplore the wreckage of his dream.

In the Smith House, the town's only hotel, you hear the gush and plaint of unfettered plumbing, while from the dining room downstairs comes the scent of coffee and country sausage.

Outside, the timbered mountain crests are brushed by the sun. Laurel and rhododendron take color. Chickens step high in the dew, and the smoke from a moonshiner's still is made secret by full foliage, and the moonshiner is at peace. Everywhere in the fields and forests assorted birds rejoice, and now the chimes of the Methodist Church peal forth the opening

bars of *Onward, Christian Soldiers.* Thus, to the town of Dahlonega, Georgia, comes morning.

Dahlonega is Cherokee for yellow metal. You pronounce it
Dah-*lon*-ega. County seat of railroadless Lumpkin County, it
lies seventy-five miles north of Atlanta, snug beside gold-bear-
ing Crown Mountain in North Georgia's Blue Ridge region.

Hereabouts, in 1829, our country's first important gold
strike was made—twenty years before Sutter's Mill. Dahlonega
is the site of one of the earliest U. S. gold mints. And here are
the buildings of high-ranking North Georgia College, our
only coeducational military college, whose enrollment swells
Dahlonega's population to over 2,000.

Once Dahlonega was much larger. But California gold
news hit the town like a ton of iron pyrites, and in 1850 local
miners struck westward, overland. This movement gave first
echo to a phrase renowned in our language, when, seeking to
check the exodus, Dahlonega's immortal Dr. Stephenson rose
up in the courthouse, gestured toward Crown Mountain, and
cried: "There's gold in those hills! Boys, there's millions in it!"

But the boys went west just the same.

Today, remembering gold is one of Dahlonega's leading
industries. Another, more profitable, is producing broilers, for
which Lumpkin County is famous. A third is the college.
Around town, in Lipscomb's drug store, in Henry Moore's
hardware, in the Smith House dining room, you see the students, lean, clean and keen in their uniforms.

The *Dahlonega Nugget,* weekly, is noted throughout the
land as one of the nation's leading country newspapers. Apply-
ing impartially to the editor and his readers is the *Nugget's*
stated policy: "If you don't want it published in the *Nugget,*
don't let it happen."

The *Nugget* office consists of Mr. Jack Parks, editor and

owner, a supreme disarray of printer's oddments, and one type-writer—a vintage Royal with notional keys. But on the keys of this clatter-mill Jack Parks strums the homespun tune of the people. For example, on the subject of new shoes, he writes as follows:

> *A pinched foot is more distressing than a pinched pocket-book. We have heard it said that shoes that squeak are not paid for. We wish to state flatly that there is absolutely nothing to this, for ours don't squeak.*

Large in heart and welcome, Dahlonega runs a little shy on architecture. Its structures expound utility rather than distinction—except for the college buildings and a few others, of which the courthouse is a standout. During fishing season, you can't get a document executed in the courthouse. You can't even get tried, let alone convicted, because the officials are either tying flies or casting them. Rufe Ed Baker, the mayor, urges citizens to commit crimes out of season, if at all.

The courthouse has two dates—1833, when it was sup-posed to be built; and 1836, when it *was* built. The 1833 con-tractor used up his advance money without laying a brick. The 1836 man carried on from zero to completion.

Here is a dignified old edifice rising in the town square, a polite and patient island in the asphalt river of U.S. 19. The red brick structure has two rotund white pillars, and an out-side balcony from which to deliver orations. Withal, the court-house breathes an air of comfortable dilapidation, combining friendliness, justice, and good fishing toward one and all.

The cement sidewalks in Dahlonega are irregular, having broken spots and casual changes in altitude. You get so you like it this way, especially when you hear from Jack Parks the story of Mr. Townsend versus expenditure.

The late Mr. Townsend, who preceded Jack Parks as owner-editor of the *Nugget,* was against everything except truth and humanity. He was especially against the spending of money—his own, and even other peoples'. Above all else, he was against spending money for cement sidewalks, which he considered conspicuous waste.

So when Dahlonega's sidewalks, willy-nilly, were laid, Mr. Townsend publicly scorned them. Coming from house or store, he would spring gracefully over the sidewalk to the street with never a toe touching the leprous cement. He would then, as of yore, stalk majestically up the middle of the road, and to this day, so far as the footprints of Mr. Townsend are concerned, the sidewalks of Dahlonega remain virgin.

Dahlonega's Smith House, twenty-five rooms, is the only hotel in the world that was bought at five o'clock in the morning. One night Mr. William B. Fry had been discussing purchase with the former owner. Mr. Fry went home thinking. He went to bed and tossed. At four-thirty he was back at the owner's bedroom door. The deal was closed at five A.M.

Mr. Fry engaged Fred and Thelma Welch to run his dining room in the concrete basement. Mr. and Mrs. Welch, sometimes buoyantly assisted by their four-year-old son, place platters of food on the long tables. You help yourself, and pass a platter to your neighbor. It's like a Maine farm kitchen at harvest time. The food is bountiful, and the biscuits so hot, light and golden that lonely traveling men start reminiscing about their mothers. Toothpicks by the very moderate cash register at the foot of the stairs.

We sensed in Mr. Fry a man pent with information. So we put questions about gold panning, waterfalls, fishing, and campsites in the nearby Chattahoochee National Forest. To each question, he replied with a sentence which is probably the clearest statement of the sonata form ever voiced by man:

"I'm gonna tell you, but first I'm gonna tell you somethin' else, and that somethin' else I'm gonna tell you will lead right back to what I'm gonna tell you."

Mr. Fry then substituted substance in this formula, as follows: in the streams around Dahlonega, if you work well, you can pan three dollars' worth of gold in eight hours. Mr. Fry will personally conduct Smith House guests to crucial creeks. But if a group gets really hot for the yellow stuff, Mr. Fry will persuade old Bill Jenkins to go along. Bill Jenkins, one of the town's leading characters, has taken from prospecting only sufficient time to fight World War I, in which, as reported by himself, he slew large numbers of the Kaiser's men by conking them with frozen Irish potatoes, perhaps from Aroostook County, Maine.

Dahlonega is pleasing not only of itself, but for the good things within a few miles of it: Cane Creek Falls, Camp Wahsaga, Woody Gap, Neel's Gap, Vogel State Park, Calhoun Gold Mine, Amicalola Falls, higher than Niagara, Lakes Winfield Scott and Trahlyta.

Within seventeen miles of Dahlonega are fifteen creeks, all in the Chattahoochee National Forest. They are stocked with browns, speckles and rainbows by the Georgia Fish & Game Commission which opens a creek a week during the season. For the hidden fishing, where you catch 'em wilder and alone, we learned from Henry Moore's secretary whom to ask. "Go over to the courthouse," she said, "and ask anyone."

We left Dahlonega with accumulating reluctance, and now, six months later, we are remembering a good town. We are remembering an item in Jack Park's *Nugget,* and its appeal, and its struggle for Truth are significant to the perpetuation of home fires.

We erroneously stated last week that Leonard Tritt had suffered a head bruise while holding a lantern for his wife to cut stove wood at night. We intended to say Grady Tritt because Leonard would not think of letting his wife cut wood after dark.

We remember stories of the moonshiners in the Georgia Blue Ridge, and a conversation with a Dahlonegan of great dignity.

"Is Lumpkin County dry?" we asked.

"Lumpkin, suh, is as dry as its red clay dust in August." With a sigh, and a fond gesture toward the wooded hills, he concluded: "We are dampened only by the mountain dew."

We remember the thrilling mountain driving; the green kudzu vines climbing beside the grades; the Smith House meals; the waterfalls veiling the limestone cliffs; the possum in the persimmon tree; the deer drinking from the branch below Neel's Gap; the sound of *reveille* at morning; and by night the dream of old Bill Jenkins and his yellow nuggets.

So the fact is that, like Mr. Fry, we are so pent with memory that we want to tell it, but first comes some other memory that we want to tell, but in time, this one will lead right back to what we want to tell you—which is: Dahlonega is so good it reminds us of Shin Pond, Maine.

Greenville

YOU KNOW THE TOWN is right there below you, but you can't see it. You know the great, wilderness-reaching lake is there, too. But now, in the early morning, looking from the window of Room Number One in the Hotel Greenville on the hill, you can see nothing but the expanse of fog—dense, cotton white, as motionless as a damp giant holding his breath.

In this situation, you *hear* the town of Greenville, Maine, and you hear Moosehead Lake—before you see them. It's a strange and fascinating introduction. A loon gives its long, sad, wilderness call, and far away another answers from a cove.

A band saw whines from a mill, and you can almost smell sawdust. An outboard motor starts with a roar, and stops. The
Diesel on the Bangor & Aroostook R.R. fills the valley with a
hollow moan. A door slams, and dialogue takes place between
two men unknown, unseen, their voices a glad cry flung by the
mysterious acoustics of the fog.

"Any luck yesterday?"

"Four trout and two salmon."

"Where?"

"Off Dry Point."

You could say that the lake and the town are talking, and
that theirs is a special communion. In Sanders' store, which
is 125 years old, or maybe in Folsom's store, you hear another
bit of talk—the business essence of Greenville and the lake. A
man from Iowa, or New York, or Montana parks his car on a
mound of asphalt in front of Sanders' and steps inside.

He says: "I want to outfit for the Allagash and St. John
River trip."

This is routine for Harry Sanders. It was routine for his
father and grandfather.

"How many, and how far downriver are you going?" he
asks.

"To Fort Kent. Four of us."

"Come back in a couple of hours," says Harry; and the
voyager may rest assured that in two hours' time he will have
canoes, guides, tents, provisions and a supply of dry matches
adequate to his journey.

The wilderness region which serves and is served by
Greenville and the lake inspired Whittier's poem, "To a Pine
Tree." And a hundred years ago this summer, James Russell
Lowell savored the lake and forest on a canoe trip on which he
saw for the first time a young lady dressed in bloomers. Far

from being shocked, the poet realized that the maiden's garments were well suited to a land especially designed for hunting, fishing and camping. So he awarded his blessing to bloomers, and predicted that they might come into general use—"When women believe that sense is an equivalent of grace."

Mr. Lowell, Greenville, Moosehead Lake and women have all proved out. Today, except in black fly season, you can count a thousand or more ladies in shorts in Greenville and vicinity.

Someone has said that Greenville is the result of a collaboration between Sanders' store, Moosehead Lake, and the Great Northern Paper Company. Thanks to the Great Northern's logging operations and road building, you can drive around the lake.

Moosehead, so named because its shape resembles the antlers of a moose, is about thirty-five miles long, and from one to twenty miles wide. It is New England's largest lake—mountainous, islanded, most of it forested in spruce, fir, pine, beech and birch.

From the high hill above town, when the fog lifts in the morning, you can see Squaw Mountain and Kineo rising from the lake.

You can see boats and canoes putting out from innumerable sporting camps for the day's fishing—trout, salmon and lake trout. A little seaplane takes off, the water blown to vapor which trails from its pontoons. The pilot is George Later, Maine's first flying game warden. Another noted Greenville warden is Ed Lowell, retired. Ed is the dean of American wardens. He helped take spawn from the first trout ever to be used for artificial propagation.

Greenville's two thousand citizens have ignored the trend toward ranch type homes. They reside comfortably in clapboard houses, and every other front lawn is functionally adorned with a pile of split wood and a canoe. Wall decorations, in homes and stores, run to mounted specimens of trout, salmon, togue and game animals. The lake, incidentally, has offered up countless specimens appropriate in size and form to the most fastidious museum. A huge landlocked salmon mounted on the wall in Sanders' store is said to have caused first utterance of a now time-worn comment. On sighting the mammoth salmon, a nameless stranger remarked:

"The man who caught that fish is a liar."

It is hard to name the outstanding characteristic of the citizens of Greenville. It might be good nature. Everyone seems to be smiling—usually in memory or anticipation of fishing. It might be patient honesty. A visitor once bought a pair of moccasins in the Indian store and left them on the counter. Two years later he came back and the Indian girl who had waited on him wordlessly passed him his moccasins. Or maybe, after all, the chief characteristic is durability. An item in *The Moosehead Gazette,* weekly, tells how Gene Dupré, who runs a sporting camp on Allagash Lake, was so severely injured in World War I that in winter he has to go to Arizona to hunt mountain lions.

Good nature, patient honesty, durability—and loyalty, too. The Greenville people loved the sight and sound of the old steam engine on the Bangor & Aroostook when she pulled into the Junction. When the brand new Diesel was announced, Greenville hearts were saddened—but when on the Diesel's first run it arrived thirty-three minutes late, happiness was again restored and cheers were audible.

The sporting camps and resort hotels and inns around the lake are famous the world over, with recreation opportunities for every whim, whether you're a golfer, camper, fisherman, hunter, canoeman or boatman.

In general, the spirit of recreation prevails in Greenville-on-the-lake. This spirit is somehow crystallized and made merry by an item in *The Moosehead Gazette,* which says, in part:

> *On Sunday, August 3, the Methodist Church in this nationally known sporting community will again be host to visiting sportsmen when the parish will hold Fishermen's Sunday Service. Maine guides will act as ushers, and the Rev. George Bullens will preach on the topic: "Let's Go Fishing."*

For Eastport—Till We Meet Again

YOU KNOW HOW IT IS when for a long, enchanted time you've been communicating with a girl you've never seen. You dream of what she looks like, how her footstep sounds. One day you decide to go and see her—and that's when you get scared. She might be surrounded by a lot of large dogs with fangs. Worse yet, she might be married.

In my case, the girl in question was the city of Eastport, Maine. I'd heard from her two or three times a day for ten years. Her voice came straight from her heart over Station WLBZ, Bangor, and she talked about nothing but the weather.

"Special forecast," she'd say, "Eastport to Block Island. Small craft warnings raised at 7:00 A.M."

"Thanks, honey," I'd answer. "Thanks for the warning. I'll haul up my boat."

But one day last summer she really gave us the sweet talk. Her voice had a soft come-hither, and the dawn was fair.

"Small craft warnings lowered at sunrise," she murmured. "Gentle westerly winds."

So in the early light we crossed the lake, got our Ranch Wagon from the garage, and headed for Eastport. About ten o'clock we turned off U. S. Highway 1 onto State 190. We crossed a bridge, and entered the easternmost city in the United States, situated on an island between Cobscook and Passamaquoddy Bays, arms of the Bay of Fundy.

On that first drive down the main street, I hardly noticed the old, white houses and the elms. But they are there, and the houses have fanlights and chimneys, and are good to dwell in, or to dwell upon. You could almost see the hands and eyes of the master craftsmen who built them.

Some of the houses are a hundred and fifty years old. The southeast gales haven't annoyed them, and you know they never will. One house had a "For Sale" sign. In a matter of seconds, my wife bought it in fancy, made alterations, and moved in. Then she saw another she liked better.

I was looking for just one thing, and there she was: a gray stone building, like a fortress with windows. I read the signs at its entrance, as I climbed the stone steps: U. S. Customs; U. S. Post Office; and—U. S. Weather Bureau! My secret love.

"Please direct me to the weather bureau," I asked a man in the post office. "I have a date with her."

"Isn't here any more."

"You mean she's *gone?*"

I must have reflected dismay—because presently a lot of nice people began being helpful. Within minutes, I met Mr.

Ashton Mabee, the postmaster. He introduced me to Mr. Charles Wilson, druggist and president of the savings bank. Mr. Wilson planned to introduce me to the Reverend Mr. Colpitts, a clergyman who is also secretary of the Chamber of Commerce—but just then Mr. Wilson saw Mr. Emery on Water Street.

"There's a man you ought to know," Mr. Wilson said; and that's how I met Mr. Roscoe Emery.

If you spend any time in Eastport, you too will meet Mr. Emery. When he tells you that Eastport was settled in 1782, or that its population is currently about 3500, you feel no impulse to check his date or count his people. It is probable that Mr. Emery has uttered as few misstatements as any man in Maine— and none deliberately. You don't even question that the sea tides of Eastport reach a peak of twenty-eight feet. This astonishing fact, together with the huge ocean pools known as Passamaquoddy Bay and Cobscook Bay, caused the late Dexter Cooper to propose the celebrated Quoddy hydroelectric plan.

A working model of this immense power project is on display at Eastport's Quoddy Village, which is a complete village built for the workers on the proposed dams. Quoddy's future is one of Eastport's four main topics of conversation, the other three being the sea, the sardine industry—and the weather.

Mr. Emery's office is correctly in the Emery Building, second floor. He is deeply concerned with Eastport's history, citizens and welfare. For years he was owner and editor of the *Eastport Sentinel,* Maine's oldest newspaper, in which he published the first true account of Eddie Lee and the Masonic tomb.

Eddie Lee is a long-haired Irishman, whose cup of cheer occasionally runneth over. Eddie's father was the superintendent of grounds at the cemetery, where Eddie sometimes worked. One afternoon when he had looked upon the wine, Eddie crept into the Masonic tomb and went to sleep. At eventide, Eddie's

father, unaware of his son's predicament, closed the tomb and
went home.

When Eddie awoke, he scented masonry and remembered
where he was. He forthwith flung out a cry. A passing stranger
heard this cry, and fled the cemetery in terror wild. A short
time later, Eddie's sister-in-law came through the cemetery on
her way home. She, too, heard a voice from the tomb—and
fainted. When she finally came to and got home, Eddie's father
guessed the truth and rescued Eddie.

"To the best of my knowledge," said Eddie soberly, "this is
the only instance of an Irishman being buried in a Masonic
tomb."

Eastport is proud of the fact that in 1910 the late President
Taft arrived in the *Mayflower* to make the first speech on Canadian Reciprocity. It is also proud that the late President
Roosevelt, a sponsor of the Quoddy project, spent his summers
at nearby Campobello Island, in Passamaquoddy Bay, through
which runs the International Boundary. And at Eastport there
is at least one renowned tombstone—that of Lorenzo Sabine,
author of *The American Loyalists*. It bears the masterfully sim-
plified, one-word legend: "Transplanted."

Down in the center of town the asphalt sidewalks have a
casual lean to them. The granite curbstones also lean, and are
painted red. Any road you take leads you to the sea, because the
sea is in all directions. The headlands and promontories are
steep, dramatic cliffs, most of them grown to spruces. Todd
Head is the northeasternmost headland of the easternmost city.

At low tide, the tall, seaweed-draped piers and pilings make
you think that Eastport is a town on stilts. Six hours later, at
high tide, she seems to be a floating citadel with the boats of
the sardine fleet moored level with her garden gates.

Absorbed in these reflections I'd half forgotten what had
really lured me to Eastport. Remembering, I stopped in front of

Quoddy Motors, owned by Ivan Wyman. Hard by is the new home of my lady love, the Eastport, Maine, United States Weather Observatory.

Mr. Wyman introduced me to Mr. Walter Hicks, the weatherman; and although Mr. Hicks is not a girl—as I had dreamed he was—he is married to a very charming one. Together, with the unsolicited aid of their two small children, Mr. and Mrs. Hicks take readings from their instruments in the kitchen of their cottage home. There you see the nine-light wind indicator right near their washing machine; the baragraph; the teletype not far from their kitchen stove; the children playing about.

My visit with Mr. and Mrs. Hicks was supremely satisfying. I knew, at long last, from whom our forecasts truly came. These were the human beings who told us hours in advance when to haul up our small boat and stake our delphinium and our clematis vines against wind and storm. Having met the Hickses, we would never be in any doubt. As we drove toward home I said, inwardly—for Eastport's private ear:

"Farewell, my lovely—till we meet again."

The wind, as she had promised in the early morning, was gentle westerly, and the day still fair in the setting sun.

Poland Spring

AS YOU SWING OFF Route 26 into the groomed, spacious approach to the Poland Spring House, at Poland Spring, Maine, you are struck—almost mortally—with the wand of Victorian elegance and the witchcraft of nostalgia. The immense, turreted façade of the illustrious, old New England hostelry is overpowering. So are the memories it engenders.

Its architecture, in virtually criminal understatement, has been called uninhibited. Acutally, it is as complicated, bewildering, and magnificent as that of a Class One battleship built solely for pleasure and equipped with long range fire escapes and heavy-calibered green and white awnings. With all parasols set, the Poland Spring House seems to sail serenely on the green sea of its golf course, its balconied and yellow-clapboarded prow seeking ever westward toward the striking silhouettes of New Hampshire's White Mountains, sixty miles away.

Even if you have never before laid eyes on the Poland Spring House, everything about it is poignantly familiar. The magic is explained by the fact that here, before your eyes, is the original working model of that stately pleasure dome, the New England Summer Hotel. It is a curiously touching experience to stand face-to-face with this classic symbol of an era. Here is the

(249)

sumptuous reality of the palace you have seen since childhood depicted on colored postcards in drugstores and novelty shops throughout the land. In all probability, on a card mailed from the Poland Spring Post Office, the following phrases were first written:

> "Having wonderful time."
> "Wish you were here."
> "Sleeping under blankets."
> "Am staying another week."
> And: "X marks my room."

Driving thoughtfully up the long, curving entrance road, you notice a skilled foursome approaching the eighteenth green, which is twenty-five feet from the huge windows of the hotel dining room. What is wrong with these otherwise correct and innocent golfers? It has to do with timing—yours, not theirs. Today is certainly today. Yet, here, it is also yesterday. The trouble with those golfers is that their clubs have steel shafts, when they ought to be hickory. It is difficult to condone the golfers' visored caps, when clearly, in these surroundings, they should be wearing stovepipe hats, and eschewing numbered irons for the niblick, the cleek and the baffy.

But wait! All is well, for instead of trundling their mallets in modern-day golf carts, the foursome's bags are carried by true, living *caddies!* There is something vastly satisfying about this, especially since the caddies, dressed in green shorts, green hats and yellow T-shirts, appear to be extremely well-mannered and capable teen-agers. They are an important part of the Poland Spring saga, as you shall presently see.

Parking your car alongside green turf under a spreading oak, you step across a porch monumented with fluted Ionic pillars of white, and enter the lobby. The Poland Spring lobby sparkles with a crystal light and seems to extend for acres in all directions. Its color motif is an unusual shade of heliotrope. You feel the uneasiness you always feel when entering a lobby for the first time, and you ask yourself the age-old questions:

"Am I wearing the right clothes?"

"Have I sufficient distinction to be accepted here?"

"Why didn't I get a haircut?"

After all, this particular lobby packs a tremendous tonnage of tradition. J. P. Morgan stopped here. So did Woodrow Wilson. And so, more recently, did Averell Harriman—and our own Senator Muskie.

Your anxiety is quelled in seconds by the graciousness of a superbly trained hotel staff, from bellboys to the Resident Manager, whose name is Mr. Daniel A. Barry, Jr. You have a sudden feeling that you're home. And by way of expressing your appreciation, you mention to Mr. Barry that you saw some caddies on the eighteenth fairway, and you'd like to know if they are real. Mr. Barry will then tell you about the Poland Spring Caddy Camp, which is unique, and very heartwarming.

Each year, for almost forty years, the hotel has brought fifty-two boys from Boston's South End Settlement House to the Caddy Camp at Poland Spring. The only stipulations are that the kids must be from thirteen to seventeen, weigh at least 110 pounds, and be no less than five feet tall. They are housed, fed, given recreation facilities and caddying instructions, all at a very nominal fee. The camp director is the head football coach at Bates College, and the assistant director is the head baseball coach at the same Maine hall of learning. The triumph of this long-lasting enterprise for the commonweal is reflected not only in the happiness of visiting golfers, but in the very apparent good health, spirits and manners of the boys themselves.

"Mr. Barry," you remark to the Resident Manager, "this Caddy Camp is a wonderful institution."

"Why, yes—I think so. Thirty-odd years ago, I was attending the Caddy Camp, myself."

Obviously, the Poland Spring Caddy Camp has been instrumental in training boys into men who can hold important jobs on or off the golf course. But there is no time for further reflection, for a bellboy comes with your luggage and car keys, and with something else—a prominent quart bottle of green glass. The bottle is very cold, and its contents is declared by a label reading as follows:

POLAND WATER. NATURAL MINERAL SPRING WATER. PO-
LAND SPRING, MAINE. HIRAM RICKER & SONS.

Each guest is given a bottle of this renowned spring water on arrival. It is served at all meals in the hotel dining room, and is pictured on match pads and in hotel literature. Besides containing minerals said to be beneficial to the health of man, Poland Water has a bacteria count of Minus Two. This, for purity and perfection, is about like carding a sixty on the Poland Spring golf course—which, incidentally, is the first hotel golf course in the world.

Centered around, or inspired by the nearby spring, the hotel was built by Hiram Ricker in 1876. The original structure has been remodeled three times. The remodeling consisted of adding a story or two, extending a wing or two, and changing the original square turrets to rounded, or cone-shaped spires. There are now about three hundred rooms, or accommodations for five hundred guests.

The dominant and palatial elegance of the hotel, being sufficient unto itself, often blinds the guest to the other delights in the vicinity. No extra added attraction seems necessary, or even possible. Actually, Poland Spring is a five-thousand-acre natural recreation center, one of the most complete playgrounds in New England, if not the nation. Besides the Poland Spring House, there are two other hotels—the Mansion House, with ninety rooms. (The northwest corner of this was built by Jabez Ricker in 1794.) And the Riccar Inn, built in 1912, with eighty rooms.

There is a summer theatre, a church, riding stables, an art gallery, a library of ten thousand volumes, fishing and boating at Middle Range Lake, a Beach Club with innumerable floats and springboards, and a galaxy of games from golf and tennis to handball and horseshoe pitching. Spaciousness in grounds and activities prevails outdoors, and graciousness within.

But if you should feel cramped and confined by a mere five thousand acres, tell Mr. Newton Graffam, Head Waiter in the vast dining room, that you're restless, and would like a box lunch. Thus fortified, you can drive to the rockbound coast of Maine in about two hours for a look at the Atlantic Ocean. Or you can drive into the heart of the White Mounains of New Hampshire in less than that. You can spend a day fishing or boating on nearby Sebago Lake, and visit the little towns with old world names: Denmark, Sweden, Naples, Norway, or even Paris and China, if you want to rack up a score.

Road weary, with your eyes full of sights, you return to the Poland Spring House about four in the afternoon. There is plenty of time before supper to visit the Poland Spring itself. It is not as impressive as the great Missouri springs, nor as spectacular as Yellowstone's Old Faithful. It is not spectacular at all. Because of the grandness of the hotel, you expected something on a par with Yosemite Falls.

But if you enter the spirit of the thing, you won't be disappointed. The waters from this modest font have passed down the throats of the mighty and the minute of men in all corners of the globe for a hundred years and more. The sedate green bottles have really got around, like those of Appolonaris, Vichy, Canadian Club, and Pluto.

A short distance from the hotel, along a tree-shaded road, a simple white sign says:

THE SPRING

It—the spring—is housed in a yellowish brick structure with a green, tile roof. You can't type the architecture. One moment it resembles a mosque, the next a pagoda. That it houses Poland Spring is enough.

The floor of the spring house is of small white tile, the walls of mottled gray marble. Beside a dial phone reposes a single copy of *Holiday,* and on the tile floor, worked in blue mosaic, are the words:

SAPIENTIA DONUM DEI
(Wisdom is the gift of God)

It is now the cocktail hour, and, taking heed of the blue mosaic motto, you drift back to the hotel and into the subdued lounge. This may be the only cocktail lounge you ever saw with stained glass windows. More than that, and besides Poland Water chasers, it has a dim skylight, a firmament like Grand Central Station for a ceiling, and murals showing pine trees, wooden bridges and refined waterfalls. It's a wonderful place to end a day, and to dally a while before supper.

You would as soon expect to see Cinderella in a Bikini bathing suit as a man without jacket and tie in the dining room of the Poland Spring House. If you ventured across the threshold in shorts, a shaken committee would wait upon you—but not a waitress.

The menu is a positive torment. The bills of fare are a literature of tasties, and you are ever looking up at late golfers pitching to the eighteenth green outside the big windows, with the mountains in the background. And you are constantly aware that legions of the decent have been doing just what you are doing in this same dining room—for over eighty years. You would not be surprised to see a hoop-skirted beauty, or the umbrella stand gleaming with gold-headed canes.

In this nostalgic mood, following your dessert of lemon ice and demitasse, you stroll out onto the curving porch, and select a rocker from among the Ionic pillars. The porches, the pillars and the rockers extend for uncounted miles, and the sunset over the White Mountains is hard to equal east of the Grand Canyon. The golf course looks like soft, green fur laced with lengthening shadows, all under a twilight inspection by a few agreeable crows. The American flag—Old Glory—is lowered, the green and white awnings are furled for the night, and the orchestra is playing, "Where deep shadows fall, over purple garden walls . . ."

The cool dark hovers. Cigars glow. A spent cigarette makes a fiery arc. Voices are low. Hearts are full. On the way through the heliotrope lobby, before taking the elevator to your room, you pause to buy a stamp and a postcard depicting the Poland Spring House, Poland Spring, Maine. And on the card, as if some benevolent gentleman in an Inverness cape were guiding your hand, you write immortal words, as follows:

"X marks my room. Sleeping under blankets. Having wonderful time. Wish you were here. Am staying another week."

Part Five

MAINE VARIETY PACKAGE

Spring Drive

AT GRAND LAKE DAM, on the East Branch of Maine's historic Penobscot River, a breathless feminine observer once caroled that the river-drivers were as picturesque as questing knights of old. Happily, her comparison was muffled by the thunder of the river, the shock of logs up-ending in the sluice gates, and the bright blast of language. The lady should have left the knights out of it. River-drivers are as picturesque as themselves, which puts King Arthur's blades in place position.

Not even Sir Lancelot would char a piece of green alder and write on birch bark at Stair Falls: "Sixty-nine days to beer." And, even with the itch to go questing for grails really burning him, it is hard to imagine Sir Galahad saying to a Round Table pal: "Hey, Stub. Let's go upriver on the drive. I got ants in my pants as big as young mice."

In spring, "upriver" is a word of peculiar force and magic. Upriver is where the log drive begins—the headwaters, the source. On the Penobscot's East Branch, "upriver" means Grand Lake, Webster, Telos, and the vein-work of wild streams, all roaring white in May before the snow has died in the forests.

"Downriver" means the cities and the towns: Grindstone, Mattawamkeag, Lincoln, and that rose-tinted rendezvous of lumberjacks for 150 years, Bangor. Besides being the beginning of tidewater, Bangor is the end of the drive, and—almost simultaneously—of four months' wages.

"Why do you like to go up on the drive?" you ask the restless-footed one with the red shirt and three-inch belt buckle.

"To get down to Bangor the hard way."

"Why do you want to get to Bangor?"

"So I can go broke, go upriver, and start over."

This logic is understandable only to those who have followed the turbulent cycle for years. When they sign on, the boys know exactly what they are in for: approximately 120 days of bone labor, wet blankets, black flies, headwinds, eye-squeezing weariness, homesickness, hazard, and some of the meanest air-conditioning the Maine weatherman can think up. It's a life without sheets, Sundays, or pyjamas. The estimated saving in razor blades would endow a Bangor juke joint.

But the compensations are there. The tangibles are good wages with overtime, good food and plenty of it. The intangibles are the lure of the wild, mountain scenery; the ceaseless change of lake and river; adventure, companionship, and *esprit de corps*.

The river-driver's calling is as proud and exclusive as that of sandhog or high-steel bird. You're not really one of the boys till you've been sluiced at least once. Sluiced means losing your footing and taking a Nantucket Sleigh Ride along with a few tons of logs under the iced rapids of one of the river's hotspots, such as Haskell Rock Pitch, or the Hulling Machine.

In lumbering's early days, the same men who felled the timber drove it to the mills. Today, in Maine pulpwood and logging operations, there is generally a distinct line between woodsmen and rivermen. A riverman views an axe with a dismay equal to that of a cowboy facing a long walk, or a motorist with an empty gas tank.

If he's driving long logs, the tool of his trade is a peavey, often called cantdog. If he's driving pulpwood, he uses a pick pole—never called "pike" pole except by visiting Bostonians, or the white flannel set. A pick pole is a slender, springy, dry-spruce shaft about twelve feet long, sharp-shod, with iron point and pick. Handling picks with great skill, the boys jab, tug and steer the four-foot pulp logs in the tricky river currents. The pole also helps the riverman balance on the murderous footing.

The East Branch drive of the Eastern Corporation of Brewer, Maine, makers of high grade writing paper, is typical of the best. River crews like to sign on with the Eastern. Bill Eggleston, Woods Manager of the company's far-flung operations; Walter Scott, Walking Boss of the Grand Lake area; Walter Clement, Operation Superintendent; and Louis Rowe, River Boss, have been in and through the mill most of their lives. They know the woods, watersheds, winds, and the backgrounds and temperaments of men. But it is possible that their combined talents would accomplish little if it weren't for one key man—the cook!

On the East Branch, you hear the boys say: "The Eastern feeds good." When the drive moves downriver from headquarters camp on Grand Lake, Clayt, Smitty, and old Jack Riley say farewell to stoves. These men are the cook, cookee, or bull cook, and the fire-, wood- and water-tender. Henceforth, they perform in the open, moving their wangan, or outfit, apace with the drive. If necessary, they cook with wet wood in a swamp, and serve hot meals in a downpour, or in sweltering heat and black flies, wherever the crew happens to be at meal-time. What they used to say of old Marvin Allen, the Eastern's late, famed cook, applies to the current crew:

"He can strike a match in mud, and build a pie with nothing but sawdust and wet cement."

Louis Rowe, the River Boss, is a quiet-spoken, respected, and even-tempered man. He has the knack of reflecting or transmitting no anxiety or impatience whatever, and his voice —never raised—would soothe the tantrums of a yearling bear. His judgment has averted an unknown number of accidents, and taken the starch out of some that happened anyway. He usually wears dark glasses, not because of eye trouble, but because: "Some day the sun might shine, and startle me."

Louis, who is crowding sixty on one side or the other, refers to his crew of from twenty to sixty men as his "boys." They range in age from an Oldtown Indian lad of twenty, to Jack Riley of the cook crew, who is seventy-three.

Early in spring, when the Eastern is hiring for the drive, the crew trickles in to headquarters camp on Grand Lake, above the big dam. They are winter-pale. The young men's stomachs lie flat under their belts, and in their hip pockets the wallets are limp and thin. As Louis greets them, they nod, smile, or remain silent in memory of a last night in Bangor.

The young men wear their hats on a slant. Their shin-high boots are spiked to give footing on the slippery logs and ledges. Their pants, cut off just below their boot tops, are known as "highwater pants."

The oldtimers, whose belt buckles once were also bright, now wear suspenders. Their shirts are chain-store black, and their stomachs lean out a little in profile. But there is experience in the eyes of the old men, and in the shape of their scarred hands is the history of forty spring drives.

Headquarters camp consists of a cook shack and bunkhouse on a knoll in the shadow of Horse Mountain, with the rolling, thoughtful peaks of Traveller beyond. Down the rugged truck road a piece is a storehouse, a splintery dock on the lake, and the bookkeeper's office and quarters. A red Ford truck, one of the Big Boys, rolls in with a load of beef, potatoes, flour, a few drums of oil, and about a mile of heavy warp for towing booms.

Brock Linscott, the driver, has been trucking for the Eastern over 10 years. He is the only known truck driver whose shoe size is five. Brock is sensitive about this, but it does not seem a deficiency to those who know him. He has red hair, and can throw an anvil as far as anyone wearing size 12. He and his truck have been places that would discourage a bulldozer.

You can smell woodsmoke, and the smoke of pitch heating in the pots. The pitch flows black and glistening over the seams of the long, peak-ended bateaus, turned up on shore for caulking.

There is also a white boat, the *Albert Doran,* used for towing booms of floating logs. But the real towboat, a character of dignity on Grand Lake, is the *Meadow Hen,* pronounced "Medderhen." She's painted yellow, where she's painted at all—a side-wheeler with decks and towing gear. She looks like a cross between a Mississippi steamboat and a scow. The *Medderhen* had just been launched after a lonely winter, and the boys greet her with unprintable affection.

In the morning, probably in rain or snow, the crew starts "booming out." A boom is a rope of long logs chained end to end. It can be broken, or opened, at any joint. Within the boom the four-foot pulpwood is gathered for towing on the lakes— 800 or 900 cords to the boom, or about 2,500 tons.

The drive divides itself into distinct operations: driving the brooks; that is, feeding the pulpwood into the brooks which carry it to the lakes. Next, booming out and towing. The towboats warp the booms, one by one, down through the lake to the dam, swing them on the wind, and "roll 'em in." Rolling a boom is a neat trick, interesting to see.

Louis Rowe ties one side of a boom solid to an iron ring on Anchor Point just above the dam. As it swings slowly down in the wind, the towboats hook onto the opposite side. Louis casts loose his end, and in she rolls. It's like snapping a 2,500-ton whip in very slow motion.

Sluicing is running the logs through the sluice gate in the dam. The crew strings out with their pick poles above the gate on each side, and keeps the logs moving. The logs run through, tumble end-over-end into the great pool below, circle in the big eddy, and finally start downriver.

The last boom to go through the sluice gate is called the "rear." When the rear is down, headquarters camp is abandoned—usually towards the last of June. From then till September, it's tents and blankets.

On each bank there are points where the pulpwood lodges on shore, or ledge, building up in stacks sometimes as neatly as if piled by hand. Louis stations his boys at these points to keep things moving. You don't stand at a point, nor are you stationed there in the lingo. You're "tendin' out."

A fleet of bateaus goes down with the drive to move men across the river from point to point, and to transport the wangan, or supplies. But the young lads often scorn the bateaus. To get from point to point, they sometimes hook the picks of their poles in their belts, jump in, and "ride the bubbles."

The whole countryside takes an interest in the progress of the drive. Pat Steen, at the dam, controls the water, cooperating with Louis Rowe, and adjusting the big gates to the desired flow. When the drive ties up somewhere downriver for the night, Pat shuts off the water. The dam, built by the Bangor Hydro-Electric Company, is pretty much the pulsebeat of the log driving process.

Somehow, as you watch the flash and motion of the log-

laden river, you are struck with the potential in a single, far-travelled stick of pulpwood. Along the waterway, turbulent or still, this stick may have been lost and found a dozen times. It has rolled under a riverman's foot, and sluiced him. It has slipped out from under a boom and wandered, water-logged, in the lake for weeks. It has started at the head end of the drive, and wound up in the rear. It has been scarred and stabbed by a dozen pick poles, and loomed out of the early morning fog across the bow of an unwary canoe. In midlake, in the wind-ripped waves, gulls have casually perched upon it. It may even have caused fights, and upset the equanimity of fifty men. That's what they sometimes call a "rogue spruce."

Looking at such a stick, four feet long, its ends splashed with yellow paint—the Eastern drive brand—you wonder what words will one day be written on the paper made from it? Something seems to vitalize the stick. What will be its end result? A death warrant? An old man's will? The deed to home? A poem? Or a police report?

You almost never know—but once in a while you do. For a few fibers of one such stick once made the paper on which the following letter was written. The letter was found on the river-bank near Grindstone. It was addressed to a young river-driver. It bore the watermark EASTCO, which is an Eastern brand, and read as follows:

Dere Joe, the baby come the 16th an is so beautifull an soft an got your hair too Joe, an we miss you so terrible. O, wen will the drive get down so we can be together agin the three of us? O, Joe I cant wait to have you come an see our baby, an pray you will love him like I do. Love from me an the baby, your wife

Mayme

The Genteel Interval

IN AN ATTEMPT to restore a semblance of the gracious life, and to reduce the incidence of ulcer in our workaday world, a simple device, or social discipline, is here proposed for one and all. I have named this discipline "the genteel interval," and its functions, besides the above-mentioned, are to exhume courtesy from the slag heaps of commerce and preserve the identity of individual man. Briefly, the genteel interval is the lapse of time between the moment of one's introduction to a stranger and the moment when it is decent to call the stranger by his nickname.

In many marts in many parts of the country the genteel interval is lacking entirely, with results which I consider disturbing. Let us say your name is John Winthrop Worthington. You are introduced to a man named Henry Wadsworth Osgood. In acknowledgment of the introduction—you have never met before—Mr. Osgood clasps your hand in a firm, enthusiastic grip, and says:

"Pleesa meetcha, Jack."

And you respond with:

"Gladda knowya, Hank."

Here, in a matter of seconds, Mr. Worthington has been reduced to anonymity as "Jack," while Mr. Osgood, as "Hank," has become a human shard, a white chip at best. Both men have lost dignity as well as identity. At least two of the initials on their suitcases are rendered superfluous. Stripped of all reserve, they stand figuratively naked, as though they had been long users of the same swimming hole or bathtub, or members for years in a poker club in the back room of a tavern in the town.

It would be far finer, it seems to me, if Jack remained Mr. Worthington for a few minutes, and if he in turn allowed Hank to pose briefly as himself, to wit, Henry Wadsworth Osgood. Thus each man could proudly assume that he had a surname, and by inference a father and mother, perhaps even ancestors and a life of his own.

The idea behind the electrically-instant use of nicknames is, of course, to abolish privacy and reticence and get right to business. When members of opposite sexes fail to observe the genteel interval, this same idea probably obtains in the mind of one or both parties, which could constitute a hazard.

Of course, the time of the interval, when put into effect, will vary with the nature, stature and character of the strangers involved—and also with the geographical location. In the South, the interval is fairly well observed, or at least remembered. Throughout, deponent is addressed as, "sir,"—a more genuine "sir" than the one used by prep school boys to their elders, or by enlisted men to officers—but once across the northerly Ohio border, the wayfarer becomes "Mac," "Joe," or, "Hey, you," and is one with the masses, his ancestry for naught.

It is difficult in any case to stipulate a maximum or minimum time lapse for the genteel interval. For the Middle West, a five-minute minimum is suggested as not being too revolutionary for a beginning. This would allow Mr. Worthington and Mr. Osgood to call each other Mr. Worthington and Mr. Osgood perhaps twice immediately following the grip. They would thus enjoy a moment of reserve and would then get into the hard core of their business deal as happily and mercilessly as of yore.

In some cases, the interval might last a lifetime, as in that of the late Oliver Wendell Holmes, or of Nero Wolfe, whom by nearly everybody is called Mr. Wolfe nearly all the time.

Between doctors and patients, the genteel interval should be extended to at least three office calls and one or two house calls. After this, the patient, if he feels he is gaining nothing in health, is justified in calling the doctor "Doc." (No interval time has as yet been established for psychiatrists.)

Where the genteel interval has been wholly breached, or ignored, there is a false and invidious assumption of friendship, familiarity—or, worse, palship. The "Let's be pals" angle is the interval's worst enemy. Does Mr. Osgood truly wish to enter into a state of palship with Mr. Worthington on sight, or even after sight? I think not, especially since it is probable that the initial, tacit purpose of their meeting is a deal, which is to say a mutual cutting of throats for monetary gain. The fast car, the fast airplane, the fast palship—all inimical to the genteel interval—are all in cahoots for the fast buck; and all high factors in the following credo: the hell with you, Jack—or Hank—I got mine.

(signed) Edmund Ware (Eddie) Smith

The Outermost Henhouse

I SHALL ALWAYS CONSIDER June 18, 1954, as Judgment Day for my wilderness life in Maine. As the forest surrounding our cabin awoke to birdsong, there was no premonition of change or disaster. The weather was clear, the track fast, and my wife and I sat down to the most delicious breakfast of our lives. It was also the most expensive.

The *pièce de résistance* was a chive omelet, and it was worth the price in its engendered complacency alone. The chives came from our cabin garden, and the eggs—all five of them—from our own white chickens which, as we breakfasted, were visible from the kitchen window in their yard extending from The Outermost Henhouse.

"There never was an omelet like this," I remarked.

"Just think," said my wife. "We built the henhouse, brought the birds 'way, 'way back in here, and this feast is the result. More coffee?"

"Please."

A few minutes later, energized by omelet and coffee, and lulled by a false sense of achievement and well being, I arose to write a business letter to a farmer acquaintance down on the Maine coast.

I never should have written that letter. A man with any reticence whatever would have limited a business letter to business; but, heady with success and beguiled by self-esteem, I got my business over in a paragraph and rushed on to the poetry, as follows:

Shin Pond, Maine
June 18, 1954

Dear Mr. ———

. . . . . .

We live in this remote cabin six months a year, and spend the other six in the ghettos of Detroit, thus lending authority to those notes of yours on the bluejay, "a bird which doesn't seem to know whether to settle in a forest or a housing development."

On the path to our spring a hermit thrush is nesting on four, brilliant, blue-green eggs, her eyes full of terrible fear as we pass with the water pail. But she is now getting used to us, although I do not wish to imply that we are trying to tame her. Her wildness is part of her wonder.

This year, for fun and fresh eggs, we have built—with due respect to our friend, Henry Beston—The Outermost Henhouse. No domestic egg was ever laid within thirty miles of this spot till a few days ago, when in one of the nests appeared a fine, brown ovoid about the size of a walnut. Estimating lumber, hardware, feed, and transportation of all materiél by pontoon airplane, we figure this morning's breakfast omelet cost $167.45. It was worth every penny.

We regard our White Rock pullets as a sorority, as select and refined a group of girls as you'd come across at Spence or Miss Porter's. The view from their playground is of Thoreau's Traveller Range across the lake, and the group seems content —except that one of them crowed one morning. A sex deviate in the dormitory. Lust was the order of the day.

With no presage of evil, I signed this letter and gave it to the care of The Birdman, the bush pilot who drops in ever and anon to see how we are faring. I thought no more about it, and my wife and I went on about our gardening, wood chopping and work of life.

We had been told of a dread poultry disease called Blue Comb, that a tablespoon of molasses in a quart of water would ward it off. We dutifully followed this prescription, and the birds thrived. We had also been told that the presence of a rooster in our small group would tend to hinder the laying of eggs; and so, on a sad and harrowing day, we despatched our rooster by means of a shotgun. A day later the game warden paid us a visit, saying he had heard we were shooting birds out of season. Following our explanation of the shooting, he stayed to dinner which consisted mainly of the rooster.

Aside from this incident everything was peaceful and wilderness were paradise enow, till we went out one day to the tiny, forest hamlet of Shin Pond, and at the Post Office picked up our mail which, unfortunately, included Mr. ————'s reply to my all-but-forgotten letter.

Blank Town, Maine
June 24, 1954

Dear Mr. Smith:
    From your letter it is plain to me that the end of your wilderness life is in sight. The domestic egg is the beginning of your doom, and I can see the whole pattern unfolding— first the henhuose, then the egg, then the grainbill, then the full corn in the ear, and the bulldozer to break trail for the grain truck, and at last the green lush pasture and the white-face heifer bred by test tube arriving by Piper Cub because it's quicker than the truck. Ah, wilderness! That first egg, so deceptively beautiful, so germinal! I bought this place because it had a good anchorage for a boat. One day I noticed it had a barn. Now I don't even have a boat.

Here, in a single paragraph, our ten-year enterprise in wilderness living had been shaken to the core. On returning to the cabin, I re-read Mr. ————'s letter and then walked up the path to The Outermost Henhouse. I found six, warm, brown eggs in the nests which up to then was a near record for a single, laying day. I spoke several kind words to the birds, whom we had by now begun to call by name: Big Rosie, Stretch (who laid the huge double-yolkers), and Aunt Agnes. In both eggs and birds, in fact in the entire Outermost Henhouse project, there was no longer the full flow of satisfaction and joy. Mr. ———, with his fell creep of omniscience, had got in his work. I could reply to him only as follows:

> June 27, 1954
> a six-egg day
>
> Dear Mr. ———
> 　　Today we went the long, hard journey out to the settlements to buy beef steak, ten-penny nails, a whetstone and some gin, only to find your depressing letter of June 24th prophesying the breakdown of my wilderness life. There is some evidence in support of your prediction of my doom. For it is true that The Outermost Henhouse was delivered piecemeal by Piper Cub. It is also true that Mr. Humpy Gould, the flying plumber, flies in to fix things we can't fix, which are several. Moreover, the eggs in the hermit thrush's nest are gone, and so is the creature herself—all gone, mysteriously, into the wilds.

Shortly after signing and sealing this letter, I read in the news how a renowned university had awarded an honorary degree to my Maine coast farmer friend. This intelligence came too late for me to tear open the envelope and write some appropriate congratulations. But the award seemed to give Mr. ———'s views on everything, including my wilderness life, an added power and thrust. And one of the henhouse sorority, a thin girl named Gladys, mysteriously died that very week. I began to dread the mail, but the reply to my letter inevitably came. I quote:

Blank Town, Maine
June 30, 1954

Dear Mr. Smith:

Was shocked to learn that you have plumbing at your cabin as well as eggs. And you're not kidding me about that gin, either. It wasn't just gin you bought out there in civilization; I am betting you *also* bought a bottle of dry Vermouth or perhaps a small case of quinine water.

Never mind, I've just built a terrace. It cost three million dollars. You can see it from the little cove where I first dropped anchor so many years ago in a fog.

Yrs, ———

I was at first disarmed by what I felt was a lighter note in the above letter. But I was not long fooled. My correspondent was indeed relenting a little, but only because he knew he had me on the ropes. He was, in effect, walking to a neutral corner while the count was being taken. Rallying, I rushed to my typewriter to compose the following:

Shin Pond, Maine
July 3, 1954
a nine-egg day

Dear Mr. ———

My wilderness dream has again been nightmared by yours of June 30th. Several things need clearing up, including my plumbing. You need not be shocked by it, since it consists only of a sequestered privy overlooking the lake. On the back porch we have a gasoline pump which pumps water to the kitchen sink when it is in the mood. When it isn't, we get in touch with the Flying Plumber by Forest Service telephone. As I may have hinted, I am apprehensive about mechanical things, having but lately learned how to put a new blade in my safety razor without personal injury.

You also reached a wrong conclusion about my gin. I buy neither Vermouth nor quinine water to pour on top of it, but Coca Cola. Is anything more uncivilized than that?

About your terrace, I admit being pretty impressed with its cost. But I shall be content with the rock walls my wife has constructed right here with rocks she dug from the previously untrammeled wilderness. At this writing, I value her at *more* than three million dollars, after taxes. There goes your terrace.

I thought this would block my opponent for a while, and it did. But not for the reason I thought. He had planted the seed, and he stood aloof and let it grow, as a Maine coast farmer should.

Whether from his planting, or from the subconscious desire he suspected obtained in my mind, fine fruit has come; for in the spring of this year my wife and I bought a home full of fireplaces and modern plumbing down on the coast near Damariscotta, and there is a feeling we may withdraw there in time, tapering off our wilderness enterprise.

As for the occupants of The Outermost Henhouse, they are no more. Since we could not take them with us, we were obliged to eat them in the fall, feeling more than a little like cannibals as we did so.

Just before we crossed the lake in late October, I took a last look around at the closed and shuttered cabin. With mixed emotions, I noted several white neck-feathers adhering to the chopping block in the back dooryard. It was here that the guillotine had fallen. But, come early May, precocious robins would fly down to pluck and carry off these very feathers and with them line a nest in which to lay eggs which would hatch into little robins; and ere long the young birds together with their parents would fill the wilderness with the glory of song and new life—a thought my farmer friend would be the first to encourage and appreciate.

America's Voice Has Changed

TO THE COTERIE of mellowing Americans who can lay claim to having slept once upon a time on a corn husk mattress, today's dustless, durable product of foam rubber lacks but one thing—to wit, the power of self-expression. Foam rubber is mute. Corn husks could talk. And they did.

When, as a boy, you were sent to bed in the dark, upstairs chamber, your mattress gave you an audible reception. Under your weight, however slight, the husks crackled and rustled. At times they whispered in your nether ear, reminding you of evil you had done. If you had stolen a pie or stoned a cat, the husks gave you the business—like the cry of conscience. If, perchance, you had gone through the day without sin, they would lull you to sleep like the song of the Sand Man.

The modern inner-spring mattress has all but done away with the inner-sound model of yesteryear. The whisper of the husks is stilled. This leads one to wonder what may have happened to other everyday sounds of not so long ago? During a few decades of unparalleled development in our gadgets and implements, America's voice has changed, a fact which has impelled me to compile the following inventory of sounds now gone, or seldom heard.

You might think the research required to assemble a

modest lost-sound inventory would be a mild and pleasant experience in interrogation. On the contrary, I found it rugged, if not hazardous. If you don't believe me, just make this simple experiment: select any individual old enough to recall the celluloid collar, the sulphur match and "The Perils of Pauline," and ask him if he remembers the haunting, hollow splash of a bucket in a well? His response is likely to bury you under an avalanche of nostalgia. You will emerge, much later, with a complete compendium of splashes made by buckets in all the wells of your confrere's memory, plus the earnest story of his boyhood.

I asked one of my consultants, a revered friend of sixty-three, how long it had been since he had heard an iceman's horse rattling its harness under the elms on a village street? He rewarded me with definitive character analyses of four different icemen and their horses, together with a brief history of the Studebaker Harness Co. During the interview, two hours and one tray of ice cubes from his nearly soundless electric refrigerator were melted away.

As news of my project spread around my home town, neighbors began dropping by with the cast of reminiscence in their eyes, and their ears full of echoes. One contributor opened up with:

"The sounds of an old-fashioned wood stove—iron lids clangoring. You know, the symphony of morning in yesterday's kitchen."

"I've got that," I said. "It's high on the list."

He didn't even hear me. He was off, hell for leather, into the mists of his youth—drafts and dampers clanking, grates rattling, the thud and rumble of wood being dumped in the woodbox, and the various metallic expansion noises as his totally recalled wood stoves heated up.

"First," he said, dreamfully, "you'd smell woodsmoke—then bacon frying. And the coffee smell—"

"Look, Jake," I said. "This is a sound inventory. Smells are barred. Get back on the sound track."

He did so with difficulty and a hurt look. One of his stoves was an old, six-lid "Home Clarion," made by the late Messrs. Wood & Bishop, of Bangor.

"It was," said Jake, "as heavy as nine anvils."

"Anvils," of course, is the plural of a key word in sound-memory. Jake veered from the stove gambit into the galaxy of echoes from the oldtime blacksmith's shop. He was going nicely on the hiss of redhot iron plunged into the water barrel and the music of hammers forging chain, when again I was obliged to check him.

"I've got blacksmithing covered, Jake. You were talking about a certain stove, the old Home Clarion."

The morning clatter of this stove had been the signal for Jake, then a boy, to arise, breakfast, and go forth with axe and crosscut saw to "put up" cordwood. I was afraid he was going to veer off into the "chock" of an axe in a clearing and the "wish-wish" of the crosscut saw, both now vastly diminished by the "prutt-putter-putt" of the chain saw, but he didn't. For it seems he had been cutting his cordwood in one of our vanished chestnut groves.

"Say!" he said. "Remember the sound of ripe chestnuts and chestnut burrs dropping in the dry October leaves?"

"Good!" I said. "It goes on the list right now. Thanks."

The more you question lost-sound rememberers, the clearer it becomes that each has a cherished favorite. I have found that the wail of a steam locomotive in the night time ranks high with many people. One man, previously unsuspected of a poetic streak, called it "the sound of the long journey into the unknown."

Other strong favorites are the cranking of the Model T on a cold morning, and the voice of a mother reading Dickens aloud to her children at bedtime. The self starter and radio-TV respectively have reduced these sounds to hallowed echoes.

What about the gratifying "bo-*loop*" noise made by opening the old, collapsible, self-rising, high silk hat? Or the disconcerting "pop" of a shoe button breaking loose because of too much leverage on the button hook? You wonder how the button hook business is these days of the loafer shoe and the slide fastener? And if you remember the "chock" of the buggy whip dropping home in its dash board socket, you'll be concerned about the buggy whip manufacturers. But you'll be relieved to hear that one of them, with the end in sight, changed from braiding buggy whips to braiding fishing lines, and did well.

During the early stages of my research, I wrote to a friend in the Angler's Club of New York, who composes distinguished essays under the name of "Sparse Grey Hackle." I gave Sparse a partial list of lost sounds, including the cherished "slap-slop" of a straight razor being sharpened on a leather strop. I had thought the sound obsolete except in barber shops. Sparse set me straight; but first listed several erudite contributions to my inventory, as follows:

A mule skinner's voice (with words); squeezing the slack out of a freight train in the days before Diesels and booster gears; a New York policeman rapping for assistance with his nightstick of locust wood; a steam pile driver; horse artillery at a trot; and the "ga-*dunk,* ga-*dunk,* ga-*dunk*" of a hand pump drawing water in the kitchen sink.

"And now," Sparse's letter concluded, "if you want to hear a razor being stropped, come into my bathroom any day of the week. I have thirteen straight razors, twelve of which are handmade blades of incomparable quality, and the thirteenth, a gift, is competent."

What of the wheeze of the bellows in the parlor organ? Or the call of the wandering umbrella mender, forlorn in the rain?

My father had a special affinity for umbrella menders. He explained it on the grounds that they were men apart; for, unlike ordinary mortals, they were obliged to save money for a dry spell, not for a rainy day. I suspect he really liked them because he liked all wanderers, and wanted to hear their stories, true or fanciful.

At any rate, whenever an umbrella mender was heard, my father ordered my brother and me to empty the umbrella stand and search all closets for cripples, while he, personally, signalled the mender to our door. There was one tense occasion when we found all our umbrellas in perfect repair. But my father, undismayed, cried, "Break two or three of them! Quickly!" and rushed out in the rain to hail the wanderer.

I can't remember when I last heard the sound of a horse's hooves on a wooden bridge, or their muffled thud on a stable floor at night. The bridge is now cement, and the horse has turned into a tractor. Sleigh bells! And sled runners on hard packed snow! We used to call the sled-runner sound "the frozen violins of winter." It rates well up with the creaking of a windmill, the tinkle and rattle of trace chains and double-trees, the clucking of wagon hubs, and that clean, sharp, metallic, summery "*kee*-uk, *kee*-uk, *kee*-uk" made by a man whetting a scythe in haying time.

Then there's the "ding-ding-ding" of the trolley car gong

operated by the motorman's foot; and that other "ding" from the rear of the car as the conductor rang up your five-cent fare.

Another sound you seldom if ever hear nowadays is the whistle of a willow switch in its arc of descent toward the squirming bottom of an errant boy. When the switch was on target, you could also hear the sounds of the boy. But today, the offending child is punished by curtailment of TV time, or packed off to a psychiatrist, and his outcries are no longer heard in the woodsheds throughout our land.

A final, splendid contribution to my lost-sound inventory comes from John Gould, Maine's Mark Twain. John deeply mourns the passing from our ears of the voice of the oldtime Fourth of July orator. Now that radio and TV have taken the orator from the bunting-draped hayrack and put him in a broadcasting studio, John won't go near a Fourth of July cele-bration. Dread of disappointment. He's afraid he won't hear the frock-coated orator concluding his remarks with:

> "Thou, too, sail on, O ship of State!
> Sail on, O Union, strong and great!"

The Snorkel Bird

A FORMATION OF MERGANSERS, or shelldrakes, feeding in the shallows close to a lake shore, resembles nothing so much as a group of sincere and sedulous snorklers. For when searching for minnows, their favorite food, these amusing and excitable ducks swim flat to the water's surface, their beaks and eyes half submerged, brownish-red crests prominent as a snorkel tube, attention dedicated to life below.

On sighting a school of minnows, chub or other small fish, the shelldrake formation up-ends as one, in a crash dive. Their sterns go down last, with a show of tail feathers and orange-red feet. The merganser's bill is equipped with saw teeth, the better to seize and grip its slippery prey. After a minute or two of sub-surface fishing, the ducks pop to the surface, flipping water from their crests, and chattering news of fish caught and fish lost, no doubt exaggerating size and numbers. The chattering subsides, as they flatten their beaks and eyes to the water and continue their snorkling till another school of small fry is sighted.

Except as a personality, or a "character," the merganser is not very popular among sportsmen, which is a pity. Trout fishermen dislike him because he is supposed to eat small trout. Hunters dislike him because he isn't supposed to be palatable. Both these opinions are a lot less than half correct, for a merganser certainly eats a hundred minnows to a single bill-full of trout fry; and when cleaned immediately after brought down he makes a tasty meal. The objectionable fishy flavor comes usually only after the bird has been hung for several hours, undrawn, and with its feathers left on.

I am personally very fond of shelldrakes in the live and active state. I enjoy meeting them socially. The males are handsome, head and upper neck a dark green, backs a glossy black, tapering off to gray at the tail, wings white with a black bar. Heads and necks of females are a reddish brown, bodies gray, reddish crests pert and cocky.

The shelldrake's family life ranges from sublime to ridiculous, subject to change without notice. Widely distributed over North America, coast to coast from Alaska to New Mexico, they breed in spring time, building nests of grass, dry roots and feathers—sometimes in a hollow tree, oftener under the shelter of pine or spruce branches near a lake shore.

The mother shelldrake is a living symbol of maternal worry and fussbudgetry. After hatching her clutch of eight or ten pale, buff-colored eggs, her trials begin. If her nest is in a tree, she brings her little ones to water in her bill. Otherwise, she coaxes them to the lake afoot, very soon after they hatch.

In a constant state of alarm, or semi-alarm, she gives instructions in snorkling—swimming, diving and fishing. At the slightest sound or sight of danger, she breaks into a frantic series of quacks and puts off shore, her little ones peeping shrilly, and riding high on her back, now and then tumbling off and uttering still more shrilly the shelldrake equivalent of "Wait for baby!"

For ten seasons, from our cabin on a Maine lakeshore, we have watched shelldrake families grow from walnut-sized balls of fluff to full grown birds. Mother shelldrakes are continually losing children. One day you'll see a convoy of ten, the family intact. Another day, the poor mother comes swimming forlornly with a lone feather ball tooling along in her wake. Still another day, the mother shows up with eighteen or twenty little irresponsibles, all trying to ride on her back at once. Either she has picked up a couple of lost broods, or she is baby-sitting for some other mother shelldrake. The baby-sitting theory is pleasant. Once we saw a single mother with twenty-seven babies—the offspring of probably three mothers, counting herself. It must have been a hard day.

The young shelldrakes take a long time learning to fly. They seem to prefer volplaning along the surface, wings flapping, feet paddling like crazy, little crests giving them the appearance of urchins with their hair on end. If you follow the half-grown flock in a boat, you can get very close, even within reaching distance, before the birds dive. And sometimes, in shallow water, you can see them clinging to a weed on bottom, waiting till the fancied danger has passed, before plopping to the surface again.

Sitting quietly in your boat, you watch the family get together. The frenzied quacking diminishes. Orange bills flatten to the water, and the mother takes the lead, uttering a couple of low, hoarse syllables which, translated, mean: "Resume snorkling."

Summer Hazard

A FEW YEARS AGO, after long and heartful search, my wife and I found our permanent home and moved in, rejoicing. Hard by the soothing, old, sea town of Damariscotta on the Maine coast, our house is a restored Cape Codder with an ell; and we have a red barn with an amiable sag in its ridgepole. In all our years together, we had never owned a home except our log cabin; but now, in our middle fifties, at last we had one—with an old clock, fireplaces, a weathervane, a lawn mower and two cats.

We went to work re-decorating and furnishing with a zeal which Mary called "the retarded nesting instinct." She had vast gardening projects, I vast writing projects. Together, we built pine cupboards, painted walls, sanded floors, and selected curtain materials. We bought a deep freeze in anticipation of Mary's garden produce; and I, myself, spent twenty-nine dollars for a waste basket just because it looked well in my study— a blissful extravagance you'd expect of a honeymooner.

There wasn't a cloud on our horizon till early the first Spring, when a revered neighbor told us in muted tones that, come Summer, all would not be so idyllic. He spoke darkly of an annual, ninety-day siege—he used the word "scourge"—by something, or someone, called "they." As I remember it, the conversation went like this:

"How," asked our neighbor, "will you get any work done, when they find out where you are, and start coming?"

"Who start coming?"

"Summer visitors. Dropper-inners."

"We haven't invited anyone, as yet."

"They spare you that detail," said our neighbor. "They simply arrive—with baggage."

"Who? Who are 'they'?"

"Friends, relatives, anyone you know or ever heard of— even total strangers."

"I don't believe it!"

"You will. It's a phenomenon—maybe not peculiar to the Maine coast, but especially virulent here. They hear you've got a nice little place. They want to share it with you during their summer vacation."

"But *I'm* not on vacation. I'm working."

"You won't be," said our neighbor, "not from June to September."

Feeling that this neighbor might be suffering from abnormal anxiety, we made further inquiry. All our informants corroborated the neighbor. Maurice "Jake" Day, artist friend, and long time resident, said:

"It's true. Wait and see."

"We could hang out a NO VACANCY sign," I remarked, gaily.

"It's been tried," said Jake.

"How about CLOSED FOR REPAIRS?"

"That's the one you hang out in the Fall, after they've all left."

We consulted still another resident, a man of much experience. He had very strong feelings on the matter.

"No policy or barricade ever invented," he said, "has suc-

cessfully repelled them. The only escape is to close your house, shutter it, erect tank traps in your driveway, and go visiting yourself, till after Labor Day."

As I look back on it, our friends Edward and Julia Myers, creators of Saltwater Farm, gave us the most poignant warning of all. Authorities on the subject of the casual summer visitor, Edward and Julie didn't say a word—just looked at us in sympathy, as upon dear friends about to undergo major surgery for the first time.

I regret to say that Mary and I regarded all these warnings lightly. We went on with our eager labors of home-making, smug in the belief that our house was our castle.

The belief has been shattered. Far from being our castle— or even our *own*—our house at times resembled a small, free resort hotel, a rendezvous for the Corn Roast and Clam Bake Set, featuring exquisite cuisine and personalized service at any hour of day or night, with or without notice. We had never before enjoyed—or endured—such popularity.

At this writing, we have survived three, full-scale Summer invasions by loved-ones and not-so-loved ones. And now, while convalescing from the third assault, I would like to review the experience in the hope of promoting a better understanding between our summer visitors and their host and hostess. The advice and observations offered are for the benefit and protection of both parties. Better human relations may result. On the other hand, they might cease entirely.

To begin with, if you should acquire a Maine coast home with a view, a deep dream of peace, and easy access to sea beaches, lobster pounds, a yacht club and a golf course, let me suggest that you seal off, or de-activate, all spare bedrooms and padlock the liquor cupboard as a simple precaution against the unannounced house guests who "just happen to be driving up from Boston." In this way, you reduce your over-all summer hazard to tent-pitching nieces and nephews, and old classmates travelling by in trailers.

You will find that the tent-pitchers require only lawn space and the use of your stove, refrigerator, automatic washer, clothesline, electric steam iron and bathroom.

The trailer group, usually composed of whole families, is even more self-sustaining. They are often willing to settle for your electric current, water supply, and a patch of real estate under the shade of your old apple tree, if you'll just let them cut off those lower limbs so the trailer can get under.

"But," you say, "those limbs have little apples on them."

"Just green ones," replies your guest, swinging his axe.

As the fruited limbs fall upon the grass, you ask your friend how long he plans to be with you.

"Couple weeks," he says, "maybe three—depending how the kids like it." And with a predatory glance at your wife's vegetable garden, he asks:

"How's the sweet corn coming?"

During our first summer, I divided our visitors into two, broad classifications: My Relatives, and My Wife's Relatives. This was a mistake. If one of my nieces regarded our telephone as God's gift in the field of free trans-continental communication, the fault was mine. If one of Mary's nephews ravaged my beer supply and replaced it in the refrigerator with nursing bottles full of formula for his little son, I blamed Mary. Tempers flared for the first time in years.

"Don't you love little Bo—my own grandnephew?"

"Yes. But at times he's as damp and depressing as a flooded cellar."

"Don't talk that way! Besides, whose niece left us with a twenty-dollar telephone bill for calls to Los Angeles?"

We soon decided to abandon classification by relatives. The best method of typing, or classifying your summer visitors, is by their opening remarks, or entrance lines, as they swarm from their cars and dump the contents of their luggage compartments on your doorstep.

"You didn't answer our letter, so we just thought we'd surprise you."

Visitors using this approach are usually planning a four- or five-day sojourn. It won't do you any good to recommend a nice motel. Their arrival has been timed late in the day, when all the motels are booked solid. This type will settle in, and pervade and absorb your home. One or more of them will always be in the bathroom, and their medicines, cosmetics and suntan unguents will infiltrate cabinets and shelves. They will remark that a fireplace fire is ever so cheerful, but under no circumstances would one of them think of bringing in wood and kindling. You will have trouble mowing your lawn except by night, for by day the shapely sun-bathers in this group lie about upon the sward, springing to life only at meal times.

"Oh, darlings! We've had *such* a time finding you! We all want just a *teeny* peek at your lovely new home."

This type of entrance line may mean real trouble. Chances are you are in for some late poker games in which you will lose money. Breakfasts will be served individually from seven A.M. to two P.M. One of this party will probably sleep on the sofa in your living room, and you will step around him, or her, all morning. Another member of this set is very likely to ask you:

"What do you do all day?"

What you do all day, while they are at large on your premises and in your home, is to wait upon them and clean up after them. During a time of nervous exhaustion, I once told a visitor this. He thought it was a fine joke, and laughed loudly.

"You," he said, "are a card."

Another type of visitor says, on pulling into our driveway:

"We're just stopping a moment. We don't want to bother you."

With this group, almost anything can happen. The suspense is terrific. They may, actually, stop a moment. They may, actually, not want to bother you. On the other hand, the slamming of their car door can toll the knell on you for ten days, with a possible repeat visit.

One gay, young party of nieces and nephews—mine and my wife's, in equal parts—took a look at our red barn that we had re-modeled and immediately planned to appropriate it for dancing. Refreshments, provided by us, would be served from a long, wooden bar, which I would build; and the orchestra would be composed of everyone from Satchmo Armstrong and Wild Bill Davidson to Jimmy Dorsey. I was so alarmed by the fierceness and sincerity of the young people's dream that I lost no time in filling the little barn with cordwood, rusty farm machinery and old barrels.

Once, dizzy with fatigue after a visit from a family of four, including a teething babe—never mind whose relatives they were—I said to Mary:

"Was it you who called this house 'our castle'?"

"It may have been."

"Castle! House by the side of the road, and let the world go by! 'Go by,' my eye! The world has beaten a path to our door. What we've got here is a better mouse trap."

I think it was soon after this, toward the end of our third season of philanthropy and short-order cooking, that I began to have hallucinary conversations with guests. They were Walter Mittyish in tone and concept, and I would like to quote one or two of them.

"Look," I said—in fancy, of course—to an imperious young mother who had registered at our resort along with her husband and small children, "your husband works in an office, doesn't he?"

"Yes. What are you getting at?"

"Just this: supposing I moved a crib into his office and loaded it with a live baby—and just left it there for a few days and nights?"

"That's different."

"Why is it different? He moved a crib, complete with a baby, into my study, didn't he?"

"Our baby doesn't cry."

"He will, when he wakes up and sees me at my desk."

"Oh, in that case, it will be your fault."

You see what I mean? You can't win, even in dreams. Another one of my Mitty dialogues goes like this:

"Why can't you spare us some time?" a young nephew asks me. "You're retired, aren't you?"

"What makes you think I've retired?"

"We never see you doing any work."

"No—and you never will; because the kind of work I do, you have to be alone to do it—just me and a typewriter."

For a moment, in my fantasy, I think I have scored heavily—but no—for my nephew says:

"Far be it from me to interfere, Uncle Edmund. Go ahead and get alone."

In almost any group of visitors, there is someone who gazes critically around our living room and says:

"*What?* No TV?"

When we explain that our budget is limited, and that we spent the TV money for power tools, this person usually snorts:

"Who wants power tools?"

But perhaps the real infuriators are the amateur architects who wish to re-model our home, presumably for their own convenience.

"You ought to straighten out that sag in the barn ridgepole and put up a nice cupola with a light in it. You could have a room up here."

Or, "What I'd do would be to tear out the whole front wall of the house and put in plate glass all across it. Bring you right outdoors."

It has been suggested that a large, shed dormer would make room for two more, nice, airy bedrooms; that we ought to put a widow's walk on top of our house; that we erect a few circular turrets, glassed in. If we adopted half the architectural advice that has been offered to us, gratis, our home would resemble a child's nightmare of The Alhambra.

It was in the desperate last days of the 1958 summer hazard that I drew up a set of Rules and Regulations for use in governing the behavior of the casual visitor, whether friend, foe, or relative. Just the other day I came across the list. Oddly enough, it was tucked away among the pages of Harold Lamb's, "The March of the Barbarians." It read as follows:

Rule One: From prospective visitors, a clear statement in writing—preferably notarized—of arrival and departure times.

Rule Two: A complete inventory of members making up the party, including a statement of ages and sexes, and number of babies or toddlers.

Rule Three: A substantial deposit against breakage.

Rule Four: Mandatory: a house gift, or gifts, of food and beverage, the latter not to consist of milk for the very young.

Rule Five: A sworn statement to the effect that the applicants will make their own beds, empty ash trays, help with the dishes, and stay out of the kitchen while the host and/or hostess are preparing meals.

Rule Seven: No parking in the driveway.

Rule Eight: A deposit of $5.00 (five dollars) for each book borrowed.

Rule Nine: A severe fine for entering my study, with or without knocking, while I am in it.

Rule Ten: Occupancy of the bathroom is limited to twenty minutes during the hours of eight to eleven, A.M.

Clearly, this list must have been written by a curmudgeon in a cold, white fury. But the curious thing is that as I re-read it, with the 1959 visiting season but a few months hence, I do not feel like a curmudgeon, nor can I evoke any sense of fury or diatribe. As a matter of fact, it is very lonely here in my study, and I wish a few nieces and some babies would drop in and pass the time of day. From my window I can see the apple tree from which my old classmate axed those lower limbs to admit his trailer. Good old George! That tree needed his pruning. It looks much better now.

By some strange, human phenomenon, I am pervaded by a feeling of warmth for old George and his Boy Scout axe, and this warmth slowly extends toward all the other guests, invited or otherwise. If we don't actually love these people, and long to see them again, come Summer, why did my wife ask me to build a little, pine-panelled room in the ell of the barn? And why did I take such delight in building it? What visitor will first use the new room, and when?

So it comes to pass that Summer is not a hazard after all, but a hope. Perhaps this is one of the more striking examples of "Time heals all." Visitors, please come back! All is for-given! Never mind about those Rules and Regulations. Just come. Will have TV—and maybe Hi-Fi, too. Open, June to September, 1959. Completely re-decorated, but under same management.